MW00565656

The Memory Barrel

Second Edition

*Written
By DBLorgan*

******

*AN AWAKENING FOR THE READER
OF
LIFE IN THIS REALM, AND THE NEXT
"THE BLENDING"*

First edition released March 2010

The Memory Barrel Second Edition Copyright © 2014 by DB Lorgan
All rights reserved. No part of this book may be used or reproduced,
stored in or introduced into a retrieval system, or transmitted in any form
or by any means without the express written consent of the Publisher of
this book.

Further inquiries can be addressed to DBLorgan PO Box 223, Geneseo,
New York 14454

DBLorgan is a non denominational minister creating and performing her unique
ceremonies throughout the United State. She has been ranked in the top 5% of
officiants in the USA.
She is also a public speaker for women's groups to enhance their life as she
gathers other teachers with her for her "awakening "conferences. For all to find
the joy and fun of life.

Her works include :

The Memory Barrel
The Memory Barrel Second Edition
In the Eyes of the Beholder : Coming soon

Published and printed in the
United States Of America

ISBN-13: 978-0986109799
ISBN-10: 0986109797
BISAC: Religion / Spirituality

Acknowledgements

Where does one begin to acknowledge those that love me and walked beside me as I created my world?
My parents, my children... You know me better than any.

Friends of the heart I have made all over the world. I am blessed by your presence with me. You make my life so much brighter being beside me.

I smile as I write the words as if speaking them and they make them look "appropriate" on the pages.
My dear friends:
Sharon Beller : My anam cara.
Kathy Worth : For your friendship, patience and guidance with ideas and help editing this second edition.

May life surround us all with joy.

I also say "thank you" to my angels.
I am truly blessed..

"Do it again"

"It's an Angel Thing"

By DB Lorgan

Enjoy!

DB Lorgan

Author's Note

There's a place of peace for me beneath an old oak near the water, where a story was conceived that changed my life and the life of those who read it. It began as a journal, something private, for me, my children, and their children. My pencil took on a life of its own, and The Memory Barrel was born. Words were given to me as I continued to write the story for ten years. As with most authors, some experiences written are written well if you actually participated in them. Thus, some within are of actual moments and some are from a very creative imagination quickened by the flow of life.

It became a novel that touched the lives of more than I could have imagined. This little book continued to teach me, even beyond the words that were shared inside. I had many aha moments, the ultimate was this.

The first printing began with an error that would instill fear into the heart of even the most seasoned writer; the wrong copy was sent to the publisher! It contained errors that make me see more clearly now, but made me cringe then. I look back with amazement and appreciation that even with these mistakes, a book that started out as a private journal touched the lives of literally thousands.
A little book that was released on the night of a Blue Moon in 2009, lived up to the meaning of its birth date, "Once in a Blue Moon".....a book such as this comes along. As its popularity grew, so did I, and with it the need to correct and clarify portions of the book.
With gratitude and a joyful heart, I present the second printing of The Memory Barrel.

D B Lorgan

READERS COMMENTS FROM THE FIRST EDITION

I feel so at peace while I am reading. I really love it, don't want it to end!!!!

I just finished the book, it was awesome!!!! When I found time to sit and read I forgot everything else and was immersed in the book. I came away with a peaceful feeling of life and death thank you so much for that.

Ms Lorgan, don't you realize, no one will ever "finish" reading the Memory Barrel? It's a story which lives in every heart who reads it, and will live on for as long as those who read it lives on. You finished writing it, but no one will ever finish reading it. It's one of those...how do you say it. Angel things?

When I read this I experience so many emotions. I have never read a book and had this experience.

The Memory Barrel is a book that all women should read. It is so inspiring; it teaches us to never give up our dreams. I loved it and am buying for all my daughters and daughter in laws.

This is one of those books that you will find yourself returning to time and time again. Some of the words and phrases created by the author will echo throughout your memory repeatedly as time goes on, like some of the other all-time classics. Read it once, and then read it again, and each time you read it, it will take you on a different adventure. It is truly a written journey through life so go ahead start walking down that path.

You have a way with words that touches the heart deeply.

Love, love, loving the Memory Barrel. I am hoping to finish it this weekend and let all know more about it BUT any novel that can have me deep in tears by page 20 is a great book to me!!! Keep shining!!!

Beautiful! I am a nurse and work with dementia and Alzheimer's. Our unit is called "Memory Unit" Up until now "The Notebook" has been at the top of my list. I started reading Memory Barrel yesterday. I think I just had had an "angel thing"...Thank You for making my day....

I finished the book last night. Wow. The ending was amazing.

So I'm half way through The Memory Barrel, and had to put it down for a little bit, It just hit me hard, very emotional, certain parts I feel like I'm reading about myself, and just brings me to tears...I'm truly speechless, at the strength, I know I need to find that within myself, and know it's going to take time.

The Second Edition will carry the reader even further into DBLorgan's touching story of life and believing all things are possible as she blends this realm with the next.

It continues...

A new beginning......

Chapter One

The first step is the hardest...

The first sign of winter was in the air. Their small cabin was hidden in the woods, in a place most would only dream about. The road was hard to find, and they liked it that way. Only family and friends knew where they would be and how to find them.

They lived there...

They built it together...

It was *their* special place.

Upon entering the cabin, a fireplace with a wood stove sat on the right. A handmade mantel sat above the fireplace, covered with pictures of old and young. Their home was softly decorated with a country touch filled with magic and imagination.

The air in their little cabin always held the aroma of recently extinguished scented candles.

This was their playhouse, built for two playmates and best friends.

The neighbors would smile, telling stories of hearing their bike roaring wildly through the trees as their laughter hung in the air (and is probably still echoing somewhere in the depth of those woods). They were always searching for hidden fishing holes or bushes filled with ripe berries to make their homemade jam.

They had the magic...they found it together.

My Gram loved to fish, and Poppa loved watching her as she caught them. The size of fish never concerned her, only that she caught something.

Poppa would try to explain how fun it was watching her, as

she patiently waited for a nibble on her pole. It was worth the wait to see the look on her face when she did have something. Gram's face seemed to light up with a glow. He never knew if she would keep them or not. Usually she didn't, she loved letting them go back to *their world*. That's how she would say it: *Their* world. Poppa would just sigh, knowing she had a very different way of looking at life. That's why he loved her so much.

She taught me so many things. One lesson was to write things down. *"It will help you to make sense of things,"* she would say. It wasn't only writing them down, it was important to find the right time and place to write.

"Find it," her soft voice would say. *"You need it, baby girl, everyone does."*

Her place was always by the water, resting against her old oak tree. You could find her there with her pencil and tablet nestled up to the base of it, as if the tree was her lover.

It worked for her, so I'll try...

(Journal Entry)

It's almost midnight, and everyone is sleeping. At least I think they are.

I'm trying to sort out the events of the day. Trying to sort out tomorrow, trying to sort out the minute that is coming after this one.

At least I am trying, trying to do something. Sleep is not on my list of things to do tonight. I should, but I know it won't come.

I can see across the street that the lights are still on in Mrs. Adair's house. Shar Adair and Grami have been friends for years. Grami called Shar her Anam Cara, her soul friend, a sister of her heart.

If you were ever in the same room with them as they talked about their past, you would just be still and watch them interact with each other. You could see they were true kindred spirits. They were of one heart. I know she will miss her, too.

The stories they would tell: some were fun, and others not so fun. But they always laughed, no matter what, after telling the stories. Most likely since they are older now and they probably can't believe what they went through back then! Coming from oil lamps to the terror of life to the joy for Grami...

It was really fun to listen to the story of the oil lamps. The flickering light made it hard for them to read their bibles at the dining room table, but they still did. Nothing seemed to stop them from being together. Not even the lack of electricity. Oil lamps had been placed in every room to give light when the darkness filled the sky.

Grami strived to be prepared at all times, that's how she lived her life.

Expect the unexpected. Even the lack of money to pay her bills didn't interfere with her life. At times, there was even a shortage of food, but it was never obvious to the boys. She always made the worst moments not so bad. She would bake cupcakes for the smell in the house. This way if the boys were hungry, there was always special things for them to eat. They never, EVER went without food as long as she had a breath in her body. But she did...she had gone without food. No one knew that, though...not even Great Gram.

I forgot that until now. I will remember...I remember so I can share this with my grandchildren. Make the best of every moment in life, no matter what. That's another lesson she taught me.

I can feel the cool breeze blowing through the kitchen window. I love feeling the winter air. It always makes me feel better. Well, let it work its magic tonight of all nights - I need it so much.

I can't believe she's gone.

My grandmother Debra Pratt took her last breath yesterday. I write this in disbelief, and somehow I feel like she's here.

*****

"I miss you," Barbie said as if speaking to the wind. "I will miss you." She put her pencil down and stared out the window with the soft wind still stroking her hair. She stared out the kitchen window, her words came back to her remembrance.

*****

You never die, nothing dies: It seems it does, but it just changes.
Like a seed, or a caterpillar. Remember life and life.
I wouldn't leave you. I will be right here watching over you,
whispering in your ear.

I promise.
"It's an angel thing," shrugging her shoulders with a soft conviction.
There is life here and life in the other realm.
It's just like stepping into another room.
I will let you know I am with you. You will see.

~~~

"That must be what I am feeling. She's here. She said she would be."

Barb took a deep breath. "Gram? Gram, are you here? Show me. Give me one of your signs." Being still, she scanned the room around her, sensing only the breeze and the silence. No signs were given. All she saw in front of her was her pen and tablet.

"Okay, okay! I'll write...I'll write!"

*****

I did love the way she thought. I mean I love the way she thinks. Did, or do...which one do I write now?

I'm so not prepared to walk this path without her, no matter how many words she said or how convincing she seemed to be. I want her back. I want her back now!

Her soft voice still lingers in my mind, hearing the same words as I am writing now. What would she say? Maybe I do think the same way she did. It will never be the same, though. Ever!

What about...the smell of her perfume, what about that? Her laugh, what about that?

I will never feel her touch again; her hugs or hear her whisper in my ear, "Take some energy from me."

Oh, dear God...really?

Really??

*****

A sigh came from down the hallway. The footsteps came closer to the kitchen. A swollen, sleepy-eyed sixteen-year-old squinted at the light.

"Hey, baby girl. Come here," as she patted the chair beside her. "Sit beside me."

"Mom, I miss her!" The tears came again.

Barb pulled Sarah close, thinking, "*I don't know how much I have, but what I do is yours. Take some from me.*"

"Where's Poppa, he's not alone, is he?" Her voice trembling from the tears.

"Grandpa and Uncle Danny are with him right now at the cabin."

"Where is Aunt Leah?"

"She is over at Shar's with the girls, Michael's with her."

Barb tried to roll with her questions in the hopes of calming the confusion, to soften the sadness, only to realize that there were no words to make this any easier. They just needed to hold on to each other.

Chapter Two

The building of what ifs

Cars filled the parking lot of the *what if building*.

This is one moment in life that humans dread. Why? Because the what ifs begin.

These buildings are only for the human ceremonies of saying goodbye.

Is it really necessary to say goodbye? Really? Is this all there is, no more tomorrows ever?

The concrete and wooden walls are filled with tears and sadness. They vibrate through the walls and float above them as if a rain cloud appeared from nowhere. An *unexpected storm came into their world,* when the moment before or a moment ago there was sunshine.

Who started this tradition? Where is the joy? Where is the celebration? Is it really to be done this way?

There has to be a better way.

*****

Everyone that came to Deb's moment of goodbye seemed content to share and visit with each other. The people here are in her *life circle*, and they're together again. Well, not all of them since this little building would never hold all the people in her life circle. She touched people all over the world. From a moment in a grocery store, to traveling to places further than she had ever imagined she would go.

Barb continued to look around at the crowd. It did seem different than other times she had come. Music was playing, and there were paintings all around the room and no casket.

No casket? There is no casket, she thought. I feel like I'm in an art gallery.

A sigh of relief came from the very depths of her soul. Her eyes smiled, seeing all the people, and then she saw Felicia, Uncle Sean's niece from the Isle in Scotland. *Goodness, she is much older than I remember! I'm glad she's here.*

Write.... I have to keep writing.

Barb lifted her pen as a tear fell to the paper. *"I don't like this celebration, Gram,"* she whispered.

{Journal entry}

I hate these buildings, especially today.

Untimely, unwanted family reunions that are filled with regret and what ifs and we should haves and never should haves. Some thinking 'I wish I had' moments. Lessons we all have to walk through. Regrets or no regrets, we walk through them in these buildings.

A celebration is what Gram wanted, not sadness.

I remember her talking to me about this, trying to make it easier.

She would say, "When you first come into this world, it is a celebration, a new beginning with overjoyed faces as the first cry comes from you as you take your first breath. Everyone is so pleased you are here to be part of their family circle. You can't remember that, but it is the way it was.

"You see, it is the same when you pass over to the next realm. Of course, in the beginning when you transition, the ones left on this side are sad and miss us. Yet, on the other side it is a new day, a new chapter, a celebration of continuing life. Try to remember, those here cry as you did when you first came. Tears bring the rainbows, angel. Soon the tears will stop, though. It will take some time for them, as they did with you when you first came. They need to adjust and feel you with them with a new set of eyes and sense you with them by the signs you will give them. Life is continuing, a never ending cycle. Do you see?"

I remember, yes, I remember. Now is when I decide if I understood what she taught me. Barb smiled as she heard words come within.

Words don't teach they guide.
Experience is the best teacher.

It was Grami's celebration. Photographs and paintings adorned on all the walls, music filled the rooms and all the people that loved her were gathered together.

The photos were taken with her silly little camera. Some of her pictures won awards, which really made her laugh. *"I was in the right place at the right time,"* was her comment. *"I click the camera, and God takes care of the rest."*

Others were examining her memory paintings, trying to share a moment again with her when she talked of capturing special experiences for each person on canvas.

She would like that. She *does* like that.

These people are in all her journals. I wonder where her journals are, and her book. Where is the book she was writing?

Someone gently touched her shoulder. Barb turned to see.

"My name is Beth," the woman said as she extended her hand. "I was told Debra was your grandmother."

"Yes," Barb said, standing and extending her hand.

"We met on her last day of radiation and my first day of radiation. Debra went through the entire room at the cancer center hugging everyone and giving them each a special gift to remember her by. It wasn't a normal sight you see in there." She laughed softly. "Knowing your grandmother, I don't think anything with her would have been said to be normal!"

Barb laughed. It felt good to laugh.

"Deb sensed my fear and told me not to be afraid, that I would be fine. Then she touched my husband's hand, gently taking him to the side of the room. I never knew until 'til later what she said to him. In fact, he didn't share it with me until after my radiation treatments were finished. But from the moment she spoke to him, his mood changed, he was so different. She told him, 'Love her, hold her and make her laugh and smile. It will bring you both through this.'

"She then came back to me and told me of her angels and mine. How they are with us from the time we are born. For me to listen to them and ask them anything, and if I do they will help.

How did she know that? But ya know, she was right. "

Beth reached into her pocket and pulled out a worn photograph. "I have looked at this often throughout the years."

"Yes, I remember this." Barb softly touched it.

Leah was walking close by and noticed them both looking at something. They seemed intrigued by a picture. "It's Mom's angel cloud!" Leah shared unintentionally loudly.

Heads turned in the room. It seemed all were aware of the angel cloud. "It appeared to her in the middle of her radiation."

"Yes," Beth said, "That's what she told me. Is the place near here? I think I should go there."

Leah smiled. "It's over by the lake. It's a small site called Indian Pines. It's not far from here."

Leah touched Barb's journal, knowing what she was doing. "I am going to be right over there if you need me, okay? I won't be long. I will be right back."

{Journal entry}

The day seemed to pass like the breeze from this morning. We all sensed her presence here. It was as if she was walking through the room, touching each of us individually. She was right, she would never leave us.

All these people will miss her, too.

My uncle is playing his guitar, as if he is serenading her from the gazebo in the past. His music always took him to the same place that Gram's writing took her. I wish I could do that. Go to that place, to be close to her one more moment. He is doing it now to sense her, I know it.

"Poppa… where is he?"

Her eyes searched the room, trying to catch a glimpse of him. There were old and young, people of all nationalities and beliefs in this building. It was like the gathering of angels in a heavenly place in this realm. Do those outside realize what is taking place in here?

Then she found him, standing off to the side with a soft smile on his face for all who shared a moment with him.

"He's not alone," she thought. "He couldn't be - look at him, he's so calm."

Then his eyes connected with Barbie. He smiled and winked.

She smiled back…"Oh my God, did he hear me? No, Gram heard me and told him. Or ___oh, God, I don't know! I think maybe I am losing my mind here!"

Again, within her words came.

"Is that such a bad thing?"

Barb laughed out loud as she realized what had taken place. She tilted her head back and smiled. "Alright I get it Gram…"

{Journal entry}

You can see it. I can see it…Gram is whispering to him, as she always did. I know Gram is whispering to him. She did it to me. God, I love her!

My Poppa - such a wonderful man. He gets like a big old bear when he's upset. Gram had or has a way of settling him down. "No growling," she would always say to him. He would laugh so hard when she said that. Then she would wrinkle her nose at him. He loved her so much, I mean, he loves her so much.

I can't help but smile thinking of the two of them together.

One look at his eyes and his smile, she would say, he had her. She said he came to her when she needed him the most. Poppa was the missing piece of her soul. They were inseparable. They called it "The Blending." They met on the Internet. We tried to figure out where she even got the idea to meet people there.

Maybe Shar suggested it.

Gram dating… that was hard to watch.

We would all laugh, but still worry. She never could stay with one very long. She always found something wrong and quickly said goodbye. At least she was smiling. "Or was she?" Maybe that was for us, too. Was she occupying herself so she wouldn't feel the pain that Tom left inside her?

We watched. Praying she would survive…

She did, she always did.

Tom left her without any signs it was going to happen. I think she felt she would die if she didn't keep walking. I know she thought he was her soul mate, and so did we.

He isn't even here.

Their marriage was what we all wanted for ourselves. When it ended, all of us were in shock, but no one as much as she. How does that happen? Maybe there was more that we didn't know or see. I was young then, but hearing the stories it was a time of mourning and finding herself then. She said it was the worst journey for her, but also the best.

Then it happened. Eleven years later, Poppa came along, seemingly from nowhere. Interesting how that word can be read as "now here". He was "now here" with her.

Gram, is that you, still teaching me as I write? It is, isn't it? {Barb continued writing, sensing her presence}

Most people could only dream of a match like theirs. We were all so relieved, not only for them, but for us, too! Gram and Poppa, they found it…"the forever".... the rainbow after the storm.

Until now.

How was he going to be after this, without her? Had he or she prepared for this to happen? How do you prepare? What do you do with the space that is so empty inside? How do you go on?

How do I go on?

Leah came from the crowd and touched her hand.

"Come on, we have something to do." She patted the journal softly.

"Where are we going?" Barb could see others going in the same direction.

Shar had a smile for them as they passed by, she knew what was happening. She touched her heart in a swooping motion with her fingers as Leah pulled her along. {It was Gram's way to say I love you.}

Barbie shrugged her shoulders and repeated the gesture. Looking like a little girl, following where she was being taken. As she continued through the crowd, her hand extended and scooped up Sarah. Taking her from the moment in her mind to bring her back to now, being with her Mom - now.

In the parking lot, Deb's last love of her life was already in his truck, waiting patiently for everyone.

He waved his hand through his opened window. "Follow me." You could hear her Celtic music playing in the truck.

Debra was right beside him.

~*~*~*~

Chapter Three

Don't let your eyes deceive you,
to what in your heart, you know is true.

The cabin that they built together was at the top of the highest hill they could find.

As the caravan of cars pulled into the driveway, you could see the sun peeking over the tree branches. Debra's favorite pastime was watching the sunsets and sunrises. Timing is everything, and how perfect this timing was.

The opened garage door revealed a green tarp covering a large object. Everyone knew it was the bike, *their* bike.

The silent march continued towards the cabin.

Rob was the first to reach the front door. His hand turned the knob, and the door creaked open. The outside air filled with the aroma coming from the woodstove inside. There was a silence, except for the beating of their hearts, pounding with anticipation. A hesitant moment of reflection: What were they doing now? What was Mom doing now?

Usually, Deb would hear the door creak and would always say, "Hi" even before seeing who was there. You never knew what you would find her doing. She might be sitting on the floor reading or writing as the fire crackled. Sometimes she would be in the kitchen with her Celtic music playing loudly, serenading her as she created something special.

From time to time, you might even catch her dancing. When she spotted you, she would run over and start dancing around, like an Irish Fairy, playing you into her world.

Her magic, she loved sharing her magic.

Now what will fill in those moments? What are we going to experience walking into this world again without her? Will the music and laughter continue? How?

Questioning eyes looked at each other for an answer.

Leah spoke up. "Well, who's going to say what, she always said, must be I am?"

Expect the unexpected...everything always works out.

Mom loved to take us away from the world of reality for a moment to dream. "Memories are the past filled with laughter and tears. Sunshine and rain bring the rainbows. Remember this," Leah said, quoting her mother word for word.

Then continuing with her soft voice, "Dreams," as her voice paused for a moment. "Dreams are the future, filled with magic and imagination that is their way." It was her way.

Turning towards the trees, she closed her eyes and took a deep breath. The moment was surreal. It was the chatter, the chatter of Deb, coming through Leah, trying to make the moment easier.

"Mom!" Leah called out to the wind and over the tops of the trees that surrounded this moment. "Mom, we're waiting for the rainbow!"

~

"All right, that's my cue!" Pop's deep voice bellowed, bringing them back. "Get in here! Move it or lose it."

Debra stood to the side of the door, still trying to adjust to the moment she was in.
As each of them passed her, she wanted to reach out and touch them.
She knew, they knew she was there.
How would she, could she touch them?
Questions began streaming through her thoughts.
So many questions.
Then, a breeze blew through her hair as if comforting her, too.

Everyone entered *their* little cabin, hesitantly looking and sensing. The huge pillows were tossed on the floor around the room. The cabin seemed the same; the wood was crackling in the fireplace. Their Christmas tree was set up in the corner by the window, with presents placed neatly beneath it.

It was always on Thanksgiving they found their tree and decorated it.

Thanksgiving? Leah's mind wandered, "It was only a few days ago." {Leah's husband Michael listened}

"Mom was talking about how she and Pop slept under the Christmas tree on Christmas Eve every year since they had been together. They shared gifts with each other, some not of the unwrapping kind.

Leah smiled, thinking of how her Mom giggled, sharing those intimate moments with Pop.

"Mom and I did this every year after Dad left. We opened our gifts at midnight, or close to it - depending on how well I could convince her to let me open them sooner. It was so easy to convince her. She loved giving her special gifts. I think at times it was harder for her to hold out. Then we ended the night by sleeping under the tree. It was our tradition, now modified for her and Pop."

Leah smiled as she remembered about one specific year. Her voice came alive as she shared the story. "Our tree was sooo tall, we had to take a panel out of the drop ceiling to fit it upright. We both tried to saw the bottom off the trunk, but a small steak knife didn't work very well! We laughed trying to get this thing upright. But we did it! The angel *was in the ceiling*, sitting all comfy on the top of the tree. We laughed so hard. Mom said, 'That's perfect'... and it was for us. Such great memories! "

Deb giggled at being able to hear Leah. She always thought she would be able to. Now she was actually experiencing it for herself.
This is wonderful I can hear them. Forgetting they might not hear her, or maybe they would...

Michael put his arm around her, guiding her from the tree to the family.

They had five grown children between the two of them, plus all the grandchildren. Holidays became a banquet that she loved to prepare with her own two hands. Leah would help, but it was her gift of gifts. The dessert table could have been portrayed in a cooking magazine. She made everyone's favorite, forgetting no one. Making memories; it was her way and always on her mind.

Everyone scattered about the room, taking up every space available. Some plopped on the pillows, some on the couch. In the chairs, soothing laps were occupied. We were all family, brought together as one.

"You find it, boys?"

"Yeah, we got it." In came Rob and Dan, carrying a barrel-shaped container covered with white and blue contact paper.

Vibrant laughter rippled throughout the room as they came around the corner carrying it. It was great being there. Leah knew it was coming and stood to the side, watching the look on everyone's face as it came in. She smiled so huge, it was as if Debra herself was standing there with a young face. Deb always called her "angel face." She felt Leah was her angel.

"Mom...what is it?" Sarah asked.

"It's the memory barrel, honey, the family memory barrel."

The laughter turned to silence, and everyone seemed entranced as they waited and wondered what would take place in the next moment.

Leah watched Poppa as he sat in his chair, taking in the moment. Her mind raced from one thought to the next, trying to understand what was happening.

Mom had this planned - it was something no one else would have thought of. I know she had this planned in their discussions together for us kids. "Forever and a day," she would say. "I love you forever and a day."

This was how she would try to help us through this.

Rob stopped, with a surprised look on his face. "Who's in the kitchen? Do I smell coffee?" He started to walk towards the kitchen. Maybe he was hoping she would be in there and this was all just a bad dream. He leaned around the corner, smiled, seeing it was empty, then walked back to check on Savanna.

"I'm here." She followed him around the room.
"I wish I had a white feather that would make him laugh."

Her angel stood beside her as he watched Debra adjusting to her new life.
Hearing words now that are understood by thoughts and the emotions. She will understand soon, he thought.

*****

Leah went back to the kitchen…
"I can do this. I have to be focused," Leah thought to herself.

She continued making the coffee and muffins Pop had asked her earlier to do. Somehow she would, as she fought back the tears.

"Let's get these muffins out there and make your Mom smile, okay?"

Leah loved that Michael seemed to understand Mom.

As they came into the doorway of the living room, Leah quickly stopped. "Look at him over there playing with the girls, he is trying to keep us from coming unglued."

"She is right there with him. You can see it." Michael comforted her with his observation.

"I can't explain it, Michael, I have this uncanny calmness."

"Mom? I know you are here. I love you so much. Please never leave," Leah thought with an ache in her soul.

"I won't, angel," Deb whispered softly.
"I am here 'til you understand and beyond. I am here."

Leah hesitated for a moment, listening to a voice, a voice within herself…but she pushed it off. "I must be tired," she rationalized.

"The Memory Barrel! I can't remember when the last time was that I opened it with her." Leah strained to steady her words. Taking a deep breath, she continued toward the living room. She was strong like her Mom, always pushing forward.

"Muffins, anyone?" Handling the platter like a professional server.

"You made the muffins?" Dan asked.

"Yes, Pop put in a special request. I brought them from home. Are you okay?"

"I think so. I better get over there and calm the kiddies. I think they are going to wish that barrel open."

The sun was setting outside, and you could see her tree standing strong right on the other side of the window. The silhouette of the tree was placed perfectly in view, on the wooden floor from the setting sun.

Signs are always there you just need to watch for them.

"Mom would have taken a picture of it today. She loved that tree. When she first saw it, she knew their cabin should be built right beside it. At least that's what she said." Leah continued to chatter and Michael listened.

"It's snowing out," Robbie whispered as he was pacing the floor.

Everyone turned to see.

Leah looked in her hands and realized the plate of muffins was still waiting to be served. "Does anyone want these muffins?" as she wished someone would come take them out of her hands.

"Heck, yeah."Pop slowly stood, gathering his strength, though no one seemed to notice he was having some discomfort. He reached for the plate and whispered something to Leah. She smiled softly, and he kissed her on the cheek.

Everyone laughed as the old gent went around the room handing out muffins and teasing the little ones to make them giggle. He was so strong, yet he was so softhearted. Mom called him her mountain man. Hidden in the mountains until she found him; actually, he would say he found her. It didn't matter. They were happy.

*****

The large barrel rested in the middle of the hardwood floor, as it had done so often before.

Everyone stared at each other, waiting.

"All right," Danny spoke first. Setting his guitar down and picking up Lilly, he took a deep breath, which he had been doing a lot these days, and said, "This brings back memories for me. This old thing, it's been around since I was...hmm, probably about 5 years old."

Sarah laughed and said, "Wow, then it's really old, huh?"

Everyone laughed together. *It felt good to hear the laughter.*

The old man sat in his chair, watching the moments unfold. He was trying to be strong for the kids. He could feel his heart ache, and the heaviness was getting harder and harder to conceal. *"I'll do this, baby doll,"* he said within himself.

Danny stood solemnly with one hand on the barrel and the other holding Lilly tight. Knowing they would be walking back in time for a moment of *remembering*.

"Yes, it sure is old. All of our memories, so many moments of our life are in this barrel. It brought many smiles when we really needed them. Mom always had a way of making you smile when you didn't think you could. She would sit here on the floor with me, and we would dump it out. The treasures of the past would flow out around us. I never remember walking away from this sad. I always felt better."

"Yeah, me too" said Rob. "It was even better when she topped it off with the gobblety goops."

"The what?"

Leah couldn't contain her laughter. "They were piles of ice cream, like a sundae with everything imaginable on them. Mom bought bags of candy and had syrup, nuts, whipped cream, everything we might want to put on them was on the table to pile on. Then we would gorge ourselves, sometimes eating way too much. It always made us feel great, at least for a while."

"She always seemed to know when to pull out the gobblety time."

Sarah murmured, "We should have made them today! I could use something to make me feel better."

Rob went over to her as she sat on the floor at her mom's feet.

"I'm right here, baby girl."

"I know, Grandpa I love you."

Rob pulled Sarah close, and then continued with the moment, "My first teddy bear is in there. I loved it when we would start going through all the papers and trinkets."

"I know," Danny laughed. "Mine, too."

Rob's mind was wandering right along with them. "Remember the match box cars, Star Wars?"

"GI Joe. Mom always saved a few of the things from each of our lives at a certain time," Danny added

"Remember the cakes?" Leah joined in.

"What about the cakes?" a tiny voice from the back called out. "Is there a cake in there?"

"No, but if Mom could have she would have! I am sure there is a picture of them in there, though." Leah said.

Danny explained. "One year, she made me a tank cake when I was into GI Joe."

"Yeah, and a cake for me too. When I was able to go from seventh grade into eighth, without going through the whole year, "said Rob.

"That's not fair," Sarah piped in, elbowing her Grandpa.

"Mom really loved you guys," Leah said. "She loved all of us.

Now...hesitating for a moment, she looked across the room. "What is it we are supposed to be doing tonight? I am a little nervous here!"

Lilly called out, "Making gobblety gooos."

"Yahh," Lacey and Savanna agreed. "Poppa, can we, can we?"

"You can have them for breakfast, my little angels!"
"Dad!" "Pops!" the mothers' echoed at the same time.

Deb laughed at how the little ones
could instantly change the mood in the room.
"They still have the magic."
"Yes, they do."
Deb was surprised to hear another voice that seemed to hear hers.
She felt at peace, coming to sense not to be alone.
"Who are you?" she asked
"Oh, my sweet one, I have been with you always.
By your tree - in every step you have walked,
I have been by your side."

"Do you have a name? Is mine still as it was then with my family?"
"We all have ways of identity.
You named me so long ago."
"I did."
"Yes, as you sat on the balcony of your home, that is the first time you
mentioned my name."
"Nathaniel? Is it you?"
She glowed as she stood face to face with her companion.
Her lifelong angel, now meeting, heart to heart.
His face shined so brightly. I sensed a form, but yet not as we were in
the world of flesh.
"This is how it was always. Your human form, as theirs, is just
temporary. This is home, sweet one."
"I thought I was just losing my mind, calling to you. Hoping you were
real, since I sensed a presence with me."
"Yes, most think they have lost their mind when they converse with us.
But, it is really bringing back something you lost, while you were in
the earthly realm.
We have always been together, the true family.
The earthly is a reflection of us, the true essence of life.

But we are more real than the human form. You just need to take all veils of doubt away. Then you sense and see with your heart."

*****

A voice as an echo pulled her back to the moment in the cabin.

"I think we're doing what she wanted us to do - laugh, smile, enjoy each other, and remember. That is what she wanted all of us to do, always remember the good times and the bad. We always made it through them all together as a family. The memory barrel reflects it."

"Do you think she is here?"

They all looked at each other, smiled, and simultaneously said, "Yes, she's here."

Pops smiled and said, "Yep, you betcha. She loves all of you and wouldn't let anything stand in the way of being there for you." He paused. "She isn't gone. She hoped you would know this if we did it this way. If it had been me first, you would be doing the same thing. Only it would be her sitting here fussing over you all. We talked about it and wanted all of you to know we love you…forever and a day."

"Okay, let's go," Dan's hands gently pulled at the lid, working it off slowly. The top lifted off…

The air filled with the smell of vanilla, her favorite perfume.

"What the?"

Everyone pulled back for a moment as it took us all by surprise.

The air was empty of any sound. I think everyone was holding their breath. Then all of a sudden, there was a chorus of laughter. God, was she going to appear there in the middle of the floor like a genie in a bottle or something? We all felt she could if she wanted to. Nothing could stand in her way of doing remarkable things.

Lilly shouted, "Meme?!!! {*recognizing the aroma*} Where is she?" She tried to jump off Dan's lap to go find her.

"Where's Meme, Daddy?" Her eyes were filled with a glow of excitement.

Dan held her hand so she wouldn't run around looking for her. The soft words he spoke next came straight from his soul. "She's with the angels, baby girl. Meme wants Poppa to show us something. There is something in the barrel from Meme."

"Ohh," she said and nuzzled on his lap. "Daddy, psst, ya know what?"

He put his ear down to her...

"It's an angel thing, huh Daddy?"

Everyone, including Pop, struggled to hold back the tears.

"Yes, baby girl, it's an angel thing."

"Meme loves the angels, Daddy."

The glow was still there in her face. She understood more than they did in that moment.

The room again was filled with the silence of stirred hearts.

Lilly ran to Poppa's empty lap. She jumped in one leap across the floor because she knew he was sad, and she wanted to make him laugh. She had never seen Poppy sad before. He grunted at her, perfect landing.

"Dolly, Meme is an angel."

"I know." She took her sleeve and wiped Poppa's cheek. "I'm her angel, Poppa, and yours, too, huh?!"

"Isn't she beautiful?
We almost lost her when she was first born.
Thank you for letting her stay with us."
Nathaniel said, "It wasn't her time. She has much to show all of you.
She taught you when she walked through that moment. Do you remember?"
{Debby thought back.}
"Yes, I do. I sang to her. I put my head in her oxygen tent and sang to her.

Her little eyes connected to my soul, in that very moment."
The voice said,
"As it was before, it happened again."
{Debra understood, she smiled brightly, she understood.}

"Yes, you are, Lilly!"

"Me, too," came from Savannah.

"Me, too!"Lacey softly shared. Lacey looked up at Leah. "Me, too, huh, Momma?"

"Yes, baby, Meme loves all of you, you're all are her little angels."

"Yes, you are...I will play with you later!
I can play with them, can't I, Nathaniel?"
"In your way, you will be able to. There are no limits now, Deborah."

Pops stood and walked over to Danny, handing him Lilly, then went over to the open barrel. The lid rested on the floor beside the barrel of memories. His face showed concern as he looked inside, he seemed surprised. The large hands moved so quickly, like reaching for a butterfly before it flew away. Touching it.

Rob touched his shoulder, "Are you all right? What is it?"

He lifted a package, holding it gently in his large hands.

"What is it, Dad?" Marti (*his daughter*) seemed concerned.

"Not sure, hon, she's up to something."

It was a box, wrapped in gold paper with a gold ribbon tied around it, and a large bow. A card was attached to the outside. He walked over to his chair, holding it to his chest, silent. He began to read the card:

"Family forever and a day."

"I have to take a moment, kids." He leaned back and took a deep breath.

"He's having a hard time, can I please touch him?"

"He knows you're here. You will be with him tonight."

His eyes closed, a slight smile came over his face. It was as if she was whispering to him…

"Hey, you," Debby whispered.

"Whoa…" he growled and chuckled the way he always did with her. A chill went up his spine. It was like the moments Debra would tell him of, when she felt her angels were present with her.

He put the package on his knees and ran his hands softly across the top as if he was touching her. *"I see, baby doll. I see."*

"Dad?" Leah kneeled on the floor next to him.

He smiled, looking at her through glassy eyes, "Yes, angel, I am fine, I'm really all right. I…I just wish…" He sighed and regained his composure. He leaned forward to Leah. "She's here, do you feel it?"

Leah nodded in agreement as her eyes filled with tears.

"Is that a present for Poppa…Daddy?" Lilly said. "Ohhhhh, I know, is it an I love you gift?"

Pop laughed hearing her explain what we all were trying to accept.

"Yes, angel, Meme's I love you gifts. Do you want me to open it?"

"Yeah!!!!" the little ones squealed with excitement.

His hands started to shake.

Deb softly touched his hands. "I'm here. Take some from me."

"Now let's see what she's up to!" He slowly took the tape off the side, trying to be so careful not to tear it.

The sun had already set. The wind was blowing against the windows in the living room. It sounded like a storm was kicking up.

Continuing to unravel the package, he looked out the

window and smiled.

"Your mother and I met in a storm, ya know."

"What was it she called you?" Leah said, laughing.

A smile filled his face, and the red started to appear. He laughed that great laugh. "Aw, you know."

The wind blew outside even brisker.

Danny walked over to the window, touching the cool pane of glass. "She loved the wind."

"Yes, she did," Leah said softly. "I bet she has something to do with it, her own little angel magic. She always said the wind blew away the negativity."

Silence filled the room except for the sounds taking place outside and the crackling of the fire. All seemed to be remembering her silly ways and things she said. Or *were* they silly?

Deb sat on the floor next to the little ones.
While everyone tried to make sense of it all.

"Yes, she did have a different way of looking at things. Between the Irish and the Iroquois, her imagination and thoughts were not of this world most of the time. I couldn't tell if she was a fairy or an angel."

Leah closed her eyes for a second and put her head on Michael's lap. "The angels and my Mom together, walking us through this long, dreaded night. It was her way of comforting us through the tough times. I think this is the toughest night of my life.

Michael gently touched her, knowing she was in deep thought.

Leah sat up quickly. "Where's the baby?

"She's over there on Sarah's lap, she's fine."

Leah looked over. Sarah was playing with Lacie's long blonde hair, trying to keep her occupied.

Leah waved, and a smile filled Lacey's face. She loved her Momma. She was seven and not a baby, but that didn't stop her from referring to her this way.

Across the room, the opening of the package continued. The lid lifted easily, "Well, will you look at this?

"What is it, Pop?"

"This was going to be a Christmas surprise," Deb said
Nathaniel clarified,
*"It still is, just not the way you thought it would be shared.
Everything comes in the right time...."*

Chapter Four

The opening of my memory barrel

A smile appeared on his tired face, his eyes mesmerized by each word as he glanced over them in admiration. She did it. Her dream, she was creating it. It was here in his large hands.

Pop looked up, "Ready?"

I think he was taking a moment to catch his breath, knowing full well he was going to be a teacher tonight.

They all smiled, and a few whimpers and sniffles came from the room. Everyone was anxious to see what her gift was.

The fire was crackling in the fireplace, and the family was spread all over the room.

Large pillows were scattered all over the floor. Little heads snuggled on parents' laps. Half-filled coffee cups, and unfinished muffins sitting on plates. The blending of these two families was continuing throughout the night.

The wind was still making itself known outside. Neither the storm nor the darkness was interfering with what was taking place in this little log cabin in the woods tonight.

He began to read the rest of the card.

"To my loving storm rider," he read with a deep, playful voice.
"My best friend, I love you beyond this life and into the next."
His voice cracked as he continued,
"You found me when I was lost and guided me to the light.
Dreams do come true.
You and I share it with the world every time they hear us laugh.
To my family, may this allow you to know all things are possible in this life and the

blending into the next.

Deb stood beside him and echoed the words into the air as he read.
Could they hear her?

He had heard these words before. He knew the stories, he shared her tears and filled her with joy. He held the package tightly in his hands, not letting it slip, not for a moment.

All eyes were on him.

The first *gift* was a colorful canvas painting.

"I remember this, she was painting this for her memory paintings. This one she did before we met. It was hanging over her desk." He lifted it for everyone to see.

"Do you remember it?"

Almost everyone agreed.

"Pop there's a note on the back of it."

He turned it over. A pink piece of paper read:

This will be my cover for The Memory Barrel. I was trying to find the right picture for the cover. I painted this so many years ago, not realizing what it was for.

Now I know.

Thank you to my angels.

Everything is understood in time.

He set the painting next to his chair, propping it carefully so all could still see it. "Your Mom loved surprises; I think this is just the beginning."

The next was an envelope dated January 2010:

Dear Miss Pratt,

This is to acknowledge the receiving of your submission to us on December 31, 2009.

Our editor has reviewed your beginning transcript. We are pleased to inform you of our acceptance of The Memory Barrel for publication.

Your novel sounds inspiring. It will be an added addition to our firm, to stand beside you and as you have said, make your dream come true.

The Memory Barrel and the setting up of the processes are scheduled to begin tomorrow for publication. Our art production department will be contacting you to hear your thoughts on a design for the cover.

We look forward to hearing from you,
Congratulations

*****

"She contacted a publishing company!" Leah's voice shared with excitement

The old Scot's face just glowed with pride. "You did it, baby girl. You did it."

Everyone sat quietly, waiting for him to open the next gift.

"Well, this one's dated some time ago," as he continued to read.

October 2001

This is the beginning of my first novel.

The Memory Barrel
By Debra Pratt

The first sign of winter was in the air.

Their small cabin hidden in the woods, in a place most would only dream about.

The road was hard to find, and they liked it that way. Only family and friends knew where they would be and how to find them.

They lived there…

They built it together…

It was their special place.

Upon entering the cabin, a fireplace with a woodstove sat on the right.

A handmade mantel sat above the fireplace, covered with pictures of old and young.

Their home was softly decorated with a country touch filled with magic and imagination.

The air in their little cabin always held the aroma of recently

extinguished scented candles.

This was their playhouse, built for two playmates and best friends.

The neighbors would smile, telling stories of hearing their bike roaring wildly through the trees as their laughter hung in the air (and is probably still echoing somewhere in the depths of those woods). They were always searching to find hidden fishing holes or bushes filled with ripe berries to make homemade jam.

They had the magic…they found it together.

*****

He had to stop and take a breath as the tears came that he'd been holding back for so long. They flowed like a flood of sadness being released from within him. It had to come. It was time.

The stillness and tears flowed through them all.

Debra was writing this beginning of her story in 2001, creating in her imagination.. It was years before this moment. How could she do this?

They were sitting in the exact place, almost with the precise detail.

The wind outside blew stronger, and one candle on the mantel was blown out. There was a white feather nestled next to it. Caught by the cool air seeping through the walls, the feather gently swayed as if playfully dancing in the air above them all and then rested softly at his feet.

The room was still...no one seemed to breathe as they looked at each other, knowing this is what she tried to teach us.

They all were entranced, staring at the white soft feather.
Her laughing voice was heard within each of them, synchronized and clear

"There is no death; you go on, life and life.
There is no death, just a change.
I am smiling, watching you all."

Rob looked at Danny, and then they both looked at Leah with a question in their eyes, as if to say, *did you just hear her?* Leah's eyes and smile answered their question.

"Words don't teach, my angels, they guide.
Experience is the best teacher.
Now you see!"

"Oh, my God!" Barbie cried out. "Did you hear her?"

The old Scotsman reached for the feather. He tucked it in his shirt pocket, his hand gently rested across it, keeping it safe by his heart. "Okay, De!...okay...I get it...I get it!"

The last gift was the heaviest. It was going to be the most difficult for all of them.

He opened the box. "It's her journals." He raised them carefully, being sure to keep them safe.

Her journals: Words of joy, words of sadness, words of fear.
All of them written by a little left handed Irish, Iroquois woman.
That in time will touch the world.
It was time to share them.

"Here we go, she wants us to open them," he said loudly.

"We'll share this, and then the rainbow will appear. That's what she always said. It always appeared for us since we found each other. Now let's see it, baby doll!"

The old Scot spoke with confidence. He knew her better than most and loved how she shared of life and taught him, with her silly ways. This would be the most difficult step for him. As she said, the first step is the hardest.

He glanced over each of the journals, setting them on his lap. Each was individually dated, and pink tags with "FOR THE BOOK" written on them stuck out from certain pages.

Debby sat at his feet, listening and watching.

"These are your mother's words," he continued. "These are her journals." He held them all up again so they could see. "The pink tags in all of them read, *'for the book.'* I'm not sure if she would have read them all to you.

"I think the gift from her was to let us know the book was going to be published. She wanted us to know it was coming. It's up to all of you. Do you want to read some of the tagged areas? Since they were definitely going to be put in the book?" He needed their answer. "Or shall we call it a night and head to bed?"

The darkness outside was filling the sky. Most of the little ones were sleeping soundly on their blankets, close to the warm stove.

"I can't sleep now," Leah said. "I think I want to hear some of them, Pop, it just feels as if that is what she would want us to do. Celebrate her life."

"Yes, I agree. Now, I will stop when you say stop. We don't need these journals to celebrate your mother. All of us have been given signs that what she lived while here and shared with us is being shown today. Life and life, it continues. Do you agree?"

"Yes," they all replied.

His words were confident. "She will guide my hand, as she always has. Okay, babe," he paused for a second, "I'm ready."

His hand reached to the bottom book. He took a deep breath.

*****

Enter and walk back with me.

My name? Does it matter unless we become good friends? We meet people every day, for maybe a moment. We smile and make each other smile. Like a shooting star, it appears for a moment and then it's gone, but you remember it.

Let us start that way.

This first moment we meet face-to-face, meet mind to mind and heart to heart. We begin this, our first introduction, to understand why we have met. It will come in time, we will understand. Where shall we begin? With the yesterdays or the tomorrows? I think the yesterdays, since they make you appreciate the now and the tomorrows. Knowing where you have come from, so you can't understand and appreciate where you are going.

They say that writing things down is good for the soul. It's supposed to give you a chance to focus on your direction. I remember hearing it on Oprah. "Journal," she said. "Write things down, release and feel better. Understand by stepping outside of the situation and re-examine it."

Maybe that is true...I'll let ya know

(Journal entry)

I am in the middle of divorcing. He left, and I did not know if I could make it or not. I had to remember that I had a beautiful family, and much to live for, but my life had revolved around him. That was not a good thing, I didn't realize it at the time.

Now only a few months have passed, and I am fine and so is he. Or am I?

He's found another life so quickly, and I am genuinely trying to discover mine.

"I am fine, I am fine," was my mantra to myself and others. If I say it enough, I will believe it.

Now I begin again to learn, entering the "University of Life"...not realizing I was, or had been, unintentionally enrolled as a student, and my professor is the universe.

Apparently, I am ready. But for what?

The following are journal entries I had made over the last years.

I have learned of my success and failures, reading them again and again. It gets clearer as I walk in them from time to time. To remember, remember where I have come from, to celebrate where I am going.

My life is so different now, after walking a journey that I would not say was entirely enjoyed, but very necessary.

Why?

For clarity...now it begins. As you walk in my memory, to see why you have come to read my first novel. We will walk together and become joined within our hearts.

~*~*~*~

Chapter Five

Everything is for a time and a season.

October 2001

I left his house. The one he moved into a few weeks ago. Not a good experience, but the beginning of a new chapter in our lives, in my life at least.

"Hey," he said, answering the door with a smile on his face. "What's up?"

I was a little surprised to see his face, smiling. I remember that smile. Wait, it wasn't for me. What was he smiling about? Why is he so perky?

Why am I here? Was it to see him again? Maybe disbelief that he actually didn't love me anymore. Either way, I was here and I have to deal with it. What words will flow from me...the truth. "You're such a jerk or I miss you? or Who are you??? I screamed these questions within myself. Who are you? What have you done with my husband? I love my husband. Please, please, where is he?"

I stood silent, the silent seconds vibrating in my throat with every beat of my heart. Then words came from me, "Tom, I'm not feeling too well. Could you get Leah from school today?"

"Sure," he said quickly. I sensed he was very eager to get back to whatever he was doing. I turned to leave the porch, or had the full intention of going. I just couldn't control myself. I had to ask, my mind was taken over by the question. With a curious smirk concealing my emotions as best I could, I blurted out, "What are you doing in there?" as I slightly peered around him, remembering how he answered the door.

"Oh, chatting."

"Chatting?" I repeated his words in a bit of amazement, thinking *with who?* Because I saw no one. But then I remembered the term from the kids. "Oh, on the computer?"

We never had done this with anyone before, or I should say, I had never done this. Now is the beginning, as I am a student learning about the new Tom.

"Yeah, on the computer."

It was always so hard to get him to discuss anything, to say what was going on in his head. So, of course, my jealousy needed more words, more answers.

"With who?" I tried to hold back the sarcasm and jealousy.

"Someone I met, a friend."

His stance made it obvious that he wanted to get back to his computer screen. To his friend. I was no longer the object of his attention. Actually, I hadn't been for quite some time. I knew enough, the heaviness inside was making it clearly unbearable to remain standing. I couldn't show him that, though. I *wouldn't* show him. "Okay, please don't forget to get Leah!" I didn't want him to see me cry again, not again. I felt sicker now and wanted to bury myself in my pillow on my lonely bed.

My keys, where are the stupid keys?

{Her fingers entangled in her pocket to find them.

Her mind raced, trying to make sense.

But there was none to be found.}

That man was not the man I married nineteen years ago, or even the man I knew two years ago. He looked the same, but inside he was empty. Empty of what I once saw and loved.

She arrived home and went directly to her computer.

At least this felt better than puking…at least a little anyway, she thought.

Let's see what's out there that he thinks is so damn interesting.

~

"This was so hard, Nathaniel."

"Yes, we knew it would be, it was coming but you didn't see the signs. You had a purpose, and one of your sons told you. But you didn't listen."

"What did they tell me?"

"It was synchronized for him to come when he did.

You both were given gifts.

But he wasn't going on the same path as you.

You sensed it when he went to Africa with the bible group."

"Yes, I did."

"He was moving on, and you would, too."

Debra sighed. "Okay, I will listen."

{She was walking back and getting her answers.

Here is where the answers come.}

My heart was racing. My headache seemed to be more intense, but I couldn't, wouldn't stop. Where do I find these places? I fought against myself and continued.

"Online dating?" The empty spaces needed to be filled, they sat there on my monitor, waiting: <u>Debra</u>, she typed and quickly stopped. I should use an alias to be safe.

Maybe I should call Tom and get some pointers. She laughed but didn't really think it was funny.

"Hmm…" She sighed as she re-read what she had entered on the questionnaire. "I can do this," she whispered as if convincing herself to continue. I have to do this.

One page led to another, and another. Oh my God, this is like writing a resume to find a job, only this is to find a date, finding someone to spend some time with? Doing this isn't me, but maybe this is the *new* me. Like the new Tom, I am creating the new Debra.

My fingers trembled as they tapped the keys on the board. Was it anger that made me do it? I will show him that I don't need him. He hated that I always wanted to do things with him. I always hated going anywhere alone. I am alone now, so I better begin adjusting to being alone.

"I am alone now", she said out loud to hear the words. "I'll find my path, where I'm to go". She thought: Now if I can just keep the tears out of my eyes so I can see where the heck I am walking, I will have it made.

They say there are stages you go through in a divorce. Sadness, anger, and plain pissed off. Which one am I today? I don't care, but pissed off seems to fit this moment.

When I met Tom, it wasn't really dating. It was more of a whirlwind. It's hard to believe it was so long ago because I can still see it all so clearly. Stop, stop it!

Stay focused on the screen, don't let the chatter distract you. Match.com, I started laughing. "A match made in heaven?" That's what I thought my marriage was. I will never think that again. How could I? It was gone forever, it was dead.

My hands shook. My mind was ricocheting everywhere. The stage I was in? I took a deep breath and realized that continuously identifying it wasn't necessary. I was just doing it. Yet, fear was mixed in with the pissed off stage now.

I had never used the computer for this. To talk with someone I had never met. I was terrified. Was this a stage of online dating syndrome? I knew I was old enough to know the common sense things to keep myself safe. There were so many sites, so many faces and words to read. Going through all of them, I realized how ignorant I was, but mostly that I was wounded. I couldn't give up. Was I really looking for someone to fill his space so quickly? He did. Why shouldn't I?

Who was she, the one that caught his eye?

One click after another, one profile after another, made me see there were lots of lonely men and women out there. I looked at the faces and the things they wrote.

Some were seemingly nice people. Some you would never consider, you could see they were players. Maybe this stuff was on the computer, but you could read between the lines and see unspoken truths. Was my husband's face on one of these sites saying he was lonely and misunderstood? If I see him, I will puke for sure.

Is distance bad? Or maybe it's good? I wasn't sure. Being so new to this, I knew I had a lot to learn and definitely had the time to do it. All the free time I needed, I was alone now.

My parents, his parents, everyone was worried and shocked. Everyone was worried if I would be okay, angry that he had left me. Saying things about him they never said before. I couldn't listen; I couldn't take the sad look on their faces.

I decided what was best was to be alone. I asked them to give me thirty days to adjust and get back on track. I was trying to stay focused on keeping the kids and myself calm. I assured them I would be fine, that they shouldn't worry, but they still did.

Chapter Six

Not everything is seen with the eye.
Some things need to be seen with the heart.

He put the journal down and picked up another, opening to where the pink slip extended, guided him. Before he began, he remembered this time he was about to read. This was, of all her experiences, the most difficult to live through. She sobbed so often, her body would tremble with fear as she shared her life with me. Within himself, he said to De, *"Are you sure?"* as if asking for permission.

He felt calmness within himself but was very aware this was going to be the worst of her life moments that she would be sharing with them. *Were they ready to hear this?* Still, he felt the need, the drive to continue. Everyone could see he was hesitating.

1972

I was so thankful to find refuge in a local church group. My only son was three, and I adored him. But my husband was determined to make life a living hell for me. I was so thankful I had found this bible group. The people were so wonderful, and I needed strength outside of myself to help me endure my life. The year is 1972. I had nowhere to run, to escape. Programs weren't available in those days for battered women. Where did I get the strength? Why was this happening?

My Mom raised me in Catholicism. She never went with us, but she had promised when she married my Dad that she would keep us in the church. She kept this promise, even though he left us when I was five and she raised us by herself.

Maybe this is where I got some of my strength. My Mom is a dedicated mother, an incredibly strong woman. I love and respect her so much.

Not many of my new friends knew of my circumstances at home.

Some couldn't even begin to understand what I was walking through. I tried to hide it as much as possible. The black eyes and bruises made it obvious. I would try to cover them, but it wasn't easy. No one said anything to me when they saw them. Why? They didn't want to get involved.

It occurred to me that people who followed the Messiah never had it easy. I must be on the right path, I would say to myself. Since I didn't have it easy by any stretch of the imagination. How I endured all this, I didn't know. I thought maybe I was like the disciples, Remembering how the disciples were persecuted made me feel I needed to be silent in these moments, since God was very aware of what was going on. He would rescue me. I would be rewarded in the end. I had things to learn first so I could teach others.

Some of the friends I made in the bible group were lifelong friends. Shar, was always there, she was never afraid. Never! I will always be thankful for her in my life, my sister, my anam cara.

Life gives us the mentors and guides we need to keep our eyes open. Watch for the signs. They say that darkness hides in the light. Is that true? You be the judge.

Let me continue.

My hand shakes as I walk through this storm for the very last time. I will pick one horrific storm since all after this will seem to be like a spring time shower.

1976

I will share this for others to learn, as I did. I never thought a man in my church would create even more nightmares for me, almost beyond hope? My voice will carry through the wind because of the terror he caused me and my family.

{Boldly written across the entry in red}

THIS IS TRUE
I SURVIVED AND CHOSE TO LIVE.
KARMA RETURNS IN SOME WAY.

Debra

No one will ever control me through fear and threats again. The only way to overcome fear is to confront it. Truth takes all the power to frighten and terrorize you away. Be patient, you will succeed, and the process is very rewarding. In time, in time. You will see…I did.

Looking back, I see that people like him target individuals such as myself. My abusive marriage and hard times are what predators look for, they lie in wait for their moment. I was so young and physically and emotionally drained and victimized. I had no idea I was walking from one storm into another. This path was a double storm, how does one survive?

As I write, you will believe. Believe that there are things that exist beyond our understanding and experiences. That as we believe in the good with the angels and spirit guides, that there are black angels of darkness, demons of the night, too. I pray you never have to walk the path I have.

I was not the only one he tried to control. There were others, too. Are they well today, as well as me? I pray so.

~

I loved and respected the founder of my new church. He was a kind and loving man. I will call him Dr. K. He taught with eloquence and love, giving to all what he had received from the Creator. He was so wonderful, and everyone loved him dearly. I learned from him and was confident that my life had a purpose. In the end, it would be worth all the trials I was going through. His life ended in 1976, his life in this realm. He continues, as we all do.

One evening in particular, a week or two after my teacher had passed, the phone rang. I was alone.

"Hello," I said.

A voice at the other end was crackly and almost hard to understand. I felt fear prickle through my skin, my hair stood up on end. The man's voice on the phone sounded like someone coming from the dead. The voice said, "Listen to Devin, to all he says, and you will live."

My knees went weak.

Was he pretending to be my teacher who passed to the next realm? How could he do something so callous and cruel? He knew how much I loved and respected him. I was without words. I hung up the phone, shaking horribly. Was this true? Did he have powers like this?

My sons, were they safe? I ran to their bedroom. Yes, they are asleep. Dreaming of good things, I pray.

You're wondering how I could be so afraid, how I could believe he was capable of such terror. Well, I had seen things come true that he said he had dreamt. Others knew of his dreams. I was so young and terrified.

Devin told me of dreams he had of himself as the death angel. Yes, the death angel! He explained the power given to him to allow those he chose to live or die. In his dream, he said he rode on a great horse and people would try to reach up to him to beg for their lives. He chooses some, and others he would destroy or pluck their eyes out so they couldn't see or find the way. He said it was a power that was given to him. I know this must sound like something from the Book of Revelations. He said he was the death angel.

*****

My mind is vibrating with moments. One after the other, almost as a child chattering to share with a parent. I write this to share the truth for those that knew of me then, or thought they did. But truly, they had not even a glimmer of the horror and fear for me and my children that I lived through. You were busy with your wondrous life, and I was stroking for air to continue to be.

~

Pops looked up at all the eyes staring at him in disbelief.

"I feel your pain and sadness. If I had been there, no one would have ever hurt your mother.

These are truths she had to release. Moments that she walked through that most would never have endured. Be patient, I need to finish this part and it will be done. It will be said and shared with you, whom she loved the most.

Leah tucked her head tighter into Michael's shoulder. Rob stirred on the floor in a trance, staring at the fire. Danny laid his head back on the edge of the couch as the tears flowed down his cheek. Reesie tried to comfort him. His jaw clenched with anger.

The words continued...

*****

Another day, he came running into my home. "Oh, my God," he said, "You won't believe what was on your front porch." He began to fill my mind, with his sight of a large black bird perched on my porch. The wingspan, he said, was huge, as he extended his arms. His power allowed him to direct the bird from my home, and it flew away. "You're safe now, he was waiting for you," Devin said.

I was terrified and wanted to collapse. How much more must I take?

He knew I was trying to escape his control. He smiled wickedly, as he said no one would believe me and he was right. At times, he would force me into my own cellar with his threatening words. The dirt floor and stench of the old house resonated my nostrils. How could he do this to me? I closed my eyes and prayed. If I didn't do as he said, he told me, my life and those of my husband and sons were in his hands. My disobedience would cause terrible things to happen. I suppose you're wondering how could I believe this?

Well, fear is a very powerful tool. Some use it for control. Unless you have lived it and believed it, you can't truly comprehend it. It wasn't only Devin, it was also the fear I had with my husband.

Yet, I don't have the same anger towards him as I do Devin. I am not sure why. Maybe because I loved him at one time. My husband was in as much pain as me, maybe more. Yet, he created his pain, his choices and decisions were his. He would never listen to me. I loved my husband when we married, but as the years passed the abuse he put me through killed every ounce of love I once had for him.

I would do anything to keep my family safe. Even to the point of sacrificing myself, my very being. God would bring me through this somehow, some way. I was a victim of them both. Yet my husband never knew his life was in danger. If I told him, Devin would be dead; I just couldn't take a life. My silence was deafening.

Many more moments' of visions he had. Telling me of a vision of his nephew falling from a large cliff and becoming paralyzed. Telling me if I told what he had done to me, my son would hang himself when he was thirteen. Will he read this journal someday? Maybe so. Maybe his family will read it, and then they will realize terror in the truest sense that takes your very being from you. So much to write, so much to remember, or should I just write it this last time and let the God of the Universe do as it will...yes, this is the last time.

*****

I recall him talking often to me of a woman dressed in black. Devin said she constantly walked through my home, my life. She shared things with him. Warned of death and darkness that would happen to my family and me because I left Devin's side. I would be safe if I stayed and believed. His eyes darkened as he watched my silent reactions.

That is how I responded most of the time, in silence. I needed to protect my family.

The big old house we lived in was possessed. It had stained glass windows throughout, with pictures of the children who had been born there and died. I had no idea until I escaped what these windows represented. What is there to understand? How does one explain these real life moments? Was this house pulling him and this woman in black toward us? This isn't a movie. It is real, things like this do exist in this world.

Years later, I learned something from my son, when I told him about some of the horror of those days. He looked at me so seriously and said, "Mom? When I was little, once I woke in the night and she was there sitting next to my bed. I tried to call to you, yet the words wouldn't come out of my mouth." God, it was true. The evil was there. It was there.

"Deb," Devin would say, extending his hands in front of his chest, "You are right here in the palm of my hands."

I looked at his hands. Face up, extended and touching.

"I have the power to give you life or…" then he closed his hands together tightly "…or death," he said.

I was silent again.

I found out what evil he was capable of. He will answer for this one day. If he reads this, he knows who he is. Many will know who he is. Now you will understand as well. Don't make judgments on events until you walk in someone else's shoes. What you see with your eyes might be hiding the reality of what is really taking place.

~

Where I have grown to now is such a blessing, I don't even hate him anymore. This took years to be able to say. To say this genuinely after all that was done is growth for me, the beginning of my new life. To be in fear of him and what happened gives that power over me still, if I allow it. This is a lesson in life I wish for no one to experience.

The next step was to go on and walk with trust and faith that the Messiah would get us through it. I had to trust him, and I did. The analogy I can try to explain of this time would be as if you were walking through a dark alley with your eyes wide open, holding your breath and praying you will be safe, anxious to get to the other side. Saying a constant prayer, "Please keep me and my boys safe. Please...please..." That was my mantra.

I found the courage somewhere within my soul to finally say no. Enough is enough. I have to raise my boys in a peaceful life, no matter what. No to the physical and emotional abuse from my husband. No to Devin and his terror and intimidation.

Was it really going to be that easy? Many nights living in fear, hearing strange sounds outside. A few nights, I heard someone trying to open my front door, but it was always locked. What a relief it is locked. Would he have someone else hurt me?

Would they ever go away? Oh God, would I be okay? It was hard to sleep for years after I left him. In my new life with Tom, I would jump in my sleep, only to wake to his soft, comforting touch. He was there, and no one would hurt the boys or me.

I write this in my journal to release. Someday someone will read and see, and understand that we don't have to live through these things. Someone is there to help us.

Times have changed. It will never happen to me again. I have learned so much, becoming wise in the task of survival and maturing in life. I continued in my church group without anyone knowing. Yet, now they do.

*****

"Wait..." Leah knelt next to him with tears flowing down her face. Her shaking hand touched his leg. "Pops, what is this? What is she writing?"

The room was still with sadness and disbelief this could have taken place to their mother. Sadness none had known of until now. Why now?

He stroked her hair. "It is a storm, a nightmare she walked through. This happens to many women. It still is, but maybe one will have the courage the hope it will be over and how your mother did it. Your mother touched lives, many lives because of this. She still had the scars and hid them well. Within her soul. You saw your mom, all of you saw her, and she was strong and determined. A teacher of survival in all the storms she walked through, she taught how to dance in the rain. Remember, sunshine and rain, angel, it made her unique. There was no one I had ever met like your Momma.

"She had to write it down. Share the book, her story. With us and with the world. This is probably the hardest part to put in her book. I thought maybe that she had changed her mind about getting it published. Now look, she was going to surprise us on Christmas, I am sure."

Deb stood beside Leah, touching her hair.
It didn't move.
"Can I touch her, please...let her feel me?
This is so hard on her."

"Patience, he will make them understand."

"You never knew because she didn't want you to know until the time was right. The boys were older and had heard brief references to her past. She couldn't share these things totally with you, angel, or them. That life was finished. It was her holocaust of sorts. That door is closed, and she and the boys were survivors."

"Leah, remember how Mom would always say out of everything bad something good comes from it?" said Dan.

"Yes, you remembered."

"Yes," Leah answered.

"She kept this inside herself and kept going forward. The good was all of us and Pops. All the women she has spent time with and helped at the Women's Center. We don't understand why, but we see the end result." Danny finished. He reached for Leah across the floor, Rob came over, and they all silently embraced each other.

"Is this what the Memory Barrel is about?" she said as she tried to regain her composure as she touched the barrel.

"Not entirely. Your memory barrel doesn't have the painful

times in there, but they existed around the good times. She was always trying to shelter you from them, as you will also do for your kids." He paused for a moment. "The memory barrel is that, memories. Memories to make you smile, to look back on and remember the good times.

"This memory barrel book is hers, to share the truth and honesty…that tears, and smiles are what make you grow. She had to write this down for you and the family. Everything happens for a reason, to learn from, it's for a purpose. To know where you have come from and how much she loved you. How much she still loves you. She is here. You sense her, I sense her."

The tree branches tapped on the window.

Everyone jumped, looking in its direction.

Leah started laughing, "Okay, Mom, I see. I know I am learning. You're still teaching me, aren't you?"

Pop said, "Okay, baby doll, I know you're here, too, now let me finish this. Then come play with me in your realm tonight!"

Everyone laughed and understood what he meant.

"Thank you"
"My pleasure."

~*~*~*~

Chapter Seven

A rainbow always follows the storm.
Watch for the signs.

Everyone settled in, more intent to listen to the life of this woman they all loved. This was her life lesson to them. Live, no matter what, all for the love.

"Ok, where was I?" Pops said as he touched the journals. Looking at the tabs, they pulled him ahead in time.

*****

I have to continue moving forward; try not to relive those experiences. I need to live my life now for today and the tomorrows. Look at me trying to find Tom. What was I doing? I kept driving, and my mind was racing.

~

Rob spoke, "This is back in the early 80s, right? That's when she first met Tom, isn't it?

Pop looked at the cover of the journal, "Yes, you're right."

"I remember this story. This is a great story. It's one of her *angel things*." Danny said.

His reading continued:

Tom was the head chef at a local restaurant. In our few conversations, he mentioned he lived near work. Where is his car? I knew I would find it. But where? As I turned the corner, there it was. I no sooner spoke it, and there it was. I found it. No, I was *guided* to it. I laughed and closed my eyes, "Thank you", as I placed the note beneath his wiper blades.

The note read:

Tom,

Could you meet me at the old railroad station tomorrow in Horseheads? I will be there around 7pm.

We need to talk.

Debby

As I drove away, my heart felt like it was going to beat out of my chest. How could I tell anyone what happened today, and would they believe me if I did? I am smiling because I know it's true. It happened to me. I guess that is all that counts. I am still in shock, I can't believe I found him. In this huge town, I found his car. Was this a sign from God? Was he giving me hope that I was going to be ok?

"Did you do that for me?"
"We did that for you.
It was so strong within your heart and you just let us guide you.
We all shared in the joy and excitement with you.
You're still adjusting, but there is pleasure here in our existence.
We guide and watch over all, sometimes the humans will come so close
to their dream.
Then they go in a different direction.
We know it will come again, though.
It just takes them believing it and allowing it with no resistance.
You have learned that over the years, princess."
"Yes, I remember...Esther and Abraham...
Where is Abraham? Is he here?"
"Of course, but we all are Abraham that you knew of through Esther.
Each has a name, as you have named me Nathaniel.
To you, I have always been Nathaniel.
We, and now you, are life energy.
The life energy that was within the flesh form you were in was only a
segment of you.
The rest of the wholeness of you surrounded you.
Your fullness of you and your essence is now. What you are

experiencing now is the true essence of you.
Humans get a glimpse of us from time to time.
You will understand more as we continue.
Tonight is going to be the beginning of your clarity.
Here in this state, there is no time as the physical realm senses it.
"And no rules," Debra added.
She sensed the laughter, not just from the light beside her, but around her, too.

~~

The reading brought her back to them.

The next day came, and I arranged for the boys to be with my mom so I could go meet Tom.

I wonder what he is thinking. Will he even be there?

When I arrived home, the phone was ringing.

"Hello."

"Remember?!" the voice at the other end shouted. "Remember the dream I told you I had?! You found someone else, and your face was burned. You were unrecognizable. I saw you walking down the street. Do you remember? The old woman told me this wouldn't happen if you stayed with me. Do you remember? I saw you in your casket."

My soul trembled. It was so hard to listen. I thought he was gone. The phone just dangled in my hand. He had remarried, and I stayed hidden from his presence. Was he doing this to his new wife? Was she living in terror? How could I stop him when he was darkness in totality?

"Yes! I do! I remember everything you have said. I want you to leave me alone! Leave me alone!" I screamed.

"What about your son?" he said. "He will hang himself. It doesn't have to happen. Just do what I say, and everyone will be safe."

The silence within my soul after hearing all his threats and warnings caused a rage to come forth. "You will pay for this, Devin! You will answer for all of the things you have done to me and others."

I slammed the phone down.

Hang himself? He did say my son would hang himself. I won't allow the fear to take me again. He is demonic for saying these things to me and using my son to terrorize me.

"Nathaniel??" Her emotions flowed. Not of fear, as it was then, but for lack of understanding.
"It was difficult, but we never left your side.
As we never left your mother's when she struggled with life.
From it all, sweet one, you became a teacher. You became a guide.
A person cannot guide without knowing the path.
You lived so many experiences, to say you walked the path. That is where a true teacher comes from. The road less traveled, as is said in their realm."
"I did feel alone so often within them."
"We were there."
"He would have killed me...and my children."
"He would not have been allowed to do this.
He existed to enhance your learning.
This made your soul clear on your direction and the path you were to walk.
You made these choices before you came to that realm. Not for lessons of endurance, but of experience, to create a life most dream of.
You did this.
You believed, sweet princess that life was to be enjoyed. Yet, how would you know of joy without experiencing sorrow?
You were always strong, but had to be shown you were through moments of challenge.
It allowed your eyes and senses to be more aware of the magic of life, of your life.
With all you walked through, you had to learn to trust.
You had to learn to trust the voice within and to know those you needed would be brought to you when you were in the place to hear and listen. You had to trust your spirit of life that surrounded you. The creator of this universe adores you, and you needed to adore you, too!
We will talk more as the words of your story continue.
All answers will be given, you will understand."

Leah got up and started pacing the floor. It was hard hearing these words from her mother's journals. "How could this be? I never knew," she said to Michael. "I never knew."

The room was stirring hearing the truth of the past.

"Why didn't someone go to the police? Is he still alive? I hope not."

"Okay, everyone take a breath. It isn't only for you. She always felt this book would make others realize evil is sometimes beyond our imaginations, yet it exists. It's her words. You need to know her life lessons are in here. We'll cast this book out there like her message in a bottle. I will try to check tomorrow with her publisher to see what we have to do next," Pop said, trying to make them understand.

Leah settled next to Lacey as she slept. The night was getting colder. Dan put more wood on the fire.

His strong voice seemed to tremble as he continued to read.

I felt fear and anger cover my body. What if he makes it happen? No. God is stronger than this. It will not happen.

How was this going to stop? No one in his family believed me when I tried to tell them, but he told me they wouldn't. I never told my husband because he threatened his life, too. In any case, he was not in any condition to protect me. He was destroying himself with his drugs and with his own mind. How could he? I had to run from them both…and truly, for my life, for my sons' lives.

"Okay, okay," I thought. "Take a deep breath…"

Now it is time to just make this very clear, how this could have happened. Once and for all, as you read this it will be shared. Devin was my father-in-law. Evil revealed now, for all he did to me and others. It is time. I prayed that the angels would please help me through this.

I was terrified and should have called the police, but he had intimidated me so much over the years, how could I? I needed to let it go and hope he would eventually leave me alone.

After reliving the fear again from the call, I realized and convinced myself that I had to tell Tom, that we no longer would be able to see each other. I knew he cared for me, and I liked him, but for his own safety and mine, I had to end it.

The boys liked him, and I knew he would be good for them. Anything was better than what they had been through. I think they have blocked some of it out, and this is good. I don't want them to remember. Not all of it. I wish I could wave a magic wand and heal them of it all. I think I have blocked out some of it as well. As I write this through the tears, I cry for what I do remember.

This affected my boys, but I didn't realize how much until they got older. I am sorry. I love you so.

I regained my composure and walked into the living room, where they were watching cartoons. All was right with the world. No one would hurt them again. Not if I had anything to say about it.

"Hey, guys…let's get going. I have to get you to Grandma's."

It was a little early, but I needed to do this. When I turned the corner, Tom's car was sitting there. I was surprised. He was early, too.

My heart pounded.

How could I even begin to explain my life, my future? I went up to his car and tapped on the window.

He smiled that smile that lit up his face. "Hey," he said as I opened the car door.

"Hey, yourself."

"Are you okay? The boys?" I think he sensed a stirring inside me.

"Oh yes, we're fine…I just needed to see you and share something with you. It won't take long."

He had no idea. No one had any idea what was happening in my life or happened. I started to cry.

"Hey, hey." His hand patted mine. "What's happened? What's the matter?" Tom was very much aware of my current situation but knew nothing of the nightmares I had come through.

{I owned a video game room called Galileo's. Tom's brother worked for me. Many times, my ex-husband came in yelling, trying to scare me. It wasn't so easy for him to intimidate me there. The football players from the local high school were always looking out for the boys and me. Abusers do not like to have witnesses.}

I took a deep breath. I had to do this, to keep him safe. I hesitated. "You know I like you. And I know you like me. I love it when you come into Galileo's and play on my foosball table, knowing I get all the money. Then your flirty smiles, I love it. But in all truth, you have no idea how dangerous it is for you. The world I have come from and what I am trying to escape is filled with fear beyond your imagination. To bring you into it would be selfish of me. It would be hard for anyone to believe, so much so that I can't believe it myself."

Debby tried to laugh to convince him she was all right, but laughter wasn't going to come easy at this point and time. In time, I will understand why. 'Til then, I need to keep everyone safe that I can.

"I had to let you know how happy you made me. It was so exciting. This meeting was to let you know we can't see each other anymore and to try to explain why."

He listened with a sad and concerned look on his face.

I explained that I did not know what would happen and that I was concerned for his and his family's safety. That the people in my past were quite dangerous and I would not want anything to happen to him. When I finished, we both were crying.

"Could I ask you a favor?" I said as I reached for the handle on the door.

"Sure."

"Would you give me a goodbye kiss?" I couldn't believe the words actually came out of my mouth. It was what I had been thinking but didn't think I dared to say.

He slowly reached over, pulled me to him, and kissed me softly and gently.

I pulled back slowly and looked at him.

He had a smirk on his face.

"What? What was that? That wasn't a kiss goodbye?"

"No, it most definitely wasn't." He wiped the tears from my cheek. "Deb, go home now to those boys, and I will be over tomorrow night with dinner."

I numbly opened the door and went to my car. I had never been kissed like that. I felt a breath of fresh air, as if everything was going to be all right.

By the time I arrived home, my mom had put the boys to bed. She could see I had been crying.

"Thanks," I whispered to her. "I love you."

"I love you, too, hon."

I cried myself to sleep that night. It was partly in relief for actually telling my story to another human being.

Nathaniel could feel calmness within Debra.
"Do you see?"
"Yes, I see. It was so free writing this in my journal.
Now this will be told to the world."
"Yes, it will," Nathaniel said.
"It is time."
"Yes, this is a new beginning for me."
"Where is he, Nathaniel, is he harming anyone else?"
"He is as he is supposed to be.
Age has taken hold of many of his actions.
Now you teach others from your words being shared.
With Tom, your joy was brought back to you."
"I see."
"We will not allow any harm to you through them again."

The reading continued:

As time went on, we shared every moment we could together. My life kept flowing out like a flood of pain and tears being released. I wanted no secrets from him, he had to know everything. He was strong.

"You're going to be safe with me."

I wasn't alone anymore. I had my soul mate, my best friend. Wow...

We had been discussing marriage, and on New Year's Eve he told me his resolution was to marry me before the next year ended. Everything was shared, I had released all the sadness and terror to another person. Now life was changing so quickly, and I am so in love with him.

As we sat on the couch, it came, a thought came to me I had forgotten. It could change everything.

"Wait...I have to tell you something...this is important."

He sat there, so serious, not knowing what I was going to say.

"I won't be able to have a child." I started to cry. The words vibrated through my soul. How could I have not said this to him before we had come this far? I had my tubes tied when Danny was three. I didn't want any more children. I couldn't take care of more children or subject them to this life.

He pulled me close. "Hey, stop it. I love you and the boys. That is enough for me."

Chapter Eight

Ask, then allow, with no resistance

We were married later that year. I felt like I was in heaven. After a year, we decided to try to adopt a baby. Tom was such a good husband and stepdad, yet still I wanted more. Someday, I wanted to be able to say, "Tom, I'm pregnant." How could this even be possible? All things are possible if I believe? The adoption route seemed to be the path we were convinced to walk, so we continued. I'm smiling, though, as I write this, thinking... "I never gave up the hope that nothing is impossible." Look at how God opened the Red Sea to bring life to Israel. History proves all is possible. It was never out of my mind.

I wanted to feel his child within me. The magic that happens between a mother and child is a reflection of the magic between a husband and wife. We patiently waited for our name to move up on the adoption list. In time, we would have our baby.

Two summers came and passed. We decided to take a vacation with the boys on Keuka Lake. We found a nice cottage to rent for a week, and it wasn't too far from where we lived. This way, Tom could still work a few days to help finance this vacation. I worked at the local hospital, and this was my vacation time.

This memory is one that I stir to look back on. Thankful for the outcome, understanding we aren't in total control of our own destiny. I have lived believing that all my life. The best lessons in life are ones of experience.

~

The day was sunny, and Robby and Danny brought two friends with them. We all fished off the dock most of the morning. This was a good vacation for them. They were really enjoying themselves. It was the perfect idea, the perfect vacation for all of us.

Tom returned to the cottage after work. It was about an hour's drive for him. I was so excited to see him and share the fun the boys had been having. As we walked towards the water, he looked off the dock and saw a bobber out on the water.

"Hey, what's that?" He pointed out on the lake.

I laughed. "Oh, the boys lost it off their pole today. They had such a good time."

No sooner had I begun explaining how the day had gone, when, without hesitation, he started taking his shoes and shirt off.

"What are you doing?" I felt a bit of fear, yet I knew exactly what he was doing.

"Let's go get it." And as quick as he said it, he jumped in the water.

I laughed at his enthusiasm and half-wished that I could join him, but I couldn't swim. When he reached the bobber, about thirty feet or so away from the dock, he looked at me. A look I will never forget. Then suddenly, he went below the surface. I couldn't see him. Briefly, his head came above the water and his voice quivered...

"I can't." His voice was so faint, so hard to hear.

Panic went through my body like an electrical shock, making my legs almost give way. I screamed, "What?" as I waited to see his head surface above the water. He surfaced and said it once more, "I can't," and disappeared under the water.

The sound that came out from my soul was filled with terror, knowing I couldn't swim out. Did it occur to me to try? The seconds were like hours. My boys - I needed to live for them - I couldn't save him. His death seemed imminent. I screamed louder than I ever had in my life. "No...no!! Please, please, no!!"

Robby came running out of the cottage, hearing my scream. He ran straight past me, diving into the water.

Did I say anything to him? How did he know? I froze in time, crying and pleading to God. Then Robby came up from beneath the water, he had Tom. He was alive. I was unable to speak - all I knew was how thankful I was that my son was safe and he had saved Tom's life. Robby's friend Eric came out with as much speed as Robby, he was seconds behind him and jumped in to help.

They brought Tom to shore, and we pulled him up on the dock. His face held the stillness of one who was ready to pass on to the next realm.

Tom explained later that his legs had cramped from the cold of the water and he couldn't move them.

My son was a hero. I am honored to be his mother. "Robby," I said. "I love you so much. Thank you. Thank you."

He smiled his smile that said, "I love you, Mom."

I was so proud of him.

The moment passed so quickly. Why didn't I call an ambulance? He assured me he was okay. His legs were moving now, and he was getting color back, coming back to this world. Robby should have been honored with a medal.

He was so selfless in this rescue. He did it for me. Tom never spoke of this day, ever. Looking back, I don't even think that Tom thanked him. Could this have been a part of Tom I didn't want to see? The part that couldn't admit he did wrong or made a bad decision? I would come to understand this and see this side of him much later, though.

*****

The room filled with a soft cheer. Everyone was being careful not to wake the little ones.

"Yayy, Rob! Yayyyy Robby!"

The memory made them all so proud of him. It was good to walk back. The grandchildren had no idea this had even taken place.

Barbie gave him a big hug. "I love you, Dad!"

Rob lowered his head, remembering, walking in his own little memory moment. With stirring feelings inside.

"I love you, Robby."
He heard a small voice inside.
It made him smile...

"Nathaniel, I know I am asking so much, but why did that happen?"
"It was for Robby and Tom.
He had to see he was special, always loved and needed by you.
Tom had to learn to appreciate life, to say thank you.
"But he didn't."
"Not with words he didn't, but he did."

*****

The old gent knew he had to take a moment for himself. "Just a sec, kids. Nature call, okay?"

Everyone laughed and shifted around in the little cabin in the woods.

Danny tucked the blanket around Lilly even tighter. Michael snuggled closer to Leah. Everyone was safe and together. A piece of their life was missing, and they didn't know how to visualize their lives after tonight. But they would. It will come to them. In time.

The elderly gent struggled to stand but tried not to show his difficulty. A soft growl came out as he tried to be entertaining. He walked past the sleeping grandbabies and smiled. His life was changed now. How would he adjust to it? *I have to. It'll be fine*. He sighed to himself. *It'll be fine*.

Pops returned. He had to splash some cool water on his face to camouflage the exhaustion. "Here we go."

"Wait, Pop." Leah stood up and pulled Deb's chair close to him. "Let me read for a while."

"Okay, angel, I know your mom would like that."

Barbie called out, "Grami *does* like that!"

He smiled at Barb as he handed the journals to Leah. Her smile said everything. It was a family moment tonight. His empty hands rested in his lap. A little hand reached up softly to touch his knee.

It was Savanna… She whispered, "Can I cuddle with you, Poppy?"

"Well, I just can't think of anything I would enjoy more, little one."

She crawled up with her stuffed kitty and blanket and snuggled up under his arm.

Chapter Nine

Follow the stepping stones to your dreams

Leah's gentle voice continued the story.

The adoption quest was still in full effect. We had heard nothing but hoped it would come true someday. Tom and I were more in love than ever.

Robby and Danny had rough roads walking through their teen years. Rougher than most, I think. I had prayed that they would be okay. I think that's every mother's prayer is that for her children to grow up happy and be at peace. I saw them doing things or acting in a way that concerned me, and I would constantly blame myself. I should have taken them away from that world when they were younger. It had damaged them. The scars were there on their hearts. But there was nowhere for me to go for help back then. My husband threatened if I left, he would have my mother killed and be in church when it happened if I left him. How do you escape that thought? Then with the terror of Devon too. I am not going back; enough words have been shared in my writing, no going back.

Leah was visibly shaken as she read aloud this portion of her mother's journey.

I know they love me beyond words, and I absolutely adore them. We are going to make it. I would do everything I could to help them make it. I've always believed love can conquer all, and I had more than enough love to go around. Looking back and remembering, the words "if only" come to mind. "If only." I stir inside as I hear those words in my heart. I will write more of this memory later.

Days, weeks, and years passed. Danny was now nine, and Robby sixteen. I decided to contact my doctor to see if there was any hope of becoming pregnant again. I felt a burning desire to have another baby. It had never left me. So I called the doctor, and we met with him. I could hardly contain my excitement.

"Debby," Dr. Miller said, "I don't know if you realize how much the odds are against you to have a successful surgery. This is a relatively new procedure, having a tubal reversal. As far as the age difference between you and Tom, it's actually perfect. Perfect for the cycle you both will be going through." He explained that when I would be going through a change of cycle, Tom would be, too. He helped us understand that women usually outlive men, so this eleven year difference in age was ideal. We were both rather surprised by his enthusiasm for us.

He continued. "This is a laser surgery, and you will be in the operating room for around four hours. You have to bear in mind, you have only a five percent chance of success." He watched to see if my obvious determination changed. It didn't. If he had said one percent, I would have said let's do it.

He was very graphic. "Debby, the incision will be hip to hip," he paused.

I listened intently...

"If you don't get pregnant within one year, scar tissue will form in the tubes again and be blocked."

"I'd like to proceed, Doctor." I knew I didn't need a year. I knew it.

Tom and I agreed that we wanted to take the chance on the surgery and scheduled it for February 18th. I felt no fear at all. I knew this was in God's hands. Yet I was still a bit nervous, I had never had any operations.

On February 18th, I woke from the surgery to see my husband standing by the bed and my mom sitting in the chair next to me. My poor mom had walked beside me through everything. Now she wore such a sad face. She knew how much this meant to me.

"Hi," I said, smiling at her.

Her hand was resting on the side of the bed. Tom had left the room to talk with the doctor. The pain was intense, but I needed to keep it concealed because I could see how upset she was.

"Mom," as I touched her hand, "what are the tears for?"

"I didn't realize how much you loved him."

*****

The following morning, I was so excited, even though I was still weak. I was very anxious to get home. Tom opened our front door, and as soon as I stepped inside, I was surrounded with a lovely aroma. It was a smell I had never smelled before, like sweet soap.

"Do you smell that?

Tom said, "What?"

"That sweet smell in the air?"

"No," and walked upstairs to put my suitcase away.

I never forgot that smell; I would smell it one more time.

{Nathaniel sensed her question.}
"Yes, you were becoming aware of the signs."
"I am learning now the why of my life, aren't I?"
"Yes, you're seeing your life with a new vision.
It became a much clearer view for you, princess."

April came quickly. This was when we could try to get pregnant, and by June I was. I couldn't believe it! It was an angel thing, my dream was coming true. I had Tom's baby inside me. I never realized how powerful your thoughts could be. My heart races just to think of it again. Think it, you create it. Believe it, you will see it. I never know then what I know now. I see...I get it.

My life was changing, and all for the better. Nightmares from the past were fading, echoes of the past were buried in the archives and the stillness of my heart. This moment was one of many rainbows that would appear in my life that I cherish. To have a rainbow, you have to walk through the rain. The sun appears and turns the storm to magic...

It had been such a good life for the last four years. This was a dream come true. I was pregnant! We were pregnant!!

My baby was a gift from the angels to show me that they loved me...everything of my journey was worth it to bring me to this place.

The phone rang.

"Debby?" the voice at the other end said.

"Yes?"

"This is Mrs. Albrecht from the adoption agency. Your names are now at the top of our list. We would like to begin conducting the process now for you to receive your baby. You've waited for such a long time. I am sure you're as excited as we are for you."

I couldn't believe what I was hearing. I had forgotten to call her and tell her the good news. Three years had passed while we waited on this list, and now I was pregnant. It was all so amazing.

"Mrs. Albrecht, I'm pregnant!"

"Debby, I am so happy for you and Tom." Her laughter echoed through the phone. "Be well, and enjoy your new baby," she said.

I couldn't wait for Tom to get home to tell him about the call.

Danny overheard my excitement as I spoke to Mrs. Albrecht. "Mom, let's still take the adopted baby, too, this way we know it will be a girl and then we'll have two babies."

"Oh my," I thought. "No, Danny, we'll take what we are given."

*****

Leah was born in March. She was almost born on the highway. The drive to the hospital was over thirty minutes from where we lived, the pain was unbearable.

"Breathe, breathe!" I kept saying to myself, trying to stay focused as Tom pulled into the hospital parking lot. The doors to the emergency room seemed like they were miles away as one contraction came after another. Tom held me close as I breathed through each one and we hurried inside.

We found a wheelchair, and Tom rushed me up the elevator. We both were so overwhelmed and excited, knowing what was taking place this March night. A nurse was sitting quietly behind the desk, enjoying the solitude of the evening. She hadn't heard us exit the elevator. I stood and leaned on the desk. I laughed at her surprised look.

"Hello!" she said.

"I am so ready to have our baby!" I tried to keep taking panting breaths. I was so relieved to be there, I thought I was going to have my baby in the car.

"Well then, follow me." She walked us to a birthing room. Leah was born less than ninety minutes later. I was eight centimeters on arrival.

Then the words that came out of my doctor's mouth, "You have a baby girl."

"A girl? A little girl." I repeated it over and over. "Thank you. Thank you." My heart ached to touch her. They gave her to me wrapped in a small blanket. Her first moments in my arms were peaceful beyond words. Tom and I adored her, kissing her fingers, touching her cheeks. Then it happened…the look!

Her lower lip curled down like a pout, and out it came, the sweetest cry to my ears. "Awww," we both said, sharing the moment, one that would never come again. (That look still comes even now when she wants her way.) We love it still.

Pops said, "Let's see the look, Leah!!!"
She was surprised to hear him ask for it. "What?"
"Oh, come on, sis, you still have it."
Michael laughed. "Yes, she does. She shows it to me all the time."
With her eyes rolling and the cutest smirk, she did it. The lips puckered out, and there it was.

It was so much fun to hear everyone laugh.
That is how you get through the sadness: hold on to each other, and try to find moments to laugh about.

~

Leah continued reading...

Our neighbor brought Danny to the hospital to meet his new baby sister. It was after one o'clock in the morning. Tom and I promised him no one else would touch her after she was born until he did. To this day, they enjoy a bond that was created in that birthing room.

Robby lived in Florida with his father. A concerned choice he made, he was seventeen and quite difficult in his ways. He was walking his own life path. I had to let him go and trust he would be watched over. Our journey of life was unexpected, but for him, just loving him wasn't enough. I miss him.

Leah was born at 12:08 a.m, the first Easter baby of the year, my Leah. My little angel face. I was the happiest woman on the face of this earth. She slept so peacefully that first night beside me. She never left my side from the moment she left my body.

"Until today, I was always in her sight and she in mine."
"Yes, as it was meant to be.
She will see you clearer here than the others.
She is your anam cara and has always been with you.

Before this time as well.
She and you agreed of the meeting again.
It will always continue, you each are reflections of the other."

Leah's voice brought her back.

At 8:30 a.m. the doctor came to check on us. I was giving her a bath. I had already planned to ask if I could take her home. Take us home where we belonged.

"Hi, Debby and Leah," Dr. Miller said. "Let's get you in bed so I can see how you're doing. I have a C-section I am on my way to now. So hurry!"

"All right." I hesitated. "Can I take her home?"

"Now?" he asked. He was shocked at my asking.

"Yes, now."

"She's only eight hours old!"

"I'll be careful, and I'll bring her back for whatever you want, just please can I take her home?"

He smiled as he shook his head in disbelief. He nudged me to the bed. "Yes, yes, get over there and let me check if you're ready to go home, too."

At 9:30 a.m., we were on our way home. All of us together as a family. It was like magic, a dream come true.

As we entered the house…the smell…the sweet smell was there again, I carried Leah through the door. What was it? I looked at Tom, asking, "Do you smell that?"

Again, he shook his head no.

This was the second time it occurred. What was it? Why was I the only one that could smell it?

As time went on, I read that your angels let you know they are with you by smells and things appearing from time to time. Ah, the angels gathered to be with my angel.

It was a perfect day.

*****

"All right, it's my turn," Danny said. "Little angel Leah, it's my turn. Since I was the first to touch you when you were born, other than Mom and Tom, I will be the next reader."

"Hey, hero man over there, wanna use those amazing biceps and put some more wood on the fire?" Dan teased him.

Rob sighed. "I think that sounds like a wonderful idea, *little brother!"* he sarcastically teased.

There was calmness in the little cabin now. The experiences were allowing them to feel more at peace. That was the idea, to guide them through this. Reminisce, smile and hold on to each other and walk. You're together, not alone. If you keep walking, the trauma of life passes in time. The bond is eternal, and the veil that divided the realms is invisible when you feel the love of family.

Another little hand reached up. "Poppa, can I come up there, too?" Lilly's big brown eyes just made him melt.

"Wellllll, you betcha...let's go over to the couch, and I can have both my little ones with me. How does that sound?"

As Rob lifted Savanna, it was very obvious he was tired and Dan picked up Lilly. Pops looked a little rough around the edges.

"Now, wait a sec. I think I have four angels. Hmm, one, two...where is my other little angel?"

Lacey whispered, "I'm over here, Poppy."

He closed his eyes. "Well, maybe if I wish hard enough, I will have three angels on my lap."

He closed his eyes...

Lacey tiptoed over; clutching her teddy that Meme had given her. Just then, it started to play its music.

He opened one eye. "I think I hear music."

"Oh, it is Meme's teddy, Poppy." She tucked herself in next to him just perfectly.

"One more, I have one more. Not so small, though, a young lass. Miss Sarah, would you come beside me, too, baby girl?" A shy smile lit on her face. She was a teenager, but not too old for a Grandpa moment.

"Sure."

"There," he growled like a big old bear. "Now, Poppy is a happy bear."

The girls loved him so.

~*~*~*~

Chapter Ten

Life's unexpected surprises...

Dan picked up the blue journal. He knew that was what he
was to read from.

Memories: 1990

We moved to Rutland, Vermont, when Leah was three years old.
Danny was thirteen and starting the magnificent years of puberty.

**Danny stopped reading and laughed so loud. "Oh God, no! I
know where this is going. Mom! Funny, very funny!!!!**

Deb laughed merrily. "Gotcha!"

Do they truly have books to prepare parents for puberty? It seemed to
happen overnight. Your angel turns into a creature that thrives on
rebellion and disobedience that he calls "Independence."
    Tom and I went into the quest of puberty with Danny as students and
came out as professors. To teach him or us? What lessons were learned?
The understanding that my sons were guilty until proven innocent was
our daily mantra.

(Leah laughed)

Sex isn't an activity? Try to convince them of this. Boys don't care
about rules when they are tantalized by over-sexed teenage girls. All the
thoughts of Mom and her love disappear when they discover sex. They
seem to have the notion that they're indestructible and if it feels good, do
it. I wouldn't wish boys and puberty on any parent. One lesson I did learn
was not to make them your enemy. Always keep the lines of
communication open somehow. I can say this now with a smile, even

though back then smiles were definitely not on my face. But I loved them, and they knew it.

Football came into our life. Tom convinced Danny to play. We thought maybe it would release some excess energy and help him to understand some life lessons. He was good, really good at it. Just like lightning on the field. It was so natural for him to be there.

We all loved Rutland. Things were just good, very good for all of us. I think this was one of those peaceful times for me. My life was simple, taking care of Leah and our home. Cleaning houses occasionally, to help take the financial pinch off our lives.

We are taught in life to expect the unexpected. This was such a surprise. Was I ready for it? No!

I was pregnant again. Amazed? Lord knows I was!

My doctor had told me three years ago, if I didn't get pregnant in the first year, scar tissue would form on the inside of my tubes, making it impossible for me to conceive. We got pregnant then so quickly. I assumed, yes, assumed, that my tubes had closed by now. Boy, was I wrong!

I couldn't wait to tell Tom. He didn't show too much emotion over it, I think he was numb like me. Leah was only three, but she understood Mommy had a baby in her belly. Danny was very excited. Robby still lived in Florida, newly married with a two-year-old daughter of his own, Barbie. She was beautiful. Yes, I was a Grami, with a three-year-old and having another baby. One for the books, as far as my life had been going.

I became very active in the Headstart program in Rutland. Spending time helping whenever I could, I enrolled Leah there, too. A plus was being there for Leah to see me on occasion. I should say for me to see Leah. I loved kids, and this was so much fun for me. I met new friends and helped with the parent meetings.

My pregnancy was going fine. Everyone was so happy for us. I was four months along when I started to bleed just a bit. I called my new doctor, and he examined me.

"You have to go on bed rest immediately," he said.

I did everything he told me to do. We had already bought the crib for the baby. I always was very organized and hated to wait for the last minute to do anything. Even with the bed rest, the bleeding became worse and the doctor ordered an ultrasound. Tom was so strong for the both of us. He knew how much I wanted this baby. It was a double gift for me, a double portion from God.

"Debby," the doctor said, "there is nothing we can do. You're losing the baby."

How was I going to tell my kids, my husband, and my family?

I cried when they weren't looking. Why was it so hard for me to do in front of them? I remember my mother did this, too. I needed to learn to cry in front of them. I needed to learn that tears don't make you weak. I was learning.

I have never gone down this path. How does one get through it? I just continued to talk myself through it, as I tried to understand. Hearing the old clichéd statements people were echoing in my *ear*, "It's meant to be." "It's God's will." "Something was wrong with the baby." Words, so many words filling the air, they gave me no comfort. I wanted to scream. "Please, no words! Say no words, just hold me. Be with me and walk with me. No words...just be."

"You have to be admitted into the hospital and have surgery."

Words again...only words, but I listened and agreed. I followed a path of fear that I had to walk, with a broken heart. Learning each day of life is a gift. Each moment is precious.

~

Danny was playing in a football game that day after school. He knew I was losing the baby. The arrangements were made. I called the doctor's office and said I'll be there today, but I had one stop to make first.

"Tom, I have to go see Danny's game."

He knew how worried Danny was about me.

"I promise I won't stay long." I was bleeding badly, and I didn't know how long I could stay.

"Okay, babe."

We arranged for Leah to stay with our friends.

When we arrived at the game, the seats were filled and it was hard to find a place to sit.

Playing on the field was Danny's moment to shine. He loved to have it crowded, and the people loved him out there. I waved to him as he scanned the faces to see if I was there. I always knew how to catch his eye. He came right up to me. "Are you okay, Mom?"

"Sure, Bam," I said. That's what I called him, Bambi. I don't know how I started calling him this, it has always been. "I have to go to the hospital, though. I wanted to see you before I went."

He smiled and kissed me on the cheek.

"Now get down there and get me a homerun." I realized what I said after I had already said it.

"It's football, Mom," he said, laughing so hard. Everyone around us laughed, too.

"Woops…sorry!" I shrugged it off with a smile. My mind was on the inevitable.

Danny kept looking up from the sidelines to see if I was there. I would wave. I didn't feel like I should wait much longer. The pain was getting worse.

It was almost halftime.

"Debby," Tom said, "come on, I have to get you to the hospital."

"I will, one more minute." I knew I had to go.

Danny kept looking up from the group of players, checking on me. I needed him to see me here. I stood up and could feel the blood rushing from my body. "Tom, I have to go." How would I get through this moment? I never lost a life…I always gave it.

Tom helped me down the steps. On the way to the car, you could hear the announcer's voice. "There he goes, Danny Preston…at the 50 yard line…the 20…touchdown!" the voice shouted, the crowd roared.

"You again?"She said.
"No, he wanted it so strongly, he made it happen. Just as his love is the same for you.
He is a bright, shining star in this realm. He will shine so bright, some will try to cover it with dark clouds.
No storms last forever, he will shine again, when they least expect it.
You knew he was the son of your heart from the moment he appeared within you."
"Yes, I did…I always told him that."
"We know."
"Of course you do."
"He will see…like a caterpillar changes in hibernation, so he will take flight in time.
Be patient."

This is a memory that I will never forget. A 70-yard touchdown. I held back the tears, I was so proud of him. I cry with the thought of reliving that and feeling the moment as if it was now. His gift to me, my own special "homerun." My son Danny, I adore him. That day, they named him "Rocket." It was an angel moment.

The stillness of losing a child is one of the most difficult. No words would change what happened. No words can make it better. You need to see the people around you that love you and know they are there. This is true for all things, death, divorce, all the same. No words make it easier or better. You just have to find the strength within yourself to keep going…to keep walking.

Those that circle you give you this life force energy. It's their love. Do we humans realize this? The energy of love is the true essence of life.

We go on…somehow we do.

The old man made a noise to bring Danny's attention to him. He knew it was time for the words to be given back to him.

Danny was caught up in the moment, as was everyone else hearing the words of a woman they loved beyond words. Had they known her, the trueness of her and who she was to them and others? They were having a clearer view now.

"The journal marked 2001," he said to Danny as his hand reached out to take hold of it.

Chapter Eleven

Sometimes you have to lose to win

I remember just before Tom left, we were watching a movie and the wife in the movie said, "Sometimes you have to lose to win."

I would have prepared my daughter for the decision her dad was going to make if I had seen it coming. I knew her pretty well, and he would only dance around it. He avoided telling her, as he did so many things. I needed to be the one.

I hated to hear her cry, and the look on her face when I told her was devastating. I had to keep their relationship intact and try to let her see. It wasn't her he was leaving, it was me. He didn't love me anymore.

How do you explain that to a little girl? How do you say the love is gone? That would be something in years to come he will have to answer. I loved him, and I loved my children. I needed to think of her, all little girls need their Daddy's love. I lost my father at five years old and never wanted her to feel the emptiness I had felt over the years.

Danny has taken it with more worry of me. This man was his stepfather, he had been in his life for almost twenty years. Now he was a man of twenty-six. Leah was only sixteen. Such a delicate age for a girl to understand. She would be graduating soon. I was going to get them through this. But first I have to feel my feet holding me up.

Lose? I had lost him. How? I have no idea. Win? Win what? The pain and loneliness was deadly to me. I had to practice what I had taught my kids. Out of everything bad, something good comes from it. Now the waiting, to see what good would come.

A piece of me was missing. How could I go on without him? First, I had to decide whether I wanted to or not. Almost as the same decision I had to make when he was drowning. Well, I chose my life for my children then and I chose it again. He will live, but not as it was, as I will live, but not as it was. It will be different. An adjustment within and without. I think sometimes it would have been easier if he transitioned. He has more to do with his life, and I have more to do with mine. My angels will show me the path. Now to wipe the tears from my blurred eyes so I can see. I can do this, and I will.

This is when you learn those hard life lessons. We all have so many beginnings and endings throughout our lives. We all survive moments of sadness and live moments of pleasure that are beyond words. For what reason? Sunshine and rain…that is the reason. To grow, to be rooted as a strong old oak tree.

Maybe someday, sometime I will be able to tell another person that you will be okay. If I can make it through, then surely you can, too. Maybe I'll write a book and share my life, this journal is going to be worn out.

I probably should buy another one.

When Leah grows up, I hope she writes things down, like her memories, her dreams and imaginations, the past and the future, so she can constantly move ahead. If we all could only believe there is a reason not to let go of our dreams. You are the only one that can bring it into the world. It may take you twenty years to come to it, don't let it die.

I read these words a few days ago: Don't die with your music in you. What a great lesson. You know the tune, you know how to play it, let it be. *Your song*, it will be sung loud and clear, let it be a song of joy, not mourning.

I think I am going to be okay, I think I am discovering who I am. All the reading and listening to different spiritual teachers makes me feel I understand more fully my purpose. I finally have my own personal identity. One that isn't connected with another identity. I stand here and tell you who I am without identifying myself as a mother or a wife…but rather as a spiritual being having a human experience. I am learning.

The other day, I received an email that changed my life almost immediately. It was from a "divorcing well" site. How do you do that? It was a piece someone wrote called "The Awakening." I was never able to find out who wrote this analogy, but I'm glad they did. I have given it to many that haven't had the awakening yet, hoping they will. Hoping they will come through the night of it and wake up to the birds singing in the morn.

I remember now…*The win.*

After all this time, I finally see. I just had to wait to see, and it came. The win, the good, I found me! The gifts came as I was experiencing the sadness, the doubt. I was being strengthened, with patience and learning. Seeing with my eyes and seeing within, I would walk in confidence, seemingly alone to the eyes of the world, but I wasn't. The seeds within me *were quickened* and cultivated by seasons of life and patience. The seeds were within me all the time. They are in all of us all the time.

For them to come to life, they had to be rained on. Sunshine and rain bring the rainbow.

I do wish him well and will always love him. He is my daughter's Daddy, and she is the magic from it. For all this and the time we had together, I am thankful, for the rain, for the sunshine.

I have my children, I am alive now...I don't think I was before.

My rainbow appears

(Journal entry)

He came, not according to my time plan, but according to the universe. Years of experiences have taken place since the divorce to share with him and with you. Now I can begin living the dream with him.

Who is he? I saved the best for last, I see this now. It was all worth it.

The reading stopped as the lights in the cabin flickered and the room filled with the darkness.

"What the...?"

"Whoa, the storm hit a power line."

"Pop, where's the oil lamp or the candles?" Rob whispered.

"On the fireplace, the matches are right there next to it."

The little ones were safe as they lay on his lap, as they tried to bring the light back to the room. His large hands clenched the ribbon that had been on the gift, as if he didn't want to lose her again.

With a snap, the spark of the match lit the room, he lifted the glass dome of the oil lamp. Such a small flame made the shadows disappear.

The tired old bear whispered, "Hey, let's call it a night, whata ya say? We can read more tomorrow."

"Yeah, let's settle in."

With the electricity off, the fire in the fireplace would keep everyone warm. This happened a lot out here, they were always prepared.

Everyone gathered their little ones for a camping out night with Poppa.

He shuffled over to the window and stared out into the darkness as the rest of the family was nestling in. His hand touched the pocket where his white feather was hidden. It was his time to be alone. His face reflected that he was lonely and lost without her. Night time is the most difficult time, when you're alone.

He tiptoed past the gang, giving his occasional wink to those still awake.

"I love you, Pops," Leah said.

"I love you, too, angel face."

Deb smiled. "I love you, too, angel face."
She was still sitting on the floor, touching her babies.

He slowly walked down the hall, scuffing his slippers. Opening the door to their bedroom, his chest felt heavy. He reached for their familiar bed to hold him up. Until now, he didn't realize how he would dread this moment, the aloneness.

"I miss you, De. Do you hear me?" His heart raced.

He put on his sweatpants, shivering from the cold, and then crawled into the cold, empty bed. Tugging at the pillow on the other side of the bed, trying to smell her and feel her there, he drifted...drifted deeper and deeper...

*****

"Hey, you."
He thought he heard her soft voice behind him.
"Let's go for a ride."
He jumped up, bumping his head on the headboard.
"What the?"
Debra stood there with a smile as bright as the full moon glistening

off the snow outside.

"Baby, how?"

"Oh, don't ask questions I can't answer. They will be answered later; all the answers come later, my love. I needed to be with you, now get dressed. We have a date. I was told it would be a surprise for both of us."

Quickly, without any effort, he pulled on his jeans and sweatshirt, bundling up for the cold air outside. He kept his eyes on De, making sure he didn't lose her again.

"Brrr, it is chilly out there." He tapped the bed/ "You sure you don't want to join me in this warm bed? We could always warm it up pretty darn quick. "

"You sure you're up for this, old man?" Her laughter filled the room.

He loved to hear her laugh.

"I am always up for anything with you, arrr," he playfully growled, grabbing her and spinning her around. She felt so good, she smelled so good.

"You sure you're dressed warm enough?"

He noticed she was wearing the tan coat he bought her sometime ago. It looked new again. She always said it was her favorite; she wore it when he took her on a surprise sleigh ride at Christmas. He thought back to how much fun it was seeing her excitement by his surprises.

Deb threw her arms around his neck. "You can keep me warm, love, if I get cold."

"Babe, what's happening?"

"Us, my love, as always, no time, no rules, remember?"

"Yes," he acknowledged, still wondering how all this could be happening.

She stood at the door, waiting patiently. Her amazing smile radiated more than he remembered. Extending her hand, she walked him out the door.

{No one noticed that there was still a form lying in their bed.}

They quietly walked through the living room, her hand in his. She stopped, holding him back for a moment, to admire her family, their family. Deb gently reached down and touched Leah's hair. Leah didn't wake at her touch, a slight smile did come to her lips as she pulled Lacey closer.

"She's fine," he said, reading her thoughts as he always did.

"I know, I know she is."

Deb tugged on his hand. "Did you like the gift?"

"I loved the gift! You saw how upset they were getting. I am glad we stopped where it did."

"We felt it was time to. My friend and I, that is."

"Your friend?"

"Yes, a very nice man, his voice was so gentle. I have known him for a very long time. His name is Nathaniel. I will share more of him later.

"I felt you here…so did the kids."

"Aye, me love, right next to ya, always, right next to ya."

Even in this dream, he noticed she had her playful Irish accent.

They walked past everyone, lying so comfortably near the warmth of the fire. Lilly snuggled close to her Daddy. Reesie had Lilly covered with the blanket I made for her last year.

Everyone was safe and warm in their home. Rob was nestled near the fire, keeping the family warm.

"My family all together and walking through time. They will be fine. I will be with them."

"We will be with them."

*****

The old Scotsman guided her through the kitchen to the back door. Not really knowing what he was going to do, but just doing it.

Debra saw the muffins on the counter, pulling on his hand to make him stop for a moment. "Mmmm," she said, picking one up.

He laughed that great laugh, pulling her the rest of the way out the door.

A muffin dropped on the floor.

"Oops..."

His hand guided her closer.

She loved it when he held her close with his hand on the small of her back.

The garage door was still open. The bike sat in the darkness, covered with the tarp. They both ran to pull the cover off, giggling like teenagers, remembering how much fun they had on their toy.

"Shhhhh," she said, "we don't want to wake the kids."

"Don't you think the bike starting might wake them?"

Putting it in neutral, they pushed it out of the garage. There was a slight hill, so it was easy pushing it down the driveway. At the bottom, he got on and she stood next to him, putting her hands on his face.

"I love you forever and a day," nudging his face close to hers.

"I love you so much. I can't believe that I have you right here beside me. It's a miracle, a dream. Is it a dream, De?

"Isn't that our life, filled with dreams and imagination? I have never left your side. You knew I was here. It's been a hard time for you and the kids. We can do this together, like we always have. It will be easier very soon."

The light of the moon was full. They loved the full moon. It was their special light to play and love by. Their life seemed to surround it, filled with magic and imagination beyond this world and now blending to the next together.

"Let's go back, let's look at it again with a new vision. Let's do it again," she said softly.

"To where?"

"I'll show you, that's the best way! Our memories and our life are what we give to our children. They will learn in time, all we said was true. Anything is possible, my love, remember? You will see it when you believe it.

Let's go to the beginning and play. The kids are fine, all nestled in and safe. We can entertain them later. Now is our time."

They rode up the hillside. There was a thin layer of snow on the ground. The moon filled the sky with its radiant light, with its reflection on the snow. It seemed almost like daylight. You could see everything. The trees glistened with their frozen branches. Clusters of rabbits scurried as their little feet shuffled in the snow, trying to run from the roar of the bike. The stars filled the sky.

"Look," he said, pointing quickly, taking his hand off her leg,

"A shooting star."

"Yayyy," she said. "Angel magic, my love."

He nestled himself back in his seat, to feel her behind him. Patting her hands as they held his stomach snugly.

"Is this a dream…?" He didn't want to wake if it was.

Deb touched his neck with her finger as gently as she always did when they rode.

The air felt so good on my face. I loved having her arms around me again.

"Hey, what are you thinking up there?" Deb asked.

"Oh, my mind is wandering everywhere."

"I know, mine, too. I am so excited.

"I wonder what their surprise is?"

The voice said, "have fun!"

"Who was that, Deb?"

"Oh, that's my friend."

"I like how your friend thinks."

"Me, too!"

It was just before sunrise, you could see the light
appearing on the horizon.
Soon, everyone would be awake.
Finding what the next day was to bring.

****

Their bike seemed to travel through time...
They were being given a gift.
Which direction were they going?
I think, toward the yesterdays and the tomorrows.
To re-experience
life then and life now.
"Their awakening!"

Do it again..

As it was suppose to be.

Chapter Twelve

Our paths cross for a reason.
Maybe in another time or just in a dream

The machines were making their sounds, alive with action. Everything was dark.

"Where am I? Voices...I hear voices," he thought.

"Any changes?" Melody asked the nurse.

"All is the same, hon. He is holding his own."

"What do they mean, holding his own? Who is holding his own?" he thought.

"When will he wake up? Every day, it gets harder and harder."

"There is no way of telling for sure. It takes time. His vitals are really strong. I won't lie to you. Try to be patient. Can I get you a drink or call someone to be with you?"

"No, my brother will be here soon."

"Okay, I am right out in the hall if you need me."

"Thank you."

His mind struggled between the dream and reality. "De...where is De?" He wanted to reach back to her on the bike. He thought she was on the bike with him. *"Where were we going? Where is she...? I can't lose her again."* Jeff was very confused.

The room was bright from the sun shining through the window. Cards were taped and hanging all over the walls, and flowers arranged from friends and family were placed throughout the room. Everyone was praying for him. His face wasn't bruised much. He did put a gash in his head when he fell from his motorcycle.

It happened so fast, on his way to work. He left a little later than usual. Since the divorce, Jeff Nichols seemed to bury himself in his work. When the call came that he was needed at the hospital, the time of day wasn't on his mind. The combination of dusk, back roads, and deer was definitely an equation for an accident.

Jeff loved living in the country in his modest farmhouse on Holly Brook Pond. It has been his home for over twenty years. He had been married for twenty-five years, and now he was suddenly alone.

Jeff's son Paul, now thirty years old and a replica of himself, was a hardworking engineer with a wonderful girlfriend. They were planning to set a date for their marriage.

His daughter Melody, the glow in his eye, was always there, a real Daddy's girl. She is twenty-three and expecting her first child. Of course, he was a doting father and grandpa.

"His eyes are moving," Melody whispered. "Dad....Dad, can you hear me?" Her hand held his softly. She rested her head on the bed next to him.

Paul quietly tiptoed into the room. "Hey, Sis," touching her hair to comfort her. It was obvious she had been crying.

"Hey, calm down. He's tough. You know he is. Everything is good, according to the doctors. His body is only bruised: everything else is fine. Seven days aren't that long to be out of it. I talked with a lot of people about this. He'll be back to his old self in no time at all."

"Yeah, right, Paul, back to what? Maybe he doesn't want to come back! These last two years have been so hard for him."

The door opened, and Melody's face lit up. "Uncle Jake!"

"What's up, kiddos?" he said.

~

Dr. Jacob Byers, Jeff's best friend. Jeff and Jake, what a pair! They traveled through elementary and high school shoulder-to-shoulder, back to back, fist to fist, and always had each other's back.

Heads had to sneer in the little town of Fillmore when they both chose to go to medical school. They were the rebel pair memories, and moments not so memorable were made by these two.

Some still talk about the time that their high school tried to put a strict dress code into effect. Jeff and Jake, the activists that they were, wouldn't let it go into the official declaration without voicing their opinion. Oh, they didn't do it by appearing at a school board meeting. They rocked the town.

When they first got word, their minds started churning..

The Campbell family ran this small town. The citizens of Fillmore were hesitant to upset them, since they had the Town Council and the school board under their net of fear.

The guys approached every student in the school from freshman to seniors, and every student agreed. On October 5th at exactly 10 a.m., no matter what the situation, everyone would get up and walk out of his or her classroom. They would meet in the front yard of the school, where signs would already be stashed in the bushes. It was organized well.

Finally, the big day came. Jeff and Jake were anxious to get their plan into action. They had disagreements with Mrs. Campbell, who seemed to make it her life's goal to make their lives as tormented and miserable as possible.

This was the way of the 70s. Times of sit-ins, sit-outs and protesting, voicing opinions at a young age to the staunch Old World styles of thinking, children should be seen and not heard. This wasn't happening with J and J, they were definitely seen and heard.

9:45 a.m.

Their hearts were racing. In a few moments, they would all be one. One voice speaking against Mrs. Campbell and her hierarchy.

10:00 a.m.

One by one, each student rose from his seat in orderly, silent fashion and exited their classrooms. The floors of the school vibrated with the sound of marching in the halls. Everyone was moving in the same direction, to the front exit.

The teachers were trying their best to control the movement of the students as they stood on the side of the halls, knowing full well what was taking place. They all were determined to voice their opinion that day on what some would consider foolish and irrelevant. Some of the student's faces showed uncertainty, some wore smiles, while others found comfort in seeing friends beside them, still not speaking a word to each other. All walked on, following the leaders on the first floor: Jacob Byers, the Senior Class President, and Jeff Nichols, the star quarterback.

Jeff led his classmates down the stairs. He caught sight of Jake, now heading down the hall. They estimated it would take about twenty minutes to empty the school if everyone kept moving. A few students stopped to look around, unsure of whether they should be doing this. After seeing Jeff and Jake marching forward in confidence, they would continue as well, reassured of their newfound path of protest.

They all knew these two guys never would do anything to hurt anyone. They only had everyone's best interest in mind. After all, they were graduating this year and this event would only be helping the underclassmen.

"Life's lessons," a common refrain repeated by their favorite teacher, Mrs. Henry. Not all the staff was as bad as Mrs. Campbell. Many understood what was happening.

Speaking only with their eyes and silent gestures of their hands, the entire student body filled the front lawn. What an amazing sight it was for Fillmore residents! Cars driving by pulled off to the side of the road to see what was happening. Parents, after getting word by phone, came to witness the turning point for Fillmore.

The small town had been controlled by the Campbells for too long, from the mayor to the principal. The children were reflecting what the parents had thought for years. Today, the kids were taking the town back, one step at a time. Everyone should have a voice. One family shouldn't be allowed to control any town.

By now, the TV and newspaper reporters from the city of Wallace, which is on the border of Fillmore, had arrived. Jeff and Jake walked up to the front steps. The students stood quietly and watched. Some of the teachers even took their place in the lawn in support of the student body.

Mrs. Campbell and her husband, Mayor Peter Campbell, observed the sight with smirks on their faces. "Mr. Nichols, it seems you're in charge of this outrage. I strongly suggest you take this warning and come back inside. You need to think of the consequences and the involvement of the entire student body."

"Ma'am," said Jeff, "we are sorry it came to this, but it's the only way you would even consider the students to have a voice in this matter."

As the words left his mouth, all the students sat simultaneously on the ground.

"We respectfully disagree with your decision to initiate uniforms into our high school." He extended his hand with signed petitions from all the students in the school and their parents. "We will see you at the school board meeting tonight with our families." He raised a duplicate copy of the signatures for all to witness.

The crowd grew as parents and citizens accompanied the students to show their approval. An elderly gent called out, "I want my name on that petition, too, son!"

Fillmore changed that day. Parents stood behind the kids and confronted the school board and city council. Photographs of the protest appeared in newspapers across the state. What seemed insignificant to some became a moment never forgotten, especially by the powerful Campbell family. The town had been given back to the people.

*****

"Hey, kids," he said, opening his arms wide. "How's our guy?"

Melody stood quickly and ran into Jake's arms.

"Whoa, princess! It's all right, Mels. He's going to be fine. He's not leaving us."

"Uncle Jake, I thought I saw his eyes moving."

"Yes. It's a dream state you go into when you sleep called R.E.M., or Rapid Eye Movement. He's probably having a great time chasin' the ladies."

Paul laughed. It seemed strange for him to hear himself laugh. It felt good.

Melody went back to the chair next to her father's bed and touched his hand.

The sunlight coming into the small room began to dim as evening worked on making its appearance.
Most everyone had left, and the room was still. Melody had fallen asleep in the chair.

"Time to come back, Jeffrey Nichols."
A soft voice spoke to him.

Jeff stirred, coming to awareness.
The sounds of the world were strange to his ears. *"What*

happened? Stumbling through the thoughts in his mind, blurred memories, people, and moments.

He tried to explore his surroundings as his eyes focused. Jeff could see and feel that this place was familiar. *"Am I in bed? Where?". "Oh shit... I'm in the hospital."* He tried to touch the area of throbbing pain on his head and quickly realized that tubes were restricting his arm and the bed rails were up.

"Where is Deb?" he thought to himself. *"Is she ok?"* Groaning a little, he noticed someone sleeping in the chair. Their eyes met.

"Dad!" Melody screamed. "Oh my God, Daddy, you're back! Nurse, Nurse, quick!" She leaped from the chair.

Jeff slowly smiled. "Hey, baby girl, what happened? Aw, don't cry."

She sobbed, holding him as close as she could. "You're finally awake, Dad, you're awake. I thought I was going to lose you, too."

Two nurses came quickly into the room.

"Well, well, Dr. Jeff, you decided to return to the land of the living?" Mary said.

"I didn't know I left, Mary. Where is Debby? Is she all right?"

"Who? Dad, you were in a motorcycle accident. Who's Debby?" Melody asked.

"No one was with you. We don't know a Debby, Dad." She quickly turned to Mary, "Is he all right?"

"Sure, honey, he's fine, a little groggy is all. He will adjust in a few minutes." Jeff tried to gather his thoughts enough to form words. Mumbling, "Um yeah, I think, I think I, oh hell. What the hell happened? How did I...."

"Settle down and give it a few minutes. You're fine," Mary reassured him. "It sure is great to see those big baby blues." She loosened some of the wires that seemed to limit his movement. "You're in the hospital, and if it's any consolation, you look better than the deer and your bike."

"My bike?" His mind started to clear, "Yeah, my bike. What the hell happened to my bike? A deer?" He started to remember. Yet the memory of her sitting behind him was still fresh. *I felt her, heard her laugh.*

Paul came in holding two coffees from the cafeteria, almost dropping them when he saw his dad's eyes looking at him.

"Does one of those have a shot of scotch? I have a headache like you wouldn't believe."

"Dad, holy shit, you're awake!" The three of them embraced.

Paul picked up the phone to call Jake.

Mary put her hand on his, stopping him. "I called him already. He's on his way."

Jeff smiled as his long-time friend entered the room.

"Now, Jeffy," Jake said sarcastically, "want to tell me what you were doing for a week? Or was that the vacation you've been saying you were going to take, where no one could find you?"

He shook Jeff's hand with their special hit and tap shake. Jake held back the tears; he was relieved to see him awake too.

"I won't be riding my bike anytime soon, from the sound of it. The deer made that decision for me. I don't remember how it happened. The last thing I remember was being home and listening to some music and I think reading."

"Yeah, right, reading what...the articles in Playboy?" Jake's usual sarcastic humor was welcomed.

Melody laughed.

"No, I don't know. I can't remember right now," as he rubbed his head. "Gimme a break, Byers. I feel like I'm grasping for straws here, trying to remember."

*****

The season quickly turned from the cold, snowy nights of winter, passing faster than he ever remembered. It had been five months since the wreck, and spring was around the corner.

The house seemed lonely and still tonight. The windows rattled from the gusting wind and rain doing their dance outside.

"The wind? The window...the tree..." He walked to the

window, touching the pane...there wasn't any tree. *"I think I'm losing my mind,"* he said to himself. As he walked into the den, the fire was cracking from the fireplace. His body was healing quickly. His mind was still a little shaken from the life he experienced while in the coma. Jeff seemed to remember everything so clearly. It all seemed so real.

A knock came at the front door.

"I'm coming, I'm coming!" He glanced out the window as he passed through the den to the front door. Smiling, he opened the door. "Now what the hell are you doing driving on a night like this? You should be home with your family."

"Right...and since when aren't you family?" Jake growled, grabbing Jeff with a bear hug.

"Why is the house so dark? What are you doing in here? Got company?" He said, bobbing around Jeff and peeking around the corners of the room, laughing.

"Hardly," Jeff said.

"Why the hell not? It's not like you haven't been getting signals in every direction at the hospital."

"I know. I'm just not up to it yet. Jake, can you stay a bit?"

"Sure."

"Want a beer?"

"If you're having one, it sounds good to me." Jake tuned in a bit, realizing something was on Jeff's mind. "God, it's been a while since I've been here. Nothing's changed. It's a great ladies trap though, a nice touch of bachelor here and there." He raised a dirty dish from the sink. "That special woman will say, he needs to be taken care of," Jake teased.

"Is that all you think of, fixing me up with someone?" Jeff said, chuckling. "I'm not ready for that, Bud. Not yet."

Jeff wanted to talk to Jake about Debby, but he couldn't seem to find the words. It was a stupid dream. It wasn't real. She wasn't real.

They took their beers into the den.

Doc, Jeff's dog, was sleeping by the fireplace. Jake laughed as Doc spotted him, jumping up like a puppy, wagging his tail and going crazy.

"Hey, boy, hey, boy," Jake said as he scratched his head. "What are ya doin,' old boy? Are you taking care of this old fart?"

Jeff laughed and sat in the chair by the fire.

Doc settled down next to him, nuzzling his hand before dozing off again.

"So, how's work going?" Jake asked.

"Pretty good. It was hard at first, getting back into the swing of things, but it's coming along. It feels good to be back, I missed it. The patients keep me focused."

"Hear anything from your ex?" Jake jokingly pressed.

"No, she appeared a couple times after the accident, she's found a new life for herself and seems content." Jeff shrugged it off.

"Any chance of you and her hooking back up?" The question seemed ridiculous, but Jake could see it still bothered him that she left.

Jeff hesitated. "Sometimes it's good to look forward, not back." In his mind, he was thinking of Debby. God, who was she? Why can't he get her out of his mind?

"I can tell ya this," Jake said, "you should acknowledge some of these ladies at work. If you did, you could have your pick. I hear them talking. They don't think I do, but I do. There are many hot prospects out there waiting to be picked off the tree, if ya know what I mean. I heard one of them say you had nice buns." He raised his beer to toast to that.

"Oh... yeahhh." They hooted together as they tapped their beer bottles.

"Melody and Paul have been pretty concerned about you. Actually, she called this morning to see what I thought about your hibernating state. Seems she feels you've been in a little bit of a daze and thought work would give you a push back into the human race."

"Oh, she's trying to play mother to her old man, is all," Jeff said. "She needs to focus on her life and husband. I'm fine. Not to change the subject, but I 'm going to the bike shop tomorrow. I miss my lady. I can't wait to get back on her, feel her rumble under me."

They clanked their bottles and growled. "Oh yeah, I hear that."

Chapter Thirteen

The Old Scotsman

"What a mess this house is! How the hell did it get so messy?" Jeff turned on his stereo for motivation as he worked to get his man cave cleaned up.

Doc was sleeping by the sliding glass doors that led to the outside deck. Jeff stared at the view of the woods that circled his property. It captivated him and took him back to a special time in his life, a trip he had taken to Scotland. His mother's family was from the Isle of Skye. He went there when he was a teenager, before graduation. The small village was untouched by the outside, fast-paced world.

He went back:
"Hey, Laddie, ya lookin' for some lassies?" a deep voice called out.

"Ah, no sir, I'm just enjoying the view." Jeff sat on the rocks, watching the waves crash below. "This is great. In the States things are so fast, there doesn't seem to be time to breathe and enjoy the calmness."

"I was gonna tell ya, if ya were looking for a lassie, they aren't to be found here on these rocks!" His uncle Sean smacked him on the back, almost knocking him forward.

Jeff got his balance, and both of them laughed.

Sean slowly crouched down beside him, looking out over the water, too. "I'm glad your mother brought ya here. I never wanted to go to the States, wouldn't want to get trapped there, ya know."

Jeff continued to listen.

"It's good ya came here to see your roots, son. Ya don't know where yer goin' until ya see where ya came from."

His Uncle Sean was a few years younger than Jeff's mother was. He married young, and sadly his wife died unexpectedly. They didn't have any children, so Jeff was filling in some empty spaces for him. Sean loved sharing his unforgettable creative quotes with his attentive nephew.

"So, you're 18 years old now?"

"Yes sir, I graduated from high school."

"What are your plans for the future?"

"A doctor, sir, I want to be a doctor. My friend Jake and I are entering medical school together. We start in September. Mom thought it would be a good opportunity to take a month off to visit the Isle. That is, before I get buried in school. Once I start, there's no telling when I would have this opportunity again."

"Aye, laddie, the calm before the storm, aye?"

"Yes sir, I guess that's a way to look at it," Jeff said, smiling.

"Is this the lad yer mom told me about, that you caused such a ruckus with at the school?"

"Yes sir, he is. We have been side by side since elementary school."

"Good seed ya come from. Not afraid to speak yer mind, son. Who knows, maybe the Isle will plant a seed in ya, so you won't be able to stay away. She has a way of doin' that, ya know."

Jeff listened intently.

"She is made for lovers," Sean said with a touch of magic and memory that brought his voice down to a whisper.

"Did ya hear of the Glenora Castle?"

"No, I don't think I have."

"So, ya up for a short walk?" Sean asked.

"Sure."

"Great! Run to the Inn and tell Felicia we are off."

Felicia was Sean's niece, although she wasn't much younger than Sean. She was a surprise baby for Sean's sister Margaret and the light of her Mum's eye.

Jeff found her in the kitchen. She was sorting through some recipes, trying to decide what to make for the evening dinner special. They ran the Inn on the Isle, and it was tourist season and every room was taken.

"Felicia," said Jeff, "I'm not sure where Mom is, or your mother. Uncle Sean and I are going to take a short walk. Could you let them know?"

"Aye, Jeff. Where are ya goin'?"

"Oh, something of a castle…"

"Ah, the castle…it's a wonderful place, even though the story of her is sad. The Castle Glenora is the heart of the Isle, love."

"Really?" said Jeff.

"Aye, 'tis a love story. Yer Uncle will tell ya. Count on that fer sure."

As Jeff left the kitchen, Felicia giggled. "Short walk, me eye, 'bout 3 kilometers."

She continued thumbing through her recipes, laughing at her uncle's way of playing with Jeff.

They started walking down a stony path, sharing moments they will always remember. They bonded that day. Sean told some of the most wonderful stories. One would almost think they were fables, but he swore on the sprites and fairies they were true.

Finally, they reached the crest of the mountain and the view was unbelievable.

"There she be, Glenora. In the States, you build lighthouses to guide you. Here on the Isle, we have Glenora. She brings hope and comfort to all. Knowing she is there and her magic reaches out to us from time to time. Maybe you will see it someday. Maybe."

Jeff smiled. He wasn't going to negate or debate anything his Uncle said. Even his idea of a short walk wasn't to be questioned. They were connected, joined at the heart now.

*****

"Dad, where are you?" a voice called from the front hall.

Jeff snapped back as quick as he went there.

Jumping out of the chair he had settled into. "Here I'm, here."

"What are you doing?" Melody asked as she saw him leap up.

"I was reminiscing, baby. Every time I listen to that music and the trees are starting to bud, it reminds me of the Isle." He pointed out the window. "You can see the green starting."

"Yes, I know. It was something that you spoke of so often that I felt I was there with you. Paul and I talked about the Isle while you were in the hospital. We said that when you were better we would all go over. Maybe we can go after the baby is born?"

(Melody was almost four months pregnant.)

"How does that sound, Dad? I know you miss it."

Jeff smiled, touching her belly. "Someday angel, what brings you here on this wonderful sunny day?"

"You mentioned you were going to do some cleaning," she sighed, "and four hands are better than two."

"Cool, your dad can use all the help he can get!" He cranked up the volume on the stereo and handed her a cloth. Melody danced around the room, methodically picking up, swiping and wiping. She was so happy her dad was home.

He watched her do her dance. Even in his house, she was nesting. He remembered the look on her face when he woke in the hospital. Her saying she thought she was losing him, too. I know she misses her mom. She won't admit it, but she does. He tried to keep himself occupied so he wouldn't dig into the topic any deeper. She would talk when she wanted, that was her way.

Mel called out as she moved the cushions on the couch. "Uncle Jake said he stopped over the other night."

"Yep, we downed a few brewskys."

Her smile lit up her face. "Like old times?"

"Oh yeah, he's the man, all right. We talked a lot, and I told him I have to replace my lady."

"What?" Melody looked confused.

"Yeah, I know where I have to find her. She's really high class and only requires a little attention. Wanna meet her?" He said with a snicker.

Melody stood staring with her hands on her hips. "What's her name? Did you decide to see someone, Daddy?"

"Oh, I haven't named her yet." He started laughing.

"Haven't named her? Dad, what are you talking about?"

"I'm going to get another bike, Mels."

"Daddy, no!" Melody pleaded.

Doc jumped off his cushion, startled by her high-pitched screech. His head tilted from side to side as he watched Melody jumping around.

Jeff reached to tickle her as he made his growling sound, "Ah, yah need some cheese to go with that whine, lassie? I'll be fine. Besides, it's a chick magnet."

"Oh no, Dad!" She laughed, yet fear remained in her eyes.

Jeff released her from his Dad hug. Doc's tail was wagging everywhere as he leaped around the two of them, saying in his dog language, "Let me play, too!"

"Now, Cinderella, let's get this castle cleaned, and don't be worrying that pretty little head."

They both began shuffling around the living room, picking up and tossing things.

"What's this?" Melody said, reaching under his chair by the fireplace.

"What?"

"Hiding your reading material now, Dad?"

He laughed. "Yeah, right," as he came closer.

She read the words on the cover. "The Memory Barrel. This doesn't seem like your normal reading material. Actually, I didn't even know you liked to read!"

"Yeah, let me see that." He went serious in an instant. "I...I don't know." He felt a haunting twinge of familiarity. *The Memory Barrel, by Debra Pratt* . His own voice echoed the words, it sounded strange in his head... *Debra? Debby?* His face froze for a moment as he stared at the book. He handed it back to Melody quickly.

"What's the matter, Dad? You look like you've seen a ghost." She took a step towards him. "Are you okay?"

"I remembered something. Have you ever experienced a moment when you thought something was real and then you realize it wasn't?"

"Yes, I have. Why? What does the book have to do with it?"

"Everything," he said. "It all makes sense now! I was reading this before the accident. It must have been nudged under the chair. It was the last thing I remember. God, I remember!"

"What, Dad...what are you talking about?"

His mind was relieved as he saw how things could have seemed real to him. He tried to explain to Melody where it came from. "Someone at work had the book. It seems she knows the author. Her name is Shar, she's in the office below ours. Nice lady. We met at a hospital meeting."

Melody listened intently.

"Somehow, we got on the topic of your mom leaving. She had heard that I was having a hard time from all the rumors floating around the hospital. We all know how people love to talk."

Melody nodded and observed her father trying to calm himself.

"She told me it could be worse. Men seem to handle this stuff a lot better than the ladies do. Personally, I think she got that from Dr. Phil or something." Jeff rolled his eyes with humor to make light of this, or hoping to.

Melody laughed.

"Then she told me about her friend who wrote a book about life and walking through some pretty tough moments, from a woman's point of view. She even started laughing, saying that she was in it. I was intrigued, to say the least. So the next day, she brought it to me. It's even signed by the author."

"Since when are you interested in a woman's point of view?"

Jeff laughed. "I know, crazy, huh? I just set it down on the table when I came home, and one night, I cracked it open along with my Bud..."

She looked at him, curious.

"My Budweiser..."

"Ohhh yahh, of course."

Melody opened the cover, and the inscription read:

To Shar:
My friend, my anam cara
Remember our oil lamp days and save the best always for last.
This small book was my best counselor.
Dreams and memories of life.
Now I understand most of it, the rest will come in time.
See ya in the morning
Love,
Deb

Jeff watched Melody for her reaction.

"Wow, that's cool. So did you read it?"

"Yeah, some of it." He pointed to the book. There was a card slightly extending from one of the pages.

"You didn't read very much." Melody handed the book to

her Dad. "It looks like you still have some reading to do."

He stepped back, pulling his hand back, refusing to take it.

"What? What's the matter?"

He knew this was crazy and must have looked curious to his daughter.

"It's stupid," as he took it in his hands. "It's...do you remember when I was in the hospital and I asked for Debby?"

"We don't know a....oh my God, Dad. Is this who you were asking for in the hospital? You said you didn't know her?"

"Well, I guess I don't know her personally," he said with an uneasy look on his face. "I've never met her. I guess reading the book sort of swept me up and, well...it must have been in my subconscious or something.

"Pops, it's only a book."Melody dropped into the chair, putting her hand on her belly. "What's it about?"

"If I recall, she or the main character in the book and her husband rode a bike a lot. It wasn't about her; at least I don't think it was. I'm not sure. You know how authors are always making you guess how they know information so descriptively." He seemed to be stammering now. "This woman died and, well, her family found her journals and other things after she had passed. "I don't want to talk about it now, okay?"He rubbed his face with both hands.

"Okay, Pops, but it wasn't an autobiography, was it? I mean, is this Debby still alive?"

"Yes, I think so...when Shar gave it to me, she said some was true, but most of it was just her creating a story. It's kind of an inspirational guide book with a story surrounding it all."

He knew what he felt and what happened to him. He fell in love with her, or thought he had. The loss made him ache inside. He thought to himself...."Maybe I died and was actually there with her. Maybe we knew each other before, some say that's possible. Stop, stop it wasn't real. It's a fricken book," he thought. "It has absolutely nothing to do with me."

He set it on the mantle, trying to make light of it.

"Well, you should read it again. You definitely need some

inspiration!"

"I'll inspire you with this rag." Winding it up and smacking her on the butt. "I feel the magic, I feel the inspiration," he sang out as he sprayed the polish on the table.

"Okay," Melody laughed, "enough said."

They continued with the cleaning, but Melody could see her father was in another place. Eventually, they completed their task.

As she got ready to leave, she went over and picked up the book. "Can I read it?" she said, holding it in the air. "Maybe Shar will introduce me to her. I have never met an author."

"Sure, sure," he hesitated, "how about I take another look at it , then I'll bring it over to you."

*****

"So you found her?" Jake yelled as he pulled up to the dock. He knew he could always find Jeff by the water, either fishing or just watching the waves splash into the shore.

Jeff nodded without turning around, waved his hand in the air, and then smacked the ground beside him, signaling Jake to come sit.

Found her? Jeff thought. *Yeah, I did, she was just in my imagination. How stupid is that?*

"What are you doing here, Jeff? I thought you were going back to work?"

"Yeah, I will. I had to take a ride, to try to make some decisions. I called the office; they're covering for me this afternoon." He cast his line out further.

Jake smiled, raising his eyebrows. He knew Jeff loved to ride. "Where'd you go to?"

"It's not important. I needed time, time to think. I'm glad you came, or was this just a fluke you finding me?"

"No, Mel called me. Told me you were going today to get your Harley. She's pretty nervous about it."

"Jake, I need some time off. I know I'm putting you in a pinch again. But coming here, seeing the water, watching the boats, I have someplace that I need to go. I'm aiming in that direction,

I want to return to the Isle of Skye for a visit."
"How long do you plan to go for?"
"I don't know. No rules, no time. That's what my Uncle Sean on the Isle always said."
"Yes, nice imaginary world for the people on the Isle of Skye." He shuffled his foot on the rocks.
"Here, Jeff, we have time and rules."
"I know. I just want to see him and make sure he is okay. I need this, Jake."
"Alright, so when are you planning to go?"
"I'm kind of taking the long way around. I want to take a few weeks, put the bike in the pickup and heading east. I'll make my plane reservation from wherever I end up."
"Heading east, to anywhere special?"
"No, plans as of yet. I'll go where the wind takes me."
"Byers, you sound like you're trying to turn back time to your hippy days."
"That might not be a bad idea, Jake, but I am actually looking ahead."
"When are you going?"
"Tomorrow, if everything works out…"

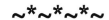

Chapter Fourteen

Everyone needs a happy place

Debby was so excited. It was the book signing that she had seen in her mind so many times over the years. She was really looking forward to this one.

"Are you about ready?"

"Yes, almost." Deb started to sing. "On the road again, I can't wait to get on the road again…"

"Did you pack everything?" as Dan tried to ignore her silly song and dance.

"What do you mean, pack? I don't think I've unpacked my things since the book was published last spring. How about you, did you call home?"

"Yes, I did. So you're sure you're going to be all right, Mom?

"I'll be fine. I guess I'm feeling like it's all a dream. Maybe I'll wake up tomorrow and it will be."

They both laughed thinking, *anything is possible*.

"I know," Danny said. "How crazy would that be?"

Deb sat on the couch, not in a hurry to get going. She was like this sometimes. Her mind take her to another place. " I came from sitting beside an old oak tree in Penn Yan, New York, writing, praying, wanting to share what I had learned. Praying that I wouldn't pass from the cancer. Knowing I had things to finish and begin in this realm. Now look at me, from an old oak tree to Oak Island, North Carolina. One oak to another, an angel thing, I think." She started laughing. "Hey, maybe I should buy a houseboat! Then I could live on the water and really have some amazing stories to share. A boat made of oak." She chuckled. "This ocean is the one that allowed me to discover many unanswered questions, from Maine to North Carolina. Water is truly the strongest energy for me."

"Mom, you're not lacking for stories! Your next book is already half-finished."

"Half-finished? I don't think so!"

"Did you come up with a name yet?"

"Maybe *Mother May I*. What do you think? "

"That's an interesting name, why that?"

"A game we would play.. It's played with a player asking permission, step by step. It would be a book for young women to let them know there are no rules, no time. They can be all they want to be. *We* put the limits on ourselves. I touched on it a week ago at the women's conference. I loved it, Dan, I loved it so much to be with all of them. This one woman…" *she suddenly stopped*. "Danny!! You have to stop me when I get going. I need to stay on schedule!" She jumped up from her chair and gave him a big hug.

Danny was leaning on the wall, patiently listening. She had a way to entrance you in the moment. You always wanted to hear more.

"I'm so excited to go see everyone up there. Plus the book signing, well, that's a bonus! I wasn't sure what I was doing with that book from one moment to the next. It took so long to finish. But I wanted it to be a book; I did know that from the beginning. I just never thought it would take years.

"All I know is it has helped a lot of people to look at things in a different way. When I try to explain the book at the signings, I get nervous at first, but then it flows. The moment just takes on a life of its own. The words come, just like when I was writing by the water or wherever I happened to be. The words just came.

"It's hard to explain. All the words, all the answers, all the music are there for you to capture. It's the place you go where it's peaceful. You have no distractions. Then you ask...ask, and it is given. Some say it's your angels, some say guides. Either way, it's where all will come to you. You can actually *feel* the communication that takes place within yourself. Words not spoken, yet they are understood within. A personal connection between you and your angels."

Danny started to laugh, watching his mother dancing with her words, singing her tune of life. She did it so well. He had no intention of stopping her. Her life was her time, her rules, her creation, and she was happy. That was all he could see in the sparkle of her eyes. She was happy.

Her words flowed. "People are looking for answers and guidance, and I tried to share as best I could. We all receive direction in different ways. It may be a sign as you're driving down the road. Or that still, small voice within you that shares what you need to hear. This happened to me so often by the lake or sitting at the tree. I wished, I hoped, I envisioned when it was finished that even just one person would come to me and say, 'Debby, that was amazing, it touched my heart.'

"It happens all the time now. I love it! So my wish came true.

Danny smiled hearing this, he was so proud of his mom. She had come so far to be in this moment.

"You have to see the success inside before you can see it on the outside. That is the magic of it all. Doubt is a dream snatcher, and until I was confident inside, it just wasn't going to appear. I know it sounds a bit strange, but maybe that's what's wrong with the world. It is controlled by a few close-minded people who may be unaware that what they are doing is truly holding people back."

"Is this the hippy coming out, Mom?"

"No, Danny. I am just trying to explain that everything happens in its own time. Believe, and you have a reason to not let go of your dreams."

Danny took his chance to say, "Maybe you can relax now and settle down with someone. We worry about you being alone so much. You still haven't called Bob back yet. He's a great guy, Mom, and he worries about you."

"Which one?" Deb said with a teasing laugh.

(The kids always teased her since many of the men that approached her online were named Bob.)

"Mom!"

"No, I'm kidding. I'll call him later. Will you please stop

worrying so much? I'm not worried about being alone anymore. I like who I am now. When Tom left, I had to find myself. That was a very tough time. The dating or being alone all those years were hard for me. I actually hated it, the dating, that is. Men who are single these days have so much baggage, it would take a moving van to date them. I had a lot of baggage back then, too...I pack light these days, though!" she added with a laugh as she swung her suitcase through the air.

Deb wanted to continue to play with him. "Danny, I heard Oprah..."

"Mom, please no!" *Waving his hand in the air.*

"Aww...stop it. She's my counselor at a distance. The safest kind for me! If I ever met one face to face and told them what happened over the years...(*sigh*)...*they* would need a counselor. So I am doing them a favor and took care of it all. I'm so thoughtful that way. Gotta love my life."

She snickered as she walked away from him towards the door. She spun around quickly and pointed at him. I love Oprah...someday; she and I will become best friends."

"Knowing you, Mom, I don't doubt that for a minute."

Believe it and see it...she started singing the Monkees song, "I'm a believer." Deb danced her happy dance, giggling.

"Now remember to call your sister and brother when you get home, and let me relax. Give Lilly and Reesie a kiss for me, too, and don't forget! That's what I pay you the big bucks for."

"For what?" he said with a playful look on his face.

"Not forgetting! You are much better at it now. Hey, I almost forgot to ask, is there any news from my publisher?"

"Books are selling as fast as they're put on the shelves. I heard they might have a contract coming for it to be translated."

"Well, isn't that wonderful? Now *that* is an angel thing!

I wonder how they say it's an angel thing in German?

They both laughed.

Maine, here I come! Is the car ready?"

"Yes, it's been ready. I don't know why you don't fly. I would worry less."

"Aye, laddie, it's hard to carry a pole on the plane!"She played with her Irish accent. "I might want to stop somewhere on the way. Who knows - maybe I'll go fishing. Is it in the car...my pole?"

"Mom, you have barely enough time to get there, so no stops other than the planned ones on the way up the coast. Come on, let's stick to the schedule. You can relax once you're there, okay?"

"It's the end of September. I still have a few months left of fishing if I want."

He gave in. "Did you renew your license?"

"Aye, laddie, I did, 'tis fine. I won't be getting a ticket for that again. Now ya get home, and I'm on my way. Call the kids and tell them I will call them later."

"Aye, aye, Captain," Dan saluted his mother and kissed her on the cheek.

"Remember when you used to play for me in the Gazebo and say, 'Oh Captain, my Captain', when I got out of my car?"

Dan hugged her. "I remember, Mom. I remember everything."

*****

Debra had made this drive many times over the years, but moving to the island made the trip quite a bit longer. She didn't mind it, though. It was her quiet time alone, with her music, and the road.

The small town was on the oceanfront of Maine, Pemaquid Point. She called it "her" place. The Pemaquid Inn made you feel as though you'd gone back in time. The walls were decorated with pictures of old movie stars. An old Victrola sat in the corner of the quaint living room, where the guests would mingle at night with coffee, wine, and tasty desserts. This enchanting Inn's story was quite renowned.

Stories still carried through the years of ships sinking off the coast near the lighthouse as the storms raged. The villagers would come carrying their baskets to gather the coal that found its way to the rocky shoreline. History was experienced here. If you sat still on the rocks, you could hear the whispers in the wind and feel the presence of life. Deb had found "her" place...or was she led to it?

Mr. and Mrs. Brindle were the Innkeepers. They had been there for twenty years. They met Deb when she first came here with Tom and their little girl Leah. Her visits continued yearly, though the world of Debra Pratt was changed year by year.

Meeting Charlie was one of her favorite moments at the Inn. Charlie was a colorful elderly gent with a smile and a laugh that would captivate any maiden. She made his acquaintance the last year of her marriage to Tom. He was sitting outside the small restaurant by the lighthouse, painting under a huge, brightly hued umbrella. His work reflected his love for the water, his non-concerned attitude to your stature or your appearance was evident. Charlie was there to touch your life for a moment, like Pemaquid Point.

Many faces passed him as he created his craft, yet only a few took take the time to stop and inquire of the artist. The first time Deb spotted him, it took everything she had not to stop to say hello. But her life was at the time to please and be with her husband, he continued, so she continued past. He was doing what she always wanted to do. Sitting in the sun, painting with no concern if someone decided to stop or not. Charlie was there for more than the money.

This was Debra's hidden dream that even Tom didn't share. Maybe it was so hidden that until she saw Charlie, it surfaced. To touch lives, say hello and go on with the day. I think she has discovered that she is doing it as well, but with her words, not a paint brush.

The universal spirit of life was very aware of her dreams.

Had Tom known any of her dreams at all? She wondered, thinking back. *Had he even known her at all?*

With Ol' Charlie, it was a friendship brought together by her lighthouse. She adored their conversations. He was totally fascinated by her as well. From the moment they met, they shared stories and dreams. It was as if they had known each other forever. This was Debby's way - everyone was a friend she hadn't met yet.

*****

Two days had passed since leaving the Island. Danny would be pleased to know she hadn't stopped anywhere for too long. Besides, she had arrived as quickly as she could. She wouldn't tell him that, of course. Deb loves it when he still says he is sorry for those teen years when he made her worry countless nights. *"I think a million apologies might be enough,"* she thought and giggled.

Debby turned up the long, narrow road leading to the Inn. Her heart raced, thinking of the lighthouse and the wonderful memories there. She reached to turn the volume up on her Celtic music. The music always helped her remember…

~

"Let's go to the lighthouse at sunrise, okay?"

"Sure, I'll set my alarm."

It came so early, he softly shook me. "Babe," his voice whispered, "come on. It's time."

Time? Time for what? The night mist in my mind cleared. "Oh, yes..."

"Hurry, it will be up in a minute."

"Okay." I was rushing to throw on my jacket. I couldn't find my camera. Finally, there it was lying on the floor. Taking a moment to say, "Thank you," since I knew I had help in finding it. I must have accidentally knocked it off the nightstand the night before.

"The bottle, where is the bottle?"

The previous night, we had shared a bottle of wine by the lighthouse under the Harvest Moon of October. As we sipped the last of our wine, a thought came to my mind. "Let's save the bottle - when we leave in the morning…release it into the ocean..." I was so excited.

Then the moon light touched on the pink bracelet on my arm. As we watched the harvest moon cast its light over the water, I felt within myself I had to let this bracelet go. It brought me strength during my breast cancer storm. It had to be left here by the lighthouse. I looked around and saw a post coming out from the rocks. What a great place to set it. As I slipped it carefully on the post, I could feel it was going to be a special moment. My place of magical happenings was to continue in this little cove by the ocean.

I heard his voice saying, "Hurry, the sun is coming up. Come on, babe, let's go."

"Okay, I got it, I'm coming."

The sun was starting to peek above the horizon. I stood there in the darkness, watching with excitement. I had never seen the sun come up here before. Three years ago, I had been here with another and the moon and the ocean gave me my answers. Now I was here again. I had planned to do this for some time, and now that I was in this relationship, it felt wonderful to bring him along with me. But should I have brought him?

As I walked along the edge of the rocks, a man was sitting quietly alone, watching the rising of the sun. He rose to see the wondrous view.

Where is his wife? I wondered.

I followed his example and stood, too, alone, as the sun started to show above the horizon, moment by moment. Sunrises are momentous, bringing in a new day. My heart raced as I watched the magic occur. Most humans are asleep and unaware of this wonderment. They just accept that it is going to happen and expect it. How sad.

My bracelet was still on the post where I had left it the night before.

Her creative mind commenced as her angels stood beside her.

Someone, from somewhere, will find this…

"Look," she'll say.

The woman's husband will be holding her hand as she breaks loose to reach for the bracelet. Her hands will gently lift the pink band off the post. It will be an angel moment for her.

My worn bracelet was going to be a sign to help her see she would be fine, as I was. It will be her sign of life. As my angel cloud did for me. She will survive the cancer. We will be sisters finding the rainbow after the storm.

The woman's husband brought her here to the water, to the lighthouse, to be. To celebrate their life and to help her relax and smile. Maybe she is reading this book right now. Are you?

If so, she will say to herself, "This is the person who left the bracelet for me." One day, she will make contact with me and say, "I found your bracelet…" Our friendship will begin at that moment.

*****

Today was to be our last day here.

"Let's go over there by the rocks that go further out into the water," as I pointed down the beach, carrying our bottle.

"A message in a bottle…who does this?" he said, laughing.

"I do. I do this. These are the kind of memories not soon forgotten. Angel moments…made to happen."

The note read:

> My name is Debby, and today is my birthday.
> I have come to this place often; it has become *my* place to find answers.
> If you find this bottle, please contact me. I feel that everyone meets for a reason.
> Here is my phone number and my address.
> I would love to meet you.

We went out to the rocks. The waves were gentle, yet strong enough to carry it out to the depths of the water. He walked carefully. He didn't realize the magic that would occur days from this one.

"Wait," I said, "let's take a picture of it before you throw it." The bottle rested on the rock in the final picture before it was released.

I called out, "Don't look down, just throw it."

He smiled…his hand released the bottle, and it floated through the air, seemingly in slow motion before it finally touched the ocean and lay riding on a wave. In a short amount of time, the message quickly drifted, going out further and further away…

We both smiled, content with what was done.

Days had passed, and the bottle was a fun memory. Reflecting back on this moment. We came so close to touching the light, however fear and doubt found a way to drive us apart. Both afraid, not so much of the great possibility of sharing happiness, but of the terrible possibility of losing it again, losing me again. The scales tipped, and it became only a memory. The ocean floated him afar, just as it was to be. Though at the time, we never anticipated the beginning of the end. Which had occurred twice before, at *my* special place. Maybe solo was my destiny. It was my world, my story, my life. All for clarity, but wonderful stepping stones of life and living it without limits of expectations. He will remember me...and I him.

*****

Then, it happened. My cell phone rang.

"Hello?"

"Can I speak with Debby, please?" a woman asked.

"Yes, this is Debby."

"My name is Mary, I found your bottle."

"What?" I was dumbfounded. "You're kidding!"

"No, I'm not!"

We both were laughing.

"*Oh, my God,*" I thought. "*Who is going to believe this?*"

Mary continued to explain. "My husband and I were walking along the shore, and I spotted the bottle on a rock ledge. I begged him to get it for me, and with some hesitancy, he made his way along the rocks. Before he reached it, I called to him, 'Maybe it will have a message in it to me, saying, Happy Birthday, Mary! He waved with a whatever wave, as if to say, 'You're kidding, right?' When his hand reached for the bottle, he looked at me and said, 'Mary...there is a message in it!' I was so excited."

I could tell she was almost in tears, and so was I.

She went on, "When I opened it, and it read, 'Hi, my name is Debby and today is my birthday', my husband and I were in disbelief. It was my birthday message, my own true message in a bottle."

She shared of her life. They owned an inn, located a little more inland in Maine. They kept a journal of memories that they had, of guests who stayed at the inn, hoping someday to write a book.

I said, "Mary, I'm writing a book."

"Really?"

I know I sounded a bit overly excited. "My book is called *The Memory Barrel.*"

"No way," she said.

"Yes."

We were both amazed as we shared more and more of our lives with each other. Ironically, our birthdays were only days apart. Our friendship continues to this day at a distance because we haven't been able to meet face to face yet. But we met heart to heart that day on the phone as we shared a rainbow moment together.

*****

Debby returned back to the present without missing a beat.
Experiences like these would be difficult for anyone to believe they were
real.
But then, that was her life.
Hard to believe...

Pulling into the driveway, she saw shadows moving across the window pane. Someone was watching. Deb knew it must be Helen.

"*Yes, this is a good place for me,*" Deb thought.

The back door flew open as she approached the porch and Helen ran out the door, with her arms waving in the air. "Aw, come give me a hug, sweetie! Jim and I are so proud of you. You're famous! We watched you on Oprah. It was so exciting. You did really great."

Deb laughed, "What are you talking about? I am not famous. You're so funny."

She took a deep sigh as she held Helen so tightly. "Oh, I have missed you so much. Where is that old guy?"

"He is trying to contain himself, signing some guests in. I know he's busting at the seams to see you. We've been watching you write that book for years. We are both so happy for you!"

Debby tried peeking through the door to see Jim. She and Helen held hands walking in...

"Really, love, now tell me something, did you find him?"

"Did I find who?" Deb said, repeating it with a teasing smile on her face. "Who, Helen?"

"Mr. wonderful, of course!"

"You left us hanging at the end of the book. No one knows who he is."

"I did not. The clues were always there. You need imagination. It isn't a mystery. It's fictional, maybe a fictional mystery!" she said, laughing.

"Yeah, yeah," Jim growled with a huge smile on his face as

Debby and Helen came into the lobby. "I'll give ya fictional mystery, young lady!" He grabbed her and spun her around she felt like she was ten years old.

They were like her second parents, always there for her, laughing and crying, throughout the years.

"Helen," Debby said, "in the book she finds the most important person of all, her one true love. Like her angels told her one night on the balcony of her apartment."

Remembering back:

I felt so lonely. The night sky glistened with stars as I went out onto the balcony. I sat in the doorway, staring into the night sky.
The music softly played from the opened door behind me in the apartment.
"I wish you would please bring me my one true love...?"
Then from within, the words came.
"You are your one true love."
I almost cried. "Yes," I said. "I see that. If I don't love myself, why should I expect someone to love me the way I want? You're right. Thank you."

Helen's voice brought her back to the present.
"Well...?" as her voice raised an octave. "Tell me, love, tell me!"

Deb continued to explain, "I found myself. I found out who I really am. All of those trials that I had to go through were necessary for me to become who I am today. No regrets now, Helen. Everyone has to walk that same way, realizing maybe we don't understand why things happen at the time. But we will. There is always a reason. Now my life is wonderful. I am more than fine. My kids are happy and successful, and I am here. Let's enjoy this time together. By the way, how's my lighthouse?"

"It hasn't moved," a deep voice said as Jim came up behind her. "Come on, cutie, where's your keys?" He headed for the door. "I need to get your bags. You still drive that fast little car?"

She winked at Helen and turned to Jim. "Nope, I got a faster one. The black convertible out there."

Jim glanced into the lot and with raised eyebrows gave her a smirk.

Deb scrunched her nose. "Sporty, huh?"

Jim stared out the window, examining it at a distance.

"Would you rather I have a Harley?"

"No," he growled. "I hated it when you dated that guy on the bike."

"Guy on the bike, huh? He had a name."

"Don't they all?" he sneered, scooping the keys out of her hand.

*****

Debra settled in her room, not really unpacking too many things because her mind was on the lighthouse that was only a two-minute walk from where she now stood. She could hear and smell the ocean from the inn. It was the end of tourist season now, and in a few weeks it would be closed until April. So many thoughts ran through her mind as she started toward the lighthouse. It was almost dusk. She loved it when she could witness the setting of the sun, especially in Maine. To be there and to watch it set was her way of showing thanks for another fulfilling day.

On the island, the birds always settled on the water's edge at sunrise and sunset, as if they were watching in honor of the day that was coming and at sunset giving thanks for the day that had passed. This was a daily occurrence. I wonder who truly notices. *She did.*

Thoughts, moments and memories whirled through her mind. How had she come this far? She had walked through worlds and raging storms to be here. All for now, all for this. As she came closer, she could see the lighthouse dome was lit and the parking lot was empty…*"Good,"* she sighed.

The wind was blowing softly, and the breeze whisked through her hair. Deb found her one spot on the rocks where she had sat on hundreds of occasions, contemplating, crying, asking questions with unheard answers. Then a voice could be heard, a voice inside her saying, *"You're going to be fine."*

"Thank you," she said softly. "Thank you for letting me live." Her angels were with her. She was aware that everyone knew how she thought. She never hid it.

The sun had set now, and the moon was full. She sat on the rocks' ledge, watching the water move in rhythm to a silent melody. Her mind traveled to another time. The waves and mist soothed her.

This is where her answers were given. Memories of times past floated in the waves of her mind.

She went back in her memories…

I met him online, like the others. The only difference was that this one had become a true friend. We chatted off and on for over a year, always keeping in touch, yet never meeting.

In the midst of one of our conversations, he could sense that I really needed to relax. All of the working and worrying over life and kids, I was definitely feeling drained.

"Let's have a drink," he said.

"What, meet now?"

"Yes, meet me at the club on Rt. 21."

"Oh, are you sure? Okay, I will be there around 7."

"Sounds like a plan to me," he said.

Leah sensed my nervousness. "Mom, go! It'll be fine."

"Okay, but this is friends, nothing else?"

"Right. Now go!" as she nudged me out the door.

I waited in my car in the parking lot. It was so dark. Even though I heard a storm was coming in and I hated to drive in the snow, I went anyways. A tap came on the window, my heart jumped.

"Hey, you," he said with a bright smile.

We talked and talked. It was so easy, coming away from the computer and meeting him.

Mother Nature was making the world outside a winter wonderland. The wind swirled the snow as if it was performing a dance in the air to the melody of the wind's song.

Neither one of us wanted to part, knowing we both would become storm riders in a short time as we made our way back to our separate worlds.

Months passed, and we spent as much time together as we could. He was a good teacher, sharing things of his life and showing me things I had never seen before, making me feel like I hadn't felt in a long, long time. I was falling in love.

"Let's go for a ride, Dee," as he opened his garage door.

"Whoa!" I couldn't contain myself, I was so excited. "I was on one of them last summer and I got dumped right off!"

He laughed. "Hop on! I won't dump ya."

We rode the four-wheeler through the fields and around the trees, riding on paths that hadn't been used in ages. He kept saying, "I haven't been out here in years."

It was good…

I miss him…I wonder if he misses me.
The turning point in the world of us, or the awakening was here. He and I stood in this exact same spot, at this exact same time.
Harvest moon.
Why do I keep going back, remembering?
I still see it and feel the sadness. I should just let it go. Let him go, I thought I did.
She knew she had to write…let it go…

(Journal entry)

Bob had never been here before. He always said that he loved the ocean. This was my special place, and I wanted to share it with him. We were having a bit of a rough time in our relationship after dating for eighteen months. Somehow, we seemed to have lost the magic and I wanted it back. I wanted the answers to come for me here at this place. I felt I could get the answers here.

I watched him intently as he walked the rocks the day before, looking like a young boy as he found treasures buried in the crevices of the rocky beach. His smile glowed when he saw me holding the camera ready, his uplifted hands showing newfound treasures. It was exciting to see how happy he was. Why couldn't he be like that when we were home?

We laughed together that day and also had moments of deafening silence. This night will echo in my mind forever. I saw the end in those moments. Like the very instant you realize that you are dreaming and that any second you will wake up. Still unable to escape the haunting truth, that it will be over too soon. I remember, and so does he.

Once again, the moon was full and the night was crystalline.

We stood on the cleft of these very rocks as the waves crested below.

"Look," I pointed out. Almost at the edge of the horizon, you could barely see it. "There's a sailboat!"

It was moving so slowly on the water. The small boat, going further and further from the shore. Moonlight reflected on the surface of the water, allowing the waves to guide the path of the boat. Was the moon pulling them to the fullness of its light? This is where the magic could happen for them. (My imagination began creating a dream, a wish, or was it?)

"How amazing for them to be sailing in the night, on the ocean." My voice carried across the water.

"Does Bob feel the magic being here?" The words were said silently in my mind.

The sailboat seemed to take forever to reach the moonlit rays on the water. I stood solemnly as I patiently waited, my camera in position, waiting, waiting for them to reach the light. I shared my creative story to unknowingly inattentive ears.

"As soon as it reaches the light, I'm going to take a picture. You see, there are two people on that boat." I began to create my imaginary story. "They are so much in love. He planned this moment from the beginning, to propose to her under a full moon in the light of its rays on the ocean. He knows how much she loves the ocean, how much she loves him.

"They're coming from a surprise party he gave her on the shore, with family and friends. Everyone on the shore knows he is going to propose to her this night, promising forever and a day. The true surprise!"

Bob stood silently listening, or was he?

I continued, "He has a ring in his pocket. As soon as the boat is in the moonlight, that's when he...{*I hesitated, entranced*}...watch, it's getting closer. It's almost there."

My heart was racing from my own imagination. I raised my camera and looked through the lens. "It's in the light, the boat is in the light, and he's asking her. She's crying, and with shaking hands he slipped the ring on her finger."

In that very instant, the light hid the boat, and it literally disappeared for a moment.

"Where did they go?" I couldn't see them through my lens. "They disappeared in the light." I pulled the camera away from my eyes. "Where are they? Was it a dream? Where did it go?" My imagination seemed so vivid, so real, as if I was an invisible passenger right there on the deck.

The boat was gone.

I froze, staring at the water and the light. It was there, but I couldn't capture the moment on film. I was so disappointed. Then, the boat suddenly reappeared on the other side of the light! It wasn't a dream, it was real. Did it happen? I stood silent! I wanted to take a picture of them, it would have been one in a million.

"Aw, babe, that would have been a great picture," Bob said as he started to walk away, not realizing how important that moment was, or did he?

That was all he said. That's all he could think of to say?

My eyes swelled with tears, though I tried to conceal them. I loved him and wanted to be his wife. It happened, and then disappeared, like the sailboat in the light.

The angels gave me the answer. It wasn't him. He would have known right at that moment. {I see, I said within, I see now. We weren't on the same path. We would never share the same dream and imagination.}

We walked silently back to the inn. And after we returned home, the laughter was completely gone. As it was before we left. The touch that went to my soul was gone, never to be felt again. That is why I wanted to go to the lighthouse to get it back. It didn't come.

Instead, I gave it to the ocean. Another message in a bottle. Only this one will drift too far out. He was caught in his world, and there was no room for me. I had to regroup in my mind. I loved him, but I refused to settle. I knew the hurt will go away in time, as it always does, leaving its mark in one way or another.

She tore the pages out of her journal.
"Does he miss me, does he truly miss me? I still see his smile."
Holding the written words to her heart, she rolled them in a ball and tossed it into the water.
There, let it be as it was supposed to be.
We couldn't be then, maybe in another time we were or will be.

Nathaniel said, "Let it go, angel, it is taken care of."

"Are you okay?" a male voice called out to her from a

distance.

Deb was startled. As she came back from her memory, she quickly wiped away the tears. "I'm sorry, you scared me. I thought I was alone." She could see a shadow of a man and his dog reflected in the light from the moon. *His voice is very soft, she thought.*

"Yes, I'm okay." She stood quickly, brushing off her jeans. "Reflecting, I'm just reflecting. Have a good night."

"You, too," the soft voice said.

Her swift steps on the path to her room in the inn made her heart race. Or maybe it was the memory of the unexpected guest. Either way, it didn't matter.

Then reality gradually set in. *"My book signing! Oh no, it's so late and I have to get up early...and it's already midnight."*

The sound of a motorcycle slowly passing caught her attention, and then she noticed the phone resting on the table by the window.

"I forgot to call Bob... it's better this way."

~*~*~*~

Chapter Fifteen

The Signing

They were both waiting for her to come downstairs.

She was up pretty late last night, I hope she rested well, Helen thought to herself.

"How do I look?" Deb asked as she surprised them dancing around the corner into the lobby for their approval.

"Cutie, you look like an author," Helen said.

"Oh yeah?" She laughed. "How does an author look?"

"Tired," Jim said as he pushed her gently on her shoulder. "Late one last night, huh?"

"What, are you keeping track of me? Did I break curfew?"

"Nah, worry about you is all,"

"Don't let him fool you! He heard a bike pull in last night. He was worried, all right," Helen added.

"Oh, yeah? You think I'm only drawn to men with motorcycles?"

"No, I don't," as he urged her out the door. "Get your butt moving and sign those books, young lady. Make me proud." He leaned down and kissed her forehead.

*****

It wasn't a long walk to the village square. A large white gazebo was placed strategically in the center of the park. All of the shops circled the square, and thus the gazebo. Young musicians would often come and serenade the tourists as they walked about the square. Tourism was big here. It paid for the town expenses during the off season. In fact, the shopkeepers made enough in the five months of tourist season to be comfortable for the rest of the year. It was a good life.

Deb had become familiar with many of them over the years. These folks were not impressed by the wealthy. They lived simple lives. They couldn't care less about social climbing. The whole "I live to work" mentality did not exist here. Less is more to them.

"Here she comes!" Vanessa yelled over her shoulder into the Novel Café. An older woman appeared at the door with her apron on.

"Come on, missy, get in here. I've made you your special coffee, and guess what else?"

"Hey, Hattie," Debby said, running to her open arms. "I don't care, whatever it is, I love it! Just being here and seeing your face again fills me with joy."

"Well, missy, you can smell, can't ya?"

They hugged tightly, and Vanessa watched with her huge smile on her face. Deb reached out over Hattie's shoulder to touch Vanessa's hand.

A smile spread over Debby's face as the aroma filled her soul. "Chocolate chip muffins... You made the chocolate chip muffins, they smell wonderful. You're such an angel, Hattie!"

"I know. Why do ya think my business is so successful? Plus having my own special author pay a visit doesn't hurt either. After reading your book, a lot of people have come to see the famous Novel Café. I remember you coming in here with all your writing stuff."

"Me, too. I have so many memories being here with you. Most of The Memory Barrel was critiqued here. Right on that table," Deb said as she pointed to the one by the window.

"Leah is writing now, too. Did I remember to tell you that in my letters? She is writing children's books. I think Lacey is bringing it out of her."

"Ah...an up and coming author, like her mom? Maybe the apple doesn't fall far from the tree!" Hattie shuffled Deb into the Café. "There are some pretty hard things written on those pages, young lady, I pray all of it isn't true."

"It is what it is, and isn't. My lips are sealed. I do hope you enjoyed the story," she said, laughing. "I have read and re-read the book so many times, I just hope women find some strength and direction from it. If anything, I hope they see not to give up on their dreams. Yet, and more importantly, that they truly believe they are being watched over and they aren't alone. Even though their eyes say they are, their hearts know differently. That's what I pray for."

"You have the gift to convince them if they don't, love," Hattie said lovingly. "So, the ending looks like another book will be coming?"

Debby looked surprised, though she had been hearing that a lot lately. "Oh, really? Seems you're not the only one that thinks that. I keep saying maybe. Since when am I in control of what happens? Time will tell."

"Ah...see? You are thinking of writing another."

"Yes, but this one won't be the same. Not sure if I could create a sequel to *The Memory Barrel*."

Deb stuffed the last piece of muffin in her mouth and helped clear the table.

"Are ya ready? People are out there waiting to meet ya."

"Oh, I'm ready," she said, smoothing down her skirt.

Hattie had a wireless microphone and began to attach it to Debby's blouse. "Everyone wants to hear what is happening, so say hello to your friends, angel."

People were standing inside, and some were outside, waiting to get in.

"Oh, my goodness," Deb said, backing up into Hattie.

"Steady, girl," Hattie said as she placed her hands on Deb's shoulders.

"Do we set up books, or what do I do here?" Deb was nervous.

"Yes, we did...stacked them high!" Hattie said, anticipating her concern. "Danny sent cases of books last week. It's covered."

"Ok," she said softly, with almost a squeak in her voice.

Her voice carried inside and out of the little Novel Cafe.

"Hello, everyone!"

Voices old and young responded loudly, "Hello!"

"I am so excited to be with you today."

Her face shined as the fear of the moment evaporated and she became Debra Pratt, the author.

"I have a little thought that was shown to me the other day as I was preparing to come here. I would like to share it if I may."

Everyone listened and hushed one another. None of De's thoughts were *little thoughts*.

"As you all know, I live what I say. Words are given to me from a place that all those words are available. Yes, they are available to all of you, just as they are to me. Most of the time, I am shown things when I least expect them. Like this one. Similar to all the messages I shared with you in *The Memory Barrel*, they come. From where, you might ask? You all can have your answers to this, but I say they come from my angels. This is what I was shown:

"A caterpillar crawls on the ground for a time, then by nature begins creating a cocoon. Not knowing what will be taking place. She created it and enfolds herself inside it. Do you see she created it? Please try to remember this!"

She took a moment for everyone to absorb what she was saying, as all good teachers do.

"I always have paper ready. Or I find one quickly, so I can write it down!! Toilet paper, receipts, anything you can grab works."

Everyone laughed

As Deb waved the paper in her hand that words were written on, it looked like the back of her print out of her road map to come to Maine.

"So this little caterpillar is buried inside the cocoon. She hears sounds and feels vibrations from life outside. Being still, just waiting. Listening and waiting. For what? Time will show her. As she waits, she can feel changes taking place. Something more is developing that she didn't have before a magical beauty. Then one day, a beam of light reflects through her surroundings.

She stirs since light hasn't been seen for some time. It had been so dark inside there. Now the layer that enfolded around her is thinning. She feels the space she is in growing smaller, and she knows a change is coming. Not realizing it already happened.

What is it? What's next?

She can see the true light now, but somehow it looks different than when she went in.

She came out of her space with more than she had going in.

She sits on the branch examining her surroundings. Examining her body, the newness of it.

How lovely I am now. How did this happen?

"What now?" she asks within herself, but without words and it is understood and answered by life.

"Come fly now," a voice convinces her from within it is time to do something she'd never had before.

"Fly? Wings?" She turns to see now by the light she has a beautiful presence with her. "What do I do?

I remember life with wings on others before. They soared above me."

"Now it is time for you to soar as they...trust and fly," the voice says, "it will come naturally."

She is now free. Free from what contained her...

She has more than she came with in the beginning.

Did she work for it?

NO...

It was just given, so she could be all she was to be right from the beginning.

It takes time and patience, like a seed, to grow.

Deb moved all around a lot when she spoke. The world was her stage as she entertained everyone with her expressive way of telling her stories.

She lifted her wings, and the wind swirled beneath them.

Ahhhhh, she sighed as the wind took hold of her.

The source of all that is life gave her a nudge.

"There," the voice said, and she soared.
"Now you are who you were meant to be.
Touch the light, feel the air, make those who see you smile."
Debra stood silently for just a moment, thinking of what she learned from these words that had been given to her. She put her hand on her heart. Her head rose, and a tear rolled down her cheek. Remembering before, and remembering now.

"Today I am...with you, with all of you. I am so honored and celebrate life today from where I have come from to be here now. So let's have fun and make this a day to remember!!"

Some had tears, others handing tissues. The clapping of appreciation surrounded Deb as she wiped her eyes. I see so clearly now. Deb walked straight to the table filled with her unsigned books. Suddenly, she spotted something to the side of the arrangement.

"Oh my gosh, Hattie, where did you get this?"

Hattie started laughing. Everyone was smiling. Seeing the surprise on Deb's face was priceless.

"Rob called and said the kids wanted to send you a gift."

"How did it get here?"

"Sam from the drug store was heading in Rob's direction. Since this is your first book signing here, we thought it would be wonderful to have your mascot here, too."

Debby walked over and softly touched the barrel.

The emotions rose, and all could see it written in her eyes. "Is it full?"

"Of course, everything is there, hon. No one has touched a thing."

Hattie said, "Dee, the kids called, they said there was a surprise for you in it."

"Really, do you know what it is?" She could feel her heart racing as she slowly loosened the lid. The people came closer because the group in the back was pushing forward so they could see. It lifted with some difficulty, which reminded her of when she brought it home. The lid was very tight then, too.

She couldn't help thinking back…

It had to be around 1980.

I worked at a meat processing store. Accountant, bookkeeper, but most importantly the master of peeling onions and whatever else needed to be done. One dear friend there called me Madame Secretary. We became great friends. The owner ordered seasoning in large barrels for his homemade lasagna and other Italian specialties that he sold in his store.

I came upon an empty one and saw the possibility for it...a memory barrel for my family.

"Hey, Jim, can I have this barrel?"

I knew he was throwing it out.

"Sure, Dee, take it home."

"Thanks."

I brought it home and began to work on it, covering the seasoning labels on the large canister with contact paper.

"What are you doing, Mommy?" Danny asked. *He was only five at the time.*

"I am making us a Memory Barrel, Bam."

"A what?" Robby asked.

"A memory barrel. We'll put all your special things in it, like your teddy bears that Grandma bought you and things you guys made for me. It will make us smile when you are older when we go through it and share your treasures with me."

"Not Sparky, though," Danny said with concern.

"Not Sparky, honey. For now, he needs to keep Benji company in your bed. *(Benji and Sparky were his frog and dog toys he loved)*

Both boys helped me, knowing how tired I was. They could never imagine how precious this would be in the future moments we walked through in life.

"You all right, Dee?" A soft hand touched her.

"Shar! Oh, what a wonderful surprise!"

Hattie and Vanessa stood by, quietly watching Shar and Debby embrace.

"I'm so glad to see you. Thanks for coming. How are the

girls? Did they come with you?"

"I wouldn't have missed this for anything. Remember what we always said? Out of everything bad, comes something good. This is our time, angel, I came to be with you for our time; it has been quite a while. The girls send you their love, though."

"I know, we've been patient and now look."

"I know, Dee, it's wonderful."

Someone yelled from the back, "Open the barrel!"

As she lifted the lid, the smell of vanilla filled the air. Debby stepped back away from it for a moment, taking a deep breath.

The people that were standing close to it looked at each other, remembering what was in the book.

"Oh my gosh, those kids are awesome. I feel like I'm in the first chapter of my book."

Then she saw it, a package wrapped in gold paper with a gold ribbon wrapped around it.

A card was attached. It read:
Family forever and a day
Expect nothing, but hope for everything
Love,
Dan, Rob and Leah

Her eyes filled with tears, making it difficult for her to see.

Shar touched her. "It's okay, hon."

She paused for a moment... "Wait, isn't there supposed to be a Scottish fella opening this?"

Everyone laughed. "Yahh, where is he?" someone called from the door.

Dee looked with a squintish smirk. "Well, he's in the book, aye? Ya know it to be true," she said in her playful Gaelic voice. "'Tis a wonderment, to be sure. I think he might be hidin' in the..."

Someone from the other side called, "In the mountains of New York."

Yes, he is!!" Dee laughed out loud. "Yes, he is."

"So why are you here in Maine, lassie? You should be finding him."

"Ahhh, 'tis no finding to be done. The angels and fairies will bring him if he is my love. Besides, you're my family right now."

Everyone cheered.

"When you believe it, you will see him. When you believe it, you will see him!!"

Deb did her happy dance, playing with everyone as music began to serenade their moves throughout the room. Everyone joined in with the playful dance. "I believe, I believe," they all sang and danced in the cafe and in the street.

Everyone was there to experience Debra Pratt and her world. So many lives had been touched by her already, and many more to come.

Hattie handed her a tissue. "Come on, lassie, your public awaits."

Debbie held up her album with the painting on the cover, her memory painting, and the people applauded.

"Let's get to these books," she said. Picking one up, she sat down and extended her hand. "Hello," she said to the first person. "My name is Debra Pratt. It's a pleasure to meet you."

The middle aged woman smiled. "No, the pleasure is all mine."

One person at a time, she spent hours making sure something special was said or written to every person.

Shar went back to the Inn. She wanted to leave her to the signing and personal time with the people. The two planned to meet for dinner later.

Hattie's special brew, along with her chocolate chip muffins, kept them all pumped up and fully charged.

~*~*~*~

Chapter Sixteen

Everyone meets for a reason.
Timing within the Universe brings clarity of life.

First thing the next day, Jeff started on his personal trip, marking his ledger that sat next to the armrest in his truck, May 5th.

"Today, boy, we are heading for nowhere and ending up somewhere."

Doc's ears perked up, and he barked with excitement.

Jeff drove for hours, listening to his music. The little town of Fillmore was fading in the distance as he headed east. The further he distanced himself, he felt as if a heavy weight were being lifted from him. His life had changed these last three years. Time was necessary to refocus. He stopped occasionally if something caught his eye, especially if it was a fishing hole.

His wife of thirty years had decided she wanted to find herself. They met while he was in medical school. She was interning in pediatric medicine. Their schedules were grueling, but they always found time for each other. She came back to Fillmore with Jeff, and they married there. Her family was from Boston, so moving to Fillmore and leaving her family was a big adjustment for Sarah. But she loved him, and a wife should be by her husband's side. At least that's what was taught in the early 70s.

Sarah was offered a pediatric surgeon's position in Fillmore, which wasn't hard to accept. Two beautiful children and a successful husband didn't keep her mind still. What was she looking for? Her life was what most women dream of.

Now that the children were grown, she needed to leave to expand her horizons, follow *her* passion. She felt she lost it somewhere in the married years.

This is something that happens to more families than not, living your life around the kids so when they go on their own journey, you're now just two adults living in the same house, but strangers. Both had failed to keep the relationship strong enough to endure the emptiness without the children.

It's so hard on the children to be the ingredient that makes you both happy. Maybe that's why the children blame themselves when you can't be together, not realizing whose fault the failure was. So it is.

Jeff remembered reading about this after their divorce. Trying to understand what happened. Failing to realize what was happening all along. Taking every sunrise and sunset for granted, *maybe even her. Where is she tonight? Does she know I left Fillmore? Does she even care I left?*

"Whoa, too much going back in time is not what this trip is for. I don't want to go back. Life goes on, that's what this trip is about, going on, going forward."

Doc looked at him as he rambled. He did that often, and Doc would always be by his side listening.

The days turned into months when Jeff finally reached the coast. Five months had passed since leaving Fillmore. He was a little rough around the edges but felt amazing. As he drove up Route 1, a coastline road in Maine, it led him to a special hideaway.

What he didn't realize was that he was being guided there.
In time, he will see; always, one must expect the unexpected.
There is more to this life than meets the eye.

He pulled into an inviting campsite that was half-occupied with the hardy *seasonal campers*. The leaves were starting to change. Autumn in Maine was like walking into a painting, filled with colors so crisp and radiant it would be hard to describe. He took his time; he wasn't in any hurry.

"Hey boy, let's camp here. Looks like a great place."

He pulled out his ledger

October 3rd...*October? You have to be kidding me. Where did the time go? Something is happening this month. What was it? I'll remember later,* he thought.

Jim Brindle owned the campground, as well as the Inn of Pemaquid, with his wife Helen. Jeff jumped out of the truck, and Doc followed, hoping to find a place to mark his territory.

"Not yet, boy," Jeff said.

Doc's head turned in wonderment. *"Why?"* he seemed to ask with his eyes *"That's what dogs do."*

Jeff laughed and guided him to follow.

"Nice dog," Jim said as he watched them approaching the office through the screen door. "He seemed to have a plan, then you changed it." He laughed.

"Yes, sir," Jeff laughed, "but that's life, isn't it?"

Jim liked his comeback.

"I see your plates are from Ohio. Did you come here on business?"

"No, not really. Time off that was desperately needed."

"Most of the tourists have gone home, so you'll enjoy the quiet, if that's what you're looking for."

"Yes, that will hit the spot for sure," Jeff said, reaching for Doc and ruffling his head. "Right, boy?"

Doc loved to get ruffled.

"Been here before, son?"

"No, I've always wanted to but never had the time, sir."

Jim said, "That's life sometimes, no time to take a moment for yourself. The world is a busy place. I know you're going to want to fill your appetite soon. Let's see..." Jim thought for a moment, then said, "There's a pub in the square if you'd like to have a brew. They give you a mean plate full of food, too. The price is always right, and tomorrow a local will be singing there."

"Sounds like fun."

"It certainly is." Jim stretched so he could pat Doc's head. "My wife and I run the inn up the road if you need a dog sitter.

Or if it gets a bit chilly at night, we do have cabins you can stay in."

"No, that's fine. Doc will sleep in the cab of the truck while I'm out and about. I'm never gone too long. However, thank you for the offer. I'll keep the cabins in mind. It is a bit brisk lately."

Jim glanced over Jeff's shoulder. "Nice Harley!"

"I got her a few months ago."

"I used to ride, too," Jim said. "I gave it up a long time ago."

"Oh, why is that?"

"I had a bad accident when I was younger."

"I know how that feels. I had one last year, too, in the fall. Bad timing did it on the way to work. I should have known better - but hey, life lessons."

"What do you do, son?"

"I'm a doctor."

"Really?" Jim said with a surprised look. "So, is October your normal vacation time?"

"No, sir, this is just a stop for me. I'm planning to go to a place I haven't visited in many years, The Isle of Skye. Have you ever heard of it?"

"No. Whereabouts is that?"

"In Scotland; my family's from there. I still have some relatives there. They're getting pretty old, and I'd like to see them one more time."

"Family is everything, son. Don't ever lose sight of that."

"No, sir."

"I better get back to the inn. We're expecting a special visitor tonight, too. She's like a daughter to us. I don't want to miss seeing her arrive. Gotta give her my special welcome!" he said with a hardy laugh.

"Yes, it was nice talking with you."

"Now you be careful on that bike, son."

*****

Night came quickly. Setting up the tent was getting easier every time. Jeff cleaned up a bit and loaded Doc in the truck for his nightly 'Let's meet the locals'. He had met many people over the last few months. Some he wouldn't mind forgetting; yet, here in Pemaquid it seemed different. There was a peacefulness here...a peacefulness he hadn't felt in a long time.

"What can I get you? Maybe a drink to start off?" asked the waitress.

"Sure. How about some of your special brew? It comes highly recommended."

"Coming right up!" she replied with a grin.

The atmosphere was quaintly familiar. Round, small tables with chairs set closely together. It invited good conversation and overcame the feeling of being alone. The music was soft and soothing. A young woman with an angelic voice sang Irish melodies with a flutist accompanying her and a young man playing a small mandolin. Dinner was hearty, with an Irish touch.

A stout elderly man approached. He was short in stature and had a smile that lit up his entire face.

"Can I get you another brew, lad?" he asked with an apparent Irish brogue as he reached to clear Jeff's plate in front of him. "If ya be staying around for a spell, tomorrow we have a local band coming that really draws in the crowd. My daughter will be singing her songs to get the fairies dancing about the pub, sprinkling their dust on everyone. The magic makes everyone get up and dance the night away."

His eyes sparkled....*Is he a leprechaun? This is definitely going to be a place to remember.*

"I'll be here for a few days, so I'll make sure I come back. I think I'll pass on another drink, though."

"As ya say, son. A pleasure to ave' ya come by. Make sure ya wear comfortable shoes on the morrow!" The Irish gent turned on the tips of his toes, dancing away to go entertain another customer, enjoying his life.

Doc was asleep in the front seat of the truck.

"Hey boy, I know it's been a long trip. How about we go to the camp and hit the hay?" Doc wagged his tail without moving too much except his head so Jeff could squeeze behind the wheel.

It was hard to settle in here, though, with so many thoughts running through his mind. What direction should he go from here?

I should call Uncle Sean and make sure my timing is right. Mel's...I haven't called her in a while either. I will tomorrow.

Jeff patted Doc's head. "Don't let me forget, will ya boy? It's too late to call now."

The moon was full as he lifted the flap to go into the familiar bedroom he'd created. *What a life*, he thought to himself as he lay on his mat. His mind continued to keep him occupied, not allowing him to sleep.

Doc, sensing Jeff's restlessness, sat up with his head turned sideways as if he heard Jeff's thoughts. Doc wasn't tired; he'd had a cat nap in the truck - or make that a *dog* nap...

"Want to go for a walk, boy?"

Doc jumped to his feet and quickly slid through the tent door.

"Ah, that's a yes, I see." Jeff chuckled.

The moon was bright, not a cloud in the sky. The stars were brighter than bright. It was an amazing night. Jeff could smell the salt water more distinctly now than before. He started to walk towards the road and stopped, looking back at his bike. It wasn't far to ride, and the moon lit up the night.

"Let's take the bike!" It never occurred to him that that was how he'd hurt himself before. Somehow, his mind was on other things here. As he started the engine, Doc jumped around like a puppy. He was used to the sound of the bike.

The ocean was calm, just swaying under the light of the full moon. The lighthouse beacon shined its protective light on the water. Not another human to be seen; just a man, his dog and the ocean. Doc followed quietly beside Jeff as he walked down the line of rocks to get closer to the water. It always amazed him to see the rocky shore by the ocean. Each rock seemed so perfectly placed in position over the years by the water. The mist sprayed up from each rock as the impact of the powerful rushing waves collided with their place of solitude. As your sight caught the view out from the shore, the water looked as smooth as glass.

Jeff stroked Doc's head as they sat still, being lulled into a trance by the waves' methodical rhythm. "This is what it's all about, boy. It's like being in a dream." The peacefulness allowed him to try to make sense of things.

I have to get focused on my life again, he thought. *I've lost my way until now. Here at the world's edge, I can see a path. It's time to create a new life for myself.* Time passed, and Doc was going to sleep with his head resting on Jeff's lap.

"Well, boy," Jeff said, patting Doc's head, "it's time to head back. We have a busy day tomorrow."

Doc followed him up the steep, dark, rocky path. When they reached the top of the cliff, Jeff noticed someone sitting on the edge of the rocks. A silhouette of a woman, the light of the moon reflected off her dark hair.

Without hesitation, he said, "Hey, are you okay?"

He started towards her, hoping she didn't slip. *Why is she here alone?* His physician mode kicked in, making him worry she would jump. Who would know if she did? No one was around. He continued towards her, at the same time holding Doc back by his collar. It was normal for Doc to run, wagging his huge tail. He didn't want to frighten her more than he knew he just did.

She raised her hand to her face. "I...I'm sorry," her soft voice replied, "you scared me; I thought I was alone."

Jeff wanted to come closer, but her quick response and movement didn't allow that to happen.

She was standing in a flash, brushing her hair from her face.

"Yes, I am okay," she called, then began nervously wiping her jeans from the mist. "Just reflecting. Have a good night!" She quickly walked away in the direction of the inn.

Jeff watched as she faded out of sight. Doc felt him release his collar and started to go in her direction. "Whoa boy, come here! She's not in the mood to play tonight." Looking at his watch, he saw that it was midnight. *What is a woman doing out here alone at midnight? Probably the same as you; she can't sleep.* He tried to put the thought of her out of his mind.

When he started his bike, Doc did his normal dance of excitement, a dog's happy dance. He rode by the inn slowly and as quietly as he could. He could see a light on in an upstairs window. *Maybe she's in there,* he thought. *She said she was reflecting, but she seemed to be crying.*

"Doc, let's get some shut-eye." They continued on the moonlit path to the campsite.

*****

The warmth of the sun and Doc shifting around woke Jeff quickly. Glancing at his watch, he saw it was 9:00 am. "Aw, sorry boy. Nature call, huh?"

Doc darted out for the nearest spot, and so did Jeff.

After his shower, he could only think, *Coffee!* "Let's go find a coffee shop and a dog biscuit."

He started his bike, remembering the small little town up the road. Doc ran beside him, entertaining Jeff with his playful run. It was easier riding in the daylight. He pulled into the small area by the park and was amazed at its quaintness. How could this town keep its Norman Rockwell touch? The ringing of his cell phone in his pocket made him jump.

"Hey, Peanut," he said.

"Daddy, where are you? I've been trying to call you for two days."

"Well, you got me now. Are you all right?"

"Daddy...I had the baby!" she said excitedly.

"What? You're kidding! I'm sorry I wasn't there. I lost track of time, and I just wasn't thinking," he said, scrambling for words, trying to make sense of why he wasn't there. His daughter needed him, and he should have been there. "How could I be so selfish, leaving for five months?"

Melody interrupted his garble. "Daddy! Dad!" she said with a louder voice and started laughing. "You've had so much on your mind. We're fine."

"Tell me! Tell me!" Jeff pleaded. "What...what is...what did..." He continued to try to find the words.

"Her name is Mary Margaret."

Jeff was silent, then in a soft voice repeated, "Mary Margaret?"

"Yes, Daddy. I named her after Grandma. Do you like it?"

"Mels," he said, trying to keep his voice clear. "I don't have the words," he said, choking back the tears.

"I know, Daddy. It's okay," consoling him.

"I'll be right home, baby, as quick as I can drive. Oh, my God!" he yelled. "I'm a Grandpa!"

"Yes, you are."

"Oh, my God!"

"Where are you, Daddy?"

"Oh," he thought for a minute, laughing. "I'm in Maine, on the coastline. A town called Pemaquid."

"Really? Are you looking for a mermaid or an angel by the water?" Her voice echoed with a teasing laugh. "You were in a world of imagination or should I say inspiration, after your accident about that author or whatever. I just wanted to make sure you were still thinking in reality. I've been reading the book, by the way...I found my own copy. This one you can't take from me."

"No, I wasn't looking for either, but maybe one will appear. For now, I have no time to find anyone, and the author thing...well, let's not talk about that, okay? I have an angel that's waiting for her Grandpa. Maybe I can come find her another time."

"How's Doc handling the quest?" Melody asked.

"He's having a ball. He's been leaving his mark these last five months on every tree he comes close to. We'll be heading back first thing in the morning, getting an early start. I'm sure he misses you. Give Mary Margaret a kiss from her Grandpa!" He could hear her cooing in the background. "Melody, did you tell your Mom?"

"I called her secretary; she's in Europe. She should be back by the end of the week."

He hesitated, wanting to ask more.

Melody sensed his sadness about her mother's distance.

Jeff thought, *Europe? She does have a new life for herself. I'm happy for her. She's a good woman.* He noticed that his anger and hurt seemed to be disappearing. It was time to live again.

"Mel, how is Paul?"

"He's great, Dad. He got a promotion, and Megan and Paul have set the date."

"There seems to be good news flowing out of Ohio. Tell him you found me, give him my love." Quickly, he corrected the statement. "Give *them* my love, angel."

"I will, Daddy."

"I love you, Peanut!"

"Yah, me too. Hurry home. We miss you!"

Jeff stood there, still absorbing the arrival of a new life. He remembered when Mel and Paul were born. *I should have been there more, trying to push the guilty thoughts away.* He silenced his phone before sliding it into his pocket.

"Change of plans, boy," he said, scratching Doc's head. "We have a long drive ahead of us tomorrow."

Doc's tail wagged, and he started jumping around Jeff playfully.

Jim had come into town to get his morning news from the locals. He was watching Jeff and Doc running around. *Nice kid,* he thought to himself.

Jeff caught a glimpse of Jim coming up the sidewalk. "Hello, Mr. Brindle."

"Hey, Jeff. Are you enjoying your stay?"

"Yes, sir. I have to cut it shorter than I originally planned. Have to leave first thing tomorrow."

"Oh? Are you going to Scotland so soon?"

"No, sir. Plans changed; I have a new granddaughter that's waiting to meet her Grandpa!"

"Well," Jim replied, extending his huge hand towards Jeff. "Congratulations. Family is everything, son. Family is everything!"

"Yes, they are, sir. Thank you."

"Helen and I are going to O'Connor's tonight. Why don't you stop by? I'll buy ya a brew to celebrate."

"Yes, Mr. Brindle, I would enjoy that."

"Okay, then. Seven pm?"

*****

"Seems our night is planned for us," Jeff said as he hooked Doc's leash onto his collar. "Come on, boy, let's investigate this town."

The town wasn't very far from the campsite. *Pemaquid,* he thought. What a different name. Rows of quaint little shops, all surrounding a town square, with a white gazebo nestled right in the center of the park.

There weren't too many people filling the streets now. Summer had ended, and only a few tourists were visible. Some stragglers were still there, like Jeff, loving the area. It was obvious it was hard for some of them to leave and return home to their daily lives. Walking through town made you feel as if you were walking back in time. A dream. Each business in the square was color coordinated.

It was perfect, a perfect place for Dr. Jeff Nichols to experience some magic - and he will.

Jeff kept Doc on a tight leash so he didn't bother anyone as they walked up the small sidewalks.

Doc's tail wagged as each person passed, hoping someone would pet him. *Please, one person pet me, give me a scratch behind my ear.*

The storefront windows were carefully decorated in New England style, each having its own unique splendor to entertain the passersby.

The town apothecary was called Feline's Apothecary. Pendulous crystals inside the window reflected the morning sun, casting rainbows on the walkway. The wind chimes played their melody, dancing in tune as the ocean breeze moved softly across them.

Customers coming in and out, they were all captivated by the energy that radiated by Feline. Smiles on their faces shared their amazement over the treasures they purchased. The incense radiated around old and young. You could tell Feline created this, so all visitors - or even just people passing by - would be taking a glimmer of her with them. There is no better advertisement than smiles and treasures shared with the world. *She knew what she was doing.*

The streets were paved with bricks, as if a master bricklayer molded each one with his own hands. Each fit perfectly side by side on the path that all who visit must pass over.

Not one person here was in a hurry. It was a different life, with a touch of magic filling the air. The only sound you heard was laughter or music coming from one building or another.

Was he dreaming? Could this be a dream? Jeff noticed Doc was sniffing a nearby hydrant to see if it was worthy of his mark. He quickly pulled him away and said, "Hey, not here, boy. I guess it isn't a dream," laughing at being able to entertain himself with the imagination the town seemed to be awakening within him.

As they continued up the street, Jeff was startled by an exceptionally beautiful mannequin in a clothing store window. Music played from inside the store out onto the sidewalk for people to enjoy. Doc sat and stared. She was lovely, almost lifelike, dressed in a soft, flowing yellow dress. People definitely noticed this store window. Doc's head cocked sideways; still captivated by the presence in the window, he barked.

Jeff stilled Doc. "Shhhh, boy." Glancing back at the window, the mannequin winked at him. His head jerked back with a second glance, laughing at his discovery. The woman was still composed, but you could see her lips slightly smile at him. Her stature and ability to play the part of a mannequin so well was very impressive. Jeff winked at her as he saw another family coming towards the window to be mystified by her. He waved and had to pull Doc to follow.

Turning the corner of the square, a sight he didn't expect greeted him - but nothing he had seen or experienced today was what he expected.

"What the...." Jeff said, holding Doc back.

People lined the side of the street surrounding a quaint cottage building. A soft voice filled the area of space, surrounding the cafe.

"What is happening here?" The words were muffled because he was too far away. So he took hold of Doc's leash and moved closer. "Let's check this out." Still hoping to find some coffee. Jeff reached in his pocket to make sure his phone was on silent. As he got closer, he could smell the most amazing aroma coming from the little building.

Is it a coffee shop? It must be pretty good to have that many people waiting in line, he thought.

The sign outside read: 'The Novel Café'. As he and Doc got closer, he could hear voices:

"Really!" someone said, trying to see through the window standing on her tiptoes. "Aw," another person wooed. "I love hearing her stories. I saw her last month in Meredith, New Hampshire. It was hilarious. I learn so much when I go to her seminars. I have never laughed so hard watching her on stage."

"I wish I hadn't missed it."

"There's always another."

"Oh, she has a website with all her engagements. When we were there, she was even playing with us as we waited outside. Irish music came from the speakers of the theater. Then when we were walking in, without notice someone would come up to you and hand you a small gift box."

"What was in them?"

"Different things, some had beautiful stones, some necklaces. You just didn't know when you would get a gift."

An elderly lady overheard the conversation. "She was just teaching you. Did you know that?"

"What?"

"She was showing you that special gifts come at the most unexpected times."

Everyone smiled, understanding this was Debra Pratt's way to always be present, always be a teacher, and mostly a friend. She would say the world is filled with friends you haven't met yet.

Another said, "Her book was filled with gems, too - not of the stone kind, but gems of life. I wish I could see life as she does."

"You will," an elderly woman standing in the door called out. "You will."

In time, you will...

"What? What?" Attention was drawn back to inside the Novel Cafe.

Music filled the square flowing from the Novel Cafe. Everyone started dancing around like a spell was put on them. The soft voice came along with the music...wait - isn't there supposed to be a Scottish gent opening this?

Everyone began calling out following her lead. "When you believe it, you will see him. When you believe it, you will see him!!"

"I believe! I believe!" they all sang and danced in the street.

Jeff stood with amazement. The voice...it seemed so familiar. *Well, what do we have here?* he thought to himself. *I'm Scottish...maybe I should just walk in and say...I'm Scottish,* but then he reconsidered, seeing he would be totally surrounded by crazy women dancing in the street, saying they believe in something. Plus, Doc's ears were perked up; he was ready to take part in the entire playful moment. Jeff patted his head. "I know, boy, you believe, too - huh?"

The crowd seemed to divide as someone was trying to make her way through them. Yet, the crowd wasn't moving to the side easily. It was a dark-haired woman, smiling, with a gentle determination to escape from the dancing brigade. The waiting women kept taking her by the hand, attempting to talk with her.

"Hello..."

"Is she okay?"

"Yes, she's fine; it won't be long." Her determination was successful as she escaped the crowd. She couldn't believe her eyes. "What in the world are you doing here?!" she squealed at Jeff.

Jeff almost fell over. "Shar, what're you doing here?" Doc jumped around, doing a *dog* happy dance upon recognizing her.

"Hey, boy," she said, reaching down to scratch his ears.

Finally, Doc was getting the attention he wanted as he lowered his head with pleasure.

She jumped to Jeff's open arms.

"Arrrrr," he said. "What's going on in there, and why are you here? This is so unbelievable - five hundred miles from home, and here you are!"

Shar stood back to look him over. "Where've you been? We've all been so worried, Dr. Jeff."

"Oh, you know me; avoiding responsibilities, a lone drifter," he said with a smirk.

"Right, you've been gone so long. Are you all right?"

"Sure, better than ever. I needed to take some time for myself, a little vacation."

"Jeff, it's been five months!"

"I know. I'm heading back tomorrow. I just found out I'm a new Grandpa!"

"Congratulations!"

"Yes, a little girl. Mary Margaret."

"How wonderful. How is Melody?"

"She's great. I told her I'd be home as quick as I could. I just got here last night, and we were relaxing, taking in the town a little longer. We're heading home first thing in the morning. How'd you get here?" Jeff said.

"I flew, of course. Using a rental car at the moment."

"What brings you here, of all places?" Jeff pointed up the road. "Did you see the dress shop over there?"

Shar laughed. "Yes. She fooled you, too? That's Ayden. She's a dance teacher here on the Point and organizes the local theater when the tourists are here. She's very good, isn't she?"

"Yes, Doc spotted her right away. Come on, tell me what

you're doing here. Do you want to have a cup of coffee?" He
sighed with hopeful desire that she would.

"Remember my friend, the one I told you about, the writer?"

"Yes," Jeff said with a rush that filled his head. Was it a
caffeine-needed-soon rush, or shock? He steadied himself.

"Well, she's here. This is the town she wrote most of the book
from."

"What?" Jeff said softly and hesitantly.

"They're having a party in there for her. Everyone here loves
her. She's signing some of her books, too."

He was speechless as thoughts ricocheted through his mind,
looking at the people gathered to see Debby. "I can see they love
her. Listening to these ladies out here, I thought Oprah was in
there," he laughed, "or hoping they had the most amazing
coffee."

"Let's go in." Shar grabbed him by the hand and pulled him
towards the door. "I can get you that coffee, too!"

"I don't know...what about Doc?" *What a sad excuse,* Jeff
thought to himself. He was nervous to see this Debra Pratt.

"I'll keep him here, you go ahead. Did you get a chance to
read the book? I gave it to you before your accident. I wasn't
sure if you had a chance."

"Yes...some, " he said cautiously, not wanting to share what
happened after he read the book. If he never mentioned it again,
it would be too soon.

"Deb and I have been friends forever. You have to go meet
her, Jeff, and get some coffee. This is so uncanny, Jeff, having
you here. Deb would call it 'an angel thing'."

"I know...for me, too."

Shar had no idea how true that was; no idea at all. Jeff
quickly examined his options. "Are you sure you don't mind?"
he said as he looked at the door. He knew if he didn't do it now,
he never would. It was meant to be, him being here at the same
time as Debra.

Jeff looked around hesitantly, then reached over to pat Doc's
head and handed the leash to Shar.

"Be right back, boy." He could see it would be a while before he got in.

Shar sensed his apprehension. "Come on," she said, taking him by the hand and still holding Doc's leash in the other. As they got closer to the café, she quickly led him up the side alley. "Go this way, I have connections," she teased.

"Wait, wait a minute...maybe later," Jeff said, reaching for Doc's leash. He was feeling a bit squeamish in his stomach.

Shar opened the back door. "After you," she said, pointing towards the open kitchen door.

*****

The kitchen was small in comparison to most restaurant kitchens. You could feel the excitement that radiated from the front of the café, flowing through the building. It was obvious someone had been doing a lot of preparing for the celebration that was taking place. Flour dusted all over the countertops, empty muffin tins sat on the shelf, some in the sink waiting to be washed. Boxes, boxes, and more boxes everywhere!

As Jeff got closer to the swinging door that led to the front, he hesitated. Shar came up behind him.

"What are you waiting for? Ohh, coffee! You want some coffee?"

"What? Yes, yes, the coffee. Good idea."

Shar quickly poured him some of Hattie's special brew into a large handmade ceramic cup.

"This tastes great! Thanks." Again he glanced at the door, raising his cup. "You...you want me to go in there?"

"Sure!"

Doc's tail wagged as he watched Jeff make the decision: do I, or don't I?

He stood there for what was only a moment, but it seemed like an eternity.

Suddenly, the door swung quickly open.

"Whoa!" the voice said "Ya scared the bejesus outta me!"

"Oh, sorry!" Jeff said, backing up, almost spilling his coffee on himself.

Shar started laughing. "Hattie, it's okay."

"Shar, I thought you left? Couldn't keep ya away, aye?"

Her eyes returned to Jeff. "Look at ya, boy. You always come in through the back?" She reached over to scratch Doc's ears. *Ahh*, Doc was happy again, very happy. *A little to the right, big Momma*, he thought.

"Umm, no ma'am," Jeff said, glancing over at Shar, as if expecting her to make this moment right.

"Hattie, I bumped into him out on the street."

"Ahhh, so you thought you could trap him here in the kitchen?" she said with a hearty laugh. "Keeping him away from the other ladies, all for you, aye?"

"Noooo," Shar said, resting her hand on Jeff's shoulder. "He's my boss, from back home. This is Dr. Jeff Nichols."

"Ya don't say," she said, extending her hand to Jeff with a high-pitched tone in her voice. "A doctor and a good lookin' fella, ain't he?"

Jeff's face turned a little red.

"Yes, he is." Shar continued playing along with Hattie. It was obvious they both were having a good time teasing Dr. Nichols.

"I brought him back here to see if I could get Deb to sign a book for him. Plus, to get him some of your famous brew."

Jeff smiled, acknowledging his pleasure by raising the cup.

"That won't be a problem for either. You married?" Hattie blurted out.

Shar stood there with a sly grin on her face.

Jeff wondered if this woman was for real. Doc seemed to be more quiet than usual, seemingly entertained watching Jeff squirm.

"No, ma'am, I am not."

"No, he isn't," Shar confirmed, knowing Hattie very well. She laughed, knowing what Hattie was going to do.

"Then damn, let's get ya out there. Time's a wastin'." Hattie always tried to play matchmaker for her little Dee. Bold and blunt is Hattie's way. What you see is what you get. Everyone loved her, she had a heart of gold. Most could see through her camouflage, but only those that knew her well.

Hattie flung the door open. Jeff was hoping no one would notice her literally dragging him into the room. He quickly handed his cup to Shar with a roll of his eyes and a cute, boyish smile. Not quite the entrance he wanted to make.

The line was still very long. You could see the enthusiasm in the faces as they patiently waited. Debby was taking her time with every person she met.

Hattie quickly halted her march; it wasn't time to interrupt yet. Jeff sighed with relief. They both stood there, quietly watching. He couldn't take his eyes off Debra. He felt he had seen her before...or had he?

"Thank you," a small, gentle elderly woman said as she received her signed book.

"Mrs. Browning, it is truly my pleasure to meet you."

She reached over and touched Debra's hand.

"You have a gift, my dear. You have grown to be a butterfly, now fly and share your words. Remember, playing it safe is the greatest risk you can take. You are protected; no one will touch your soul with fear again."

Deb acknowledged her with a smile. She had been told in times past that angels appear when you least expect them. She felt she was in the presence of one now. Deb bowed her head and acknowledged her wisdom. "I thank you."

"How long will you be in town, my dear?" Mrs. Browning inquired.

"I'm not sure, I haven't decided yet. This area is so peaceful for me."

"Namaste, sweet one. Soon you will adjust to all the newness that you're experiencing and more is coming your way."

This was a moment that confirmed her learning from her angels of the butterfly.

Everyone was so patient. They just listened to Debby as she

visited with each person, not rushing, sensing things. Little ones were there with their moms or dads. She smiled at them and made them giggle, giving each of them a small gift. She loved doing that, making people remember her, even just for a moment. Like a shooting star, she would say. We all cross each other's paths for a reason; some lengthy, some not, but always for a reason.

"Hi!" Deb said to the next young woman.

She was in her thirties. Debby could sense this woman was, as some would call, a kindred spirit. The young woman was holding back tears as she extended her hand.

"Hello," her voice said softly. "I...I..." She tried to search for the words.

Deb saw the pink band on her wrist.

"My name is Arabella." She hesitated.

Debby touched her bracelet softly and walked around the table. Everyone watched as the two embraced as if they were long lost friends finally finding each other. The tears flowed, the river of tears unknowing what tomorrow might bring. Deb whispered softly, "Take some from me." Arabella's face glowed as she heard the familiar words.

Debby had survived breast cancer herself two years ago, though it seemed like yesterday to her. Her conversation with Arabella revealed she was in the beginning stage. Her soul trembled; she knew this, sensed it. Sometimes words aren't necessary to know things.

"We have met for a reason. You know that, don't you?" she said as she handed Arabella a tissue.

"Yes." She smiled. "An angel thing, right?"

Debra smiled and nodded - she, too, holding back the tears. Everyone around them was doing the same. It was a moment none of them would ever forget.

The white candles burned gently on the shelf, and cinnamon incense caressed the air.

"Do you live here in Pemaquid?"

"I came home last week to be with my family, I was born

here. I have been living in Ireland for quite some time."

Deb reached for her pen. "Give me your number so we can visit and talk."

Excitedly, Arabella tried to find a piece of paper in her pocket to write the number. The woman behind her handed her paper and a pen. Their eyes met for a moment as they smiled at each other.

"Thank you," Arabella said.

The woman nodded "You're very welcome, love."

Hattie whispered softly. "She's like that with everyone, ya know."

Jeff watched silently. He knew that somehow, but how? *How lovely she is,* he thought. It was hard to take his eyes off her.

Arabella opened her worn book to a page. "This was one of my favorites. Can I read it out loud?"

"Of course." Deb sat, intently listening.

Arabella said, "I had to read it over and over again, but then all of a sudden I had one of those 'aha' moments and I got it."

Deb laughed. "I understand. Sometimes it's like that for me, too."

Arabella began to read as Deb put the microphone near her. She stirred a bit but seemed not to let it bother her; it was as if she were comfortable hearing her voice aloud.

"Make your "TODAY" all you want it to be.
By enjoying and having fun TODAY.
Tomorrows never come, you never stand in the day and say, well this day is called tomorrow!
Now examine the words and realize your tomorrows are amazing because you have the positive energy today.
I would like to continue with this mind changing thought.
You can stand in your day and say, I love this day; it was my tomorrow yesterday. But now yesterday is just a memory.
I am living well today, because of my yesterday's way of looking at things.
I created my today.
Now, go enjoy your tomorrow today...

and remember that what you did yesterday.
That's what is reflected NOW."

Everyone took a moment, some remembering reading it before but not understanding the essence until this very moment.

"I am creating my today, Debra. Will you walk with me for a time so I can get sure-footed and take my life downstream, as you say in the book?"

"I will...I would be honored to be with you for as long as you need me."

*****

The Novel Café was a place that once you enter it, you will never forget. The shelves expressively decorated with books. So much enchantment in this little building, it was magical. Trinkets, treasures, and books sitting in view for the treasure seeker. Yet knowing and finding other treasures present that weren't to be seen with the natural eye.

How fitting to meet her here. Was this a dream?
I don't want to wake if it is.

Hattie broke Jeff's entranced observation of Deb. "Come here, Doc," she said, grabbing his arm and pulling him again. As they approached the front of the café, Deb glanced up casually, watching Hattie's determined approach. She quickly looked again, noticing a man was with her. *What is she up to?* Deb thought. *Hattie always gets that look in her eyes when she's on a mission.* She glanced back at the somewhat unwilling hostage captured by Miss Hattie. Their eyes seemed to captivate each other for a moment...just a moment.

"Hey, Missy," Hattie snickered, seeing the look on Deb's face. "I made an amazing discovery moments ago. Are you curious?"

Dee laughed, loving to play with Hattie. "Curious? Why wouldn't I be? You always have amazing lessons for me,

Hattie."

"It seems that you and this handsome gent here have a mutual friend. I think it's quite surprising you've never met before."

"Oh, really?" His eyes never left hers. She extended her hand to Jeff. "Who would be our *mutual* friend?"

"It's..." He paused, still staring for a second.

Hattie laughed. "Come on, tell her!"

"Sharon and I work together back in Ohio." He felt so foolish displaying such an unprofessional answer to such a simple question. *Come on, Nichols, get a grip,* he thought.

"Yeah," Hattie said, nodding her head, unable to wait for his next reply. Patience wasn't one of Hattie's virtues. "He's Shar's boss, Dr. Jeff Nichols. Interesting, don't ya think?"

Debby could see Shar standing in the doorway to the kitchen, watching as she was introduced to Hattie's prisoner. Shar waved to acknowledge her presence, doing the little happy dance they always did for each other.

With a smile, she extended her hand again. "It's very nice to meet you, Jeff. I'm glad you came with Shar to Maine. Do you like the area?"

"No, I didn't come with Sharon," Jeff quickly corrected her. "I was already here. Somehow we wound up in the same place. We discovered each other outside a few moments ago. She did tell me about you and your book back in Ohio, though."

"Oh? How strange - or maybe not - you are meeting her here. Life is synchronized and paths brought together when you least expect it. Do you agree, Mr. Nichols?" Deb smirked. "Were you able to read it, or was it not to your liking?"

"No, I liked what I read of it."

"Oh...well, that's good. Did Shar tell you she was in my book?"

Deb was teasing and taking a moment to play with him. She sensed he was nervous, not understanding why but wanted to continue.

"Yes, she did."

"Did you find her?"

"I did."

"Did you find anything else worth reading in it?"

Now Jeff was relaxing more. "I read some of it," he continued. "I -"

Deb laughed, interrupting his remark. "Some is good. They do say less is more."

She nudged Hattie, seeing she was getting a bit frustrated with the matchmaker position. "I must correct you, though. Only a likeness to Shar is in it since it isn't an autobiography."

Hattie smacked her butt, like a parent saying, *behave yourself.*

Deb sighed, turning towards the people waiting. "Okay," she said, looking back at Jeff as if to say, *they've read it all.*

He knew what she meant but wasn't going to let this pass. Being here face-to-face, he wasn't about to just leave. "Miss Pratt, can we possibly have a drink tonight at O'Connor's?" He wanted to be with her again, if even for a moment.

Hattie shot her a look as if to say, *answer him now! What are you waiting for?*

"I'll be there. Only, please call me 'Debby'."

"Okay, see you there, around 7 or so?"

She acknowledged with a nod of her head and took her seat back at the table.

He tucked his hands in his pocket and began to head towards Shar.

Hattie grabbed him, yanking him back. She wasn't done with him yet.

"Hey, Missy, how about grabbing one of them books and signing it for the Doc?"

"Sure." Debby picked one up. Looking at Jeff, she signed it and handed it to him. Then she put a bookmark in it that she was giving to everyone.

"Thanks," he said.

"Sure, Doc, anytime."

~*~*~*~

Chapter Seventeen

The O'Connor Experience

Returning to the inn at 5:00pm, Deb was tired. Shar was sitting in a big, overstuffed chair in the lobby. Her bare feet and comfy pants said it all. Her legs dangled over the arm of the chair.

"There she is," Shar said, "our little author."

"Comfy?" Deb asked with a rouse of her eyebrow, envious that she was casually dressed and sprawled in that grand chair.

"Oh, it's all right, I guess!" She settled even deeper in the chair. "Life is good, idn it?"

Debby laughed. "Yes, it is - and you, as always, are a piece of work, my friend. I have missed you so much. Did I tell you how happy I am you're here with me?"

"I know, I missed you too but we have are never far from each other."

Deb grabbed at her feet, trying to yank her off the chair.

"Robbie called a few minutes ago." Shar winced, dodging the attack. "He wants you to call him."

"Okay." Dee gave in to the moment, kicking her shoes off and sliding into the chair next to Shar. "What a wonderful day," she moaned and collapsed. "I meet the most interesting humans." She laughed at her silly way of thinking, but she loved it, too. She was so comfortable in herself, it didn't matter if others agreed or not. She was exactly who she wanted to be.

"You must be so proud," sensing Deb's humor while still hiding her exhaustion.

Deb stared into the flames in the fireplace. "Yes, yet proud makes it seem like I did something amazing. I controlled it. I guess I am in awe, and very thankful." She took a deep breath.

Helen came from around the corner, slowly walking towards another chair, listening and feeling the calmness in the room. "Helen?" Dee whispered.

Helen looked over and smiled. "Yes, dear?"

"I love you and Jim beyond words. I know you know it, but I needed to say the words. How can I ever express what you both mean to me?"

"No need, sweetie. Sometimes words aren't necessary."

The phone rang.

"It's for you." Shar handed Dee the receiver with a goofy grin on her face. Deb rolled her eyes.

"Hello? Hi, Bob, I'm fine. Helen's right here, waving to say hi to you, too. Yes, it went well. No, I can't now. But we can talk later. Yes, Danny and Robby told me. No, no, I'm fine. The doctor said I'm fine. Yep, Shar's here, too."

Shar had a smirk on her face as she watched, waving frantically, encouraging her to tell him she said hi, too, with no success. It was obvious she was being ignored. She wasn't going to keep this going any longer than necessary.

"Yes, okay. Bye."

Shar and Helen watched to see her reaction. Staring at the phone for a moment, seeming to be in another time, she turned and said, "Hey, your friend seems very nice."

Shar knew her well enough to know she would talk when she wanted to. Until then, it would be her usual dodge-and-duck dance. "He is very nice." "I've known him for a long time."

"You never mentioned him before."

"He never came up. He went through a divorce about two years ago. Last fall, he had a bad scare. He was in a motorcycle accident, putting him in a coma for weeks. It seemed to have affected him more emotionally than physically, so he took some time off. Actually, I haven't seen him in five months until today."

"Really? Now that's interesting."

"Mm hmm. He said he needed some time. No one seemed to know where he was - and voilà! Here he is! It's a small world, I guess. He told me today his daughter Melody just had a baby. He's heading home tomorrow a new Grandpa."

"Aww," Deb and Helen said simultaneously.

"God, he was so he nervous meeting you?" Shar said.

"I don't know why. He did seem a bit uncomfortable. Maybe it was because Hattie had her hands locked around his arm and was cutting his circulation off." Both giggled remembering the Hattie moment as they tapped their wine glasses. "Gotta love her," they all cheered.

"He can't be afraid of me because of my book. He said he only read part of it. I don't think he had time to get to the Devin part." It surprised her that nothing stirred in her at the mention of his name. She was confident now, not the same woman she was so many seasons ago.

"He asked me to meet him at O'Connor's later for a drink. Are you okay with that, Shar?"

"Of course, relax, there's nothing like that between him and me."

Debby breathed a soft sigh of relief. "You are coming with me, though, right?"

"Yes, you couldn't keep me away. You don't still have that issue of going in places alone, do you? I mean, you're a new woman, and it doesn't seem as if that would still be a problem."

"Nope, I'm a big girl now," she said sarcastically.

Deb turned to Helen, the question on her face asking, *are you coming, too?*

Helen nodded. "Yes, Jim and I are coming, dear."

"Good," she said.

They all heard the roar of a motorcycle as it passed by the inn.

Debby glanced at the window.

Shar caught her reaction. So did Helen.

"That's a young man staying at the campsite," Helen said. "Jim seems to like him."

"Really?" said Deb. "I'm shocked. He usually stays away from guys on bikes."

"This one has a dog."

Deb and Shar looked at each other and laughed.

"Jeff" they said together, tapping their glasses again.

"Do you know him?" Jim said as he came into the room.

"Surprisingly enough, I do," Shar said. "I work with him back home. He's a doctor."

"Well, I'll be," Jim said. "Now what do you think of that? It's a small world."

Jim bent over to add wood to the fire to keep it going. The crisp October air chilled one to the bone. "When I first met him at the campsite, he told me he was going to Scotland. Today he said he has to leave in the morning...seems he's a new Grandpa."

"He's really close to his kids," Shar said.

"Strange you two would bump into each other all the way over here in Maine."

"I know...we all know life is anything but ordinary around the world of Debby. It seems to touch us all. By the way, that was a nice bookmark you gave to the people today."

"Oh, you liked it? Thanks."

"What was it?" Helen asked.

Deb reached in her briefcase and handed one to her. It had a picture of a butterfly carrying its cocoon.

"What a sight that is," Helen said.

"Yes, I know, but sometimes people need a visual to understand something. Not all are readers."

Helen read what it said:

Have you ever seen a butterfly carrying its cocoon when it is in flight?

NO!

It won't.

It doesn't carry the thing around with it that had encased it in bondage.

It was for a time, it was for its growth.

But they let it go

They fly above and away from it.

Now if we could just take a lesson from nature, it would be such an easier life.

"Where do you come up with this stuff?!" Jim moaned as he heard the words.

Deb and Shar looked at each other and rolled their eyes. Both at the same time said, "He didn't read the book!" The room filled with laughter from all the ladies. Jim just ignored them and kept shuffling with the logs.

"Look at the clock! I have to get ready." Debby jumped out of the chair, then nudged Shar. "Come on, let's get ready."

"For what?" Jim said. "Nothing fancy going on around here."

"Well, dear," said Helen, "she's meeting your friend, Dr. Jeff, at O'Connor's tonight."

Jim mumbled under his breath as Deb and Shar flew past him, feeling like two teenage daughters dodging Dad.

Deb remembered Jim's comment of Jeff going to Scotland.
She was even more curious now to learn of the traveling doctor.

*****

O'Connor's was the liveliest spot in this small town tonight. It was the end of the tourist season and the beginning of a long, cold winter in Pemaquid Point. The winds from the ocean and the snow flying over the land always made it difficult to socialize. You had to be made of a special breed to live in Maine.

People from town were gathering outside as Shar and Debby pulled into the square. A local singer was performing tonight. Age was of no concern; the old and young would always mingle at O'Connor's. Outsiders were always welcome, as long as they accepted the unspoken laws of the Point. This was a town where crime was almost non-existent. Debra had been coming here for eight years. She didn't quite know everyone, but most knew her, or of her. She had put Pemaquid on the map in the public eye. Some liked it, and some didn't. Especially the old folks; they were leery of all the popularity from this little book. Although they did enjoy Oprah mentioning them...it was as if she had known them all personally. The book allowed special things like that to happen.

Dee had no idea so many sayings and comments would become commonplace from her book. She would joke about going into the T-shirt business with all her silly yet sometimes unique clichés. The one she liked to hear the best was "It's an Angel Thing."

Angels made her aware of them over the years in one way or another. It's a personal thing for each of us, she often stated. In the lectures she gave, she always spoke of one needing to find that peaceful place and get away from the world of "concrete" to refocus on the important issues of life and living it well. Deb would never ever criticize anyone for their religious beliefs or thoughts. It is a personal thing between you and the Creator.

The success of the book allowed her to relax and touch lives the way she felt she was destined to do. It also allowed her to pick up her paintbrush from time to time. When the time was right, she could become completely entranced in a painting. Her every thought would be to complete it as quickly as she could so she wouldn't lose the energy she felt to create it. No fear in this life now. She was living her authentic life.

Deb and Shar walked through the crowd, occasionally glancing around, seeing smiles from familiar and unfamiliar faces. As they moved further into the pub, they could hear the fiddler strumming inside, accompanied by the clicking of shoes in unison on the old wooden floors. Everyone was so alive, it was a huge celebration.

"Aye, there ya are, lassie."

Deb grinned. "Amos, how are you?" She threw her arms around him. "I've missed you so much."

"Seems we are filled tonight with the talent of the locals." He spun her around, holding her hand high to honor her.

Shar watched her glow and revel in the moment.

"My daughter returned from Ireland, too," Amos said.

Ireland? Ireland? Could it be? She thought to herself. "I would love to meet her."

"Aye, to be sure ya will."

A soft, angelic voice serenaded the appreciative crowd. A young woman was singing an old Gaelic tale. Amos put his arm around her, turning her towards the voice and pointing as he said, "There she be, missy. There she be."

A young woman with the sweetest face and long, curly hair had a melody coming out of her like the voice of an angel. As her hand lifted the microphone, you could see a pink band on her arm. It was the young woman from the café.

"Her name is Arabella," Amos said

"Yes, I met her today at the café."

"Her mother and I are so proud of her. She took a leave from her tour in Europe to come home for a while. I love having her home again."

Arabella's eyes met with Deb. "She's beautiful, Amos, beautiful."

"That she is."

"Hey, you," a somewhat familiar voice said behind her.

Dee was a little startled. She had heard the voice before, but where?

"Ya came back." Amos recognized Jeff from the night before. "The fairy dust is flying everywhere, are ya ready, lad to have some fun?"

"I am, sir."

Amos could see his attention wasn't on him. Jeff's eyes didn't move from Debby.

"Hey, you," she said back to him.

The night passed much too quickly. The fairies definitely sprinkled their magic on them as they playfully danced to the music. They didn't notice anyone else in the room, too captivated with each other. Shar was being entertained by one of the local men. Dee occasionally heard Shar squeal; seems the guy was teaching her a few new steps.

Jim looked at Helen, snickering as he got up from the table.

He pulled on his suspenders with a stretch. "I promised the boy a drink." His eyes were on the goal. He reached Jeff, taking him by the arm, directing him to the bar. "Let me buy you that drink, son." Everyone knew Jim was concerned for Debby, but he did promise him a drink. Flasks rose between the two.

Jeff thought to himself, *Geez, arm yanking around here seems to be a regular occurrence these days.*

"Here's to your new granddaughter, son. May the wind warm her face and the sun warm her heart."

"Thank you, sir."

The two men managed to work their way back to the table, where everyone else was enjoying the music as well as the humor Hattie brought with her. Of course, Jeff was very nonchalant, trying to avoid the clutches of Hattie. He wanted to continue his visit with Debby.

"I heard you're leaving in the morning. Congratulations are in order, Grandpa."

"My family is worried; I've been on the road for some time. I knew I was forgetting something important taking place in October. There's been a lot on my mind."

"Yes, I seem to have spent a lot of time on the road the past year myself," Deb said.

Jeff continued, "As I mentioned before, I did read part of your book a while ago."

"Yes, you shared that with me earlier, but only briefly," she emphasized.

He took a deep breath. "Let me explain."

"All right, but would you like to go for a walk while you do?"

"That would be great." It seemed like everyone's eyes were on them. He wanted some time alone with her.

"Where's your dog?" she asked.

"He's probably a little restless. He's back at the campsite."

"Why don't we go get him so he isn't alone?" She took his hand as they started toward the door, waving at Shar and giving her hand sign circle over her heart. Shar smiled and signed back.

Jim pointed his finger at her as if to say, *be good.* That was *his* hand signal, one that she understood perfectly. Debby smiled and nodded, blowing him a kiss. Helen waved to her and nudged Jim.

Outside, Jeff guided her to his bike and a second helmet. "Are you up for a short ride? If not, I can leave it here and come get it later."

"Sure. I haven't been on one in a long time."

He handed her the helmet; she looked so cute putting it on.

Debby had no idea why he was so intrigued with her. He definitely wasn't about to tell her. He didn't need someone else thinking he'd lost his mind. The lines were getting long in that department.

She settled herself on the seat of the bike, her heart began to race; she remembered having felt this way before.

Old memories came back to her. She stretched her arms around Jeff's waist; he softly patted her hands as they locked on his stomach. She smiled to herself when she felt it, thinking

I remember that, too...do they all pat your hand? Is that taught in biking school? Silently chuckling. *I love my life.*

Chapter Eighteen

Is it you, or do I wait for another?

The roar of the bike brought Debra back to the present. She was uneasy thinking back on so many memories she held deep in her heart.

Jeff drove into the campsite having no idea Deb was in another place, another time, even if she appeared to be right there with him.

Doc was so excited to see them. "Hey, boy," she said. He danced around the bike, playfully touching Dee as she rode with her hand extended to him.

The guiding light glowed above the lighthouse, on the water beyond and on the dark, empty parking lot. The fullness of the Harvest Moon added to the brightness of the night.

Silence filled the air as the bike's engine was quieted. The only thing heard was echoed by the roaring waves against the rocks.

"Do you come here often?" Jeff asked as he helped her off the bike.

She removed her helmet, shaking her hair and taking in a breath of the ocean air. "Yes and no. It's my special place."

"Really?" he attempted not to analyze her way of expressing herself.

"I love it when I sit on the rocks over there," she said, walking toward the cliff in front of the lighthouse. "It helps me to make sense of the world. People come here all the time, but I don't think they appreciate it like I do."

Jeff watched her try to explain. She saw him staring at her.

"So, do you like it?" Swinging her arms in a circle, as if her own special dance to show the view.

"Yes, of course. I was here last night. Doc and I were a little restless, so we came over."

She continued, not even hearing what he'd said. Caught again, caught up in the sound of the waves, the mist filling the air and touching her skin. She continued to share her tales.

"People, I mean humans, come here clicking their cameras, catching a moment in time but not truly experiencing the essence of it. The power, the energy, you can draw to yourself from the water. Nature is alive. It isn't made of concrete or electronics; it's natural, very peaceful. This is one of my places I come to get away from the world of concrete."

Jeff continued to listen. He'd never heard anyone express life the way she did.

"The wind gives you your second breath, watching the waves entrance you." She stopped abruptly and looked at Jeff. "I 'm a people watcher."

"Are you really, or do you mean human watcher?" He laughed at her unique way of conversing. "What do you see, Miss Pratt?"

"Men, women, and children, all having such busy lives. They are looking for something they have lost when they come here. Some of them are, not all of them. They could get a glimmer if they could just be still and listen. Sometimes..." She hesitated for a moment. "Sometimes it takes coming back more than once."

"Doing it again?" Jeff confirmed her thoughts; again, she didn't hear his words.

Jeff smiled as Deb walked right to the spot where he had seen a woman sitting the night before. You could tell she knew it well. She patted the ground next to her. "Come, sit and relax."

They all just sat on the rocks and stared at the water. "I was here last night," he repeated again.

"You...you were here?"

"Yes, it was dark. I took Doc for a run; we were restless."

Debby stared at him. "Oh," she said, remembering why his

voice tonight was so familiar. "That was you?"

"Yup..."

She giggled and continued to stare at the water, sighing softly.

"I didn't mean to scare you."

"I know. It's okay. I wasn't used to anyone being here that late, is all."

"I could tell. Did you lose something?" *Remembering her comment on people coming by the water.*

She looked at him, realizing what he meant. "You have a long drive tomorrow. I probably shouldn't keep you up so late. I'm sure your kids will be so happy to see you. Five months is a long time, Mr. Nichols."

"Yes, they will," realizing she avoided his question.

"Come on," she said, tapping his arm. "We should get some rest. I'm quite a talker, and if you get me going, we'll be here all night."

"For some reason, I believe that," Jeff said, helping her up. For a moment, they stood face to face. Her eyes were so bright and alive. He softly touched her cheek. "I would like to see you again sometime."

She smiled and shyly dropped her eyes from his.

He lifted her chin up to look in her eyes. "Really, I'm serious." His heart was racing as he tried to hold back all he wanted to say to her.

"I would like that, too," Debby said.

He touched his finger to her lips.

The energy of the moment shot through her body. There was something to this man, something she couldn't understand. She handed him his helmet and walked back to the inn.

Chapter Nineteen

Experience is the best teacher

Morning came quickly.
Debby woke remembering the night before, retracing the moments, realizing Jeff was so easy to be with. Why was he so attentive to her every word? I do hope we can...

Okay, young lady, she said to herself, shower and music...get in the water and be.

Her steps continued as she dropped her robe on the path to turn the shower and her music on. The water ran down her skin, relaxing her very being, taking her to another place. The lather from her cloth softly touching her scarred breast.
Words, thoughts, moments continued passing through her mind. *Arabella, how is she? I have to remember to call her.* The chatter in her mind continued until that small voice inside said,

"Be still, you are sharing your music with the world now. Keep singing your songs; don't ever stop."

"Yes," she replied with tears flowing. "Yes, I shall."
The soft towel caressed her wet body, and she took a breath. As her eyes focused back in her room, she saw it: her journal.
Music soothed her thoughts as she reached for it, leaving wet footprints across the carpet. Sitting on the edge of the bed, holding it, she put her finger unto the edges of the written pages. This was what she would do often. She felt her angels took her to what she was to read.
They did...

*****

January 2005...

"Hello," he said as he entered the examining room. Dr. Tasbas, a soft and gentle man.

I had been through so much at this point and survived. Now I was entering another door of life to walk through: the radiation. Not knowing what effects it would have on my body and my mind. Sometimes we go through things starting out ignorant, but having a master's degree by the time it ends.

"I see you're alone?" he said, looking up at me over the rim of his glasses. He had a foreign accent that was very comforting for me to hear. "Why are you alone? Why is no one here with you?"

Never thinking he would ask, I hesitated for a moment. "I am fine. I don't want to worry my family any more than they already are."

I wish they could have been there, but I had to think of them. I didn't say this to him, but I worried about them.

"Where is your other half?"

My other half... Repeating it aloud.

"Yes, your other half?"

I quickly said, "He left." Trying to hold back my laugh, I never expected him to ask about Tom. It had been five years since he left. He wouldn't let this go and continued with concern, to ask more.

"Where did he go?"

With a little hesitation, I said, "He's in Texas with his girlfriend, and they're very happy. Doctor, we've been apart for five years now."

He looked intently at my records again. "You have three grown children?"

"Yes."

"And they let him leave you?"

I sat silent with a smile. I had no answer for him.

He shook his head in disbelief. He didn't like me being there alone.

I touched his hand. "I am fine, don't worry."

I'll never forget that moment with him. My peace had come from my angel, my spirit guide telling me at my tree, *"Don't let your eyes deceive you to what in your heart you know is true."* I wasn't alone. I never truly felt alone.

After my surgery in December, I realized how blessed I was and that I was being watched over. We all from time to time wonder, *Is there anyone watching? Am I going to be taken care of?* I got my answers quickly.

My surgeon's name was Rachel, a sweet, middle-aged woman. I had my first surgery, it was a lumpectomy. After testing the tissue taken from my breast, Rachel told me if I had taken any form of estrogen.

I would have had full-blown breast cancer in both breasts. She found my tissue was very sensitive to estrogen. I said, "you're kidding. That is an 'angel thing'."

"Yes, it is," she agreed. The week before my surgery, she told me in her entire career she had never found cancer this early in anyone. Two angel moments occurred for us.

I asked her what I should do next after this surgery, yet I worded it, "If you were me, what would you do?

Her reply was a surprise. Without any hesitation at all, she touched my hand. "I would go in again and take a little more tissue out if it was me. I would feel more comfortable if I did."

I smiled and without hesitation said, "Let's do it."

Little did I know at the time that the third sign of angels watching over me would occur in that second operating room!

One week later, I was back in pre-op, seeing the same faces and making jokes to lighten the situation.

"Hi!" I said to Susan, my nurse. "I heard they were having a two-for-one special, and I just had to come back." She laughed along with my family at my silly jesting.

My mom, my sister and Leah were all with me, waiting for me to walk through this moment one more time. I was confident it would be fine. The anaesthesiologist came in. "Well, hello again," he said.

"Hi," I said. "You and I have to stop meeting like this."

A smile lit up his face.

The doctor then said, "Would you like to walk to the operating room?"

I looked shocked, but without hesitation I asked, "Really? I can?"

"Sure, why not?" he said.

I gave a look to my family that said, *Oh boy!* I loved to make them smile; it seemed to take the fear out of the moment. I knew they were thinking, *Are you people ready for her and what she does?*

He helped me off the gurney, and I carefully pulled my gown closed as he held my IV bag. I kissed them all and said, "I'll be right back," laughing as I scooted off with my familiar and *brave* doctor friend.

As we walked down the hallway, many wondering, I am sure, *why is she walking?*

The operating room door opened as the doctor tapped the wall button. Everyone inside was busy making ready for the next patient. One of many I am sure that they would be seeing that day.

My entrance wasn't what they expected. "Honey, I'm home," I announced playfully.

With a surprised look, they all stopped what they were doing and all eyes for a few seconds were on me. Just another patient, so they thought, not realizing that we were to touch each other differently than all the others they would have in this light-filled room.

My angels kept my heart calm and gave me the words to make this moment one not of fear, but of life. My life was in their hands. They would soon put me to sleep, but I wanted them to know me. See me a wee bit clearer through their eyes and their hearts than the others.

With just a quick glance, I scanned the masked faces, drawn to approach each with a smile. I could see their smiles concealed under their masks.

"Hi, my name is Debby. I want you to know my boob is part of a set. We went through this last week, and she was quite traumatized by it all. Well, here we are again, my boob and I. We decided to give you another chance. Please be careful, just as you were last week. My doctor wanted to take just a little more tissue out of her. Now remember this," (*all were still listening to my voice as I continued my very brief entertaining gesture standing in front of each that I was directed to within my heart*) "I don't let just anyone touch my boob!"

The operating room filled with laughter and disbelief. I know they will never forget me. I didn't want to be just another human in that room. I wanted to make them see me, even if only for a brief moment. My life is precious, as are theirs.

The surgery was as successful as the first. Rachel was by my side as I woke. "Deb, I found another microscopic tissue. So very small, but it was cancerous tissue. No technology we have would have found it this early, other than being right in sight with my instruments. We got it all!"

"Thank you," I said to her, and to my angels. The medication soothed me back into sleep.

I remembered her words when the nurse touched my arm to wake me again. The smile on her face made me smile. My family by my side. I will live even stronger now. That was the band I wore on my arm. Live strong. I shall. It will be.

My breast was still intact with a little less tissue, but I don't care. What will a man think? Hmm...less is more?? It doesn't truly matter what they think. I am alive and have one more door to walk through.

Radiation.

After I healed, the radiation treatments were to take a little over six weeks. I had no idea what to expect. My emotions were springboarding everywhere.

Deb took a deep breath and held the journal to her chest. *I remember...yes, I will always remember.* **Then she continued to read...**

*****

It begins. (my next door...)

The main effect the radiation has on me...tired. I am so very tired from it. It's hard to work or focus on anything. How can this make me so weak?

What day is it? Does it matter? They all seem the same. Every day, it seems I see a new face in this cancer center. My mind chatters inside, *how are they feeling? Are they scared? What do you do to get through this feeling?*

I do have a tendency to put on a happy face, like all is well. Why do I do that? I am sure they do care, but why burden them with my thoughts and insecurities?

My kids, what are they thinking? I think they are in denial. I feel it with them.

Cancer doesn't run in our family. Not ours, yet now it does. It begins with me. It's the greatest lesson of life I had to learn. To live, to be alive and live, no matter the storm. I will learn and teach with all my heart to my children. I will live my lessons learned.

I keep thinking that I should have done something differently. I did read the other day that everyone has cancer seeds in them. What shocked me was reading that stress makes those seeds come alive. Stress? Now I understand. I am not going to get stressed anymore...Haha.

I still wear this bracelet, it's getting pretty worn. My mother wears hers faithfully. I think she believes in the magic of positive thinking, too. Leah is like me, hiding her fear, keeping herself strong. Every day, I take my rose quartz necklace off before the radiation. I love my necklace. They say that rose quartz gives strength and confidence to you. I think it does. I am learning to be...thinking positive, casting off the fear and negativity. Think it...think it...see it.

Deb kept reading:

I have much to do. Especially the book, I need to finish the book. I have new eyes now. I can see it more clearly than yesterday.

Is that why I was brought to Penn Yan to live by the water? To have a peaceful place to come home to? I've always been drawn to it. Maybe so.

Ahhh, journal, you won't believe what happened today by the water. I took a picture, it says it all.

Another angel thing moment for me!

We all should be so blessed to have at least one angel moment, once in our lifetime. I was writing in my journal, and the sun was warm on my skin. March? A bit nippy, but I still went. I am so glad I had brought my camera. Everyone would think I lost my mind if I told them this story. I think maybe they think it without the story...ha.

Leah called and said, "Mom, where are you?"

"I am at the lake at Indian Pines Park."

"How do I get to it?"

She was attending Keuka College, and I directed her on her cell phone how to find me. There were geese and ducks all around the park. People fed them all the time. It was their home. Maybe that was why I loved it there, too. It seemed to be my place, being with them.

Leah drove into the parking lot and squealed on her phone, "Oh my God! Look at the birds!"

Watching her car enter the lot slowly, so she didn't scare the geese. She kept talking on the phone, even though she could see me. She was so excited, and so was her passenger, a sweet friend from school. Maybe she will understand for a moment why I come here. She always said, "Mom, you're so weird." I knew she meant that in a good way. She loves me much.

My camera clicked away as I captured the moment. She stayed for a short time, needing money if I recall correctly. They went back to school, and I began walking back towards the shoreline. Finding my peace there, constantly having thoughts of life and convincing any angels listening I have so much more to do. I am not ready to leave this realm. Just as I was within myself, taking in the life around me - it happened.

I looked up, and there it was. The sky bright blue, without a cloud to be seen. The sun's rays reflected down through the branches of the still bare tree branches. I saw it. A small white object in the sky, seeming to be a cloud, not a cloud. It looked like a small circle with a little appendage off it. I raised my camera, catching the moment. This moment will never come again. This one was the real thing. I was thinking, *I have never seen anything like this in my life*. It was a sign from heaven...I knew it, I felt it. My angels gave me a sign that I would be fine.

I showed the picture to anyone and everyone. They all agreed it was a sign for me. Maybe they said it was, not truly realizing those things happen. Maybe they were trying to appease me. It truly doesn't matter. Each of us has moments that happen, the angel thing moments, to make us see it was there or happened for us. It doesn't matter what others think.

We all are here for a reason. To celebrate moments together as our paths cross. Whether it is helping an elderly person find a grocery cart or a young child cross the road. Moments shared in time.

*****

"Hey…." a voice called through the door. "Are you in there?"

Deb came back quickly to the room. How long have I been...? She thought, hearing the familiar voice. She called back.

"I am, just a sec." She grabbed her T-shirt and ran to the door. "Shar? Are you alone?"

"Open up, I've been banging out here for five minutes."

"Sorry!"

"Are you all right, or do you have company?"

"I'm fine. I was just taking a shower."

"A shower? Are you deaf, too?"

"Nooo! I was…"

"Are you feeling okay?"

"Yes, it's..." she hesitated, taking a deep breath.

"Well, what?"

"When I saw the scar on my breast, I went back for a moment."

"It's not a scar - it's a sign! It shows you overcame a dark storm!"

"I know. It's been three years. You would think I wouldn't let it affect me so much!"

"Debby, you're my best friend, and you always think way too deep into things, more than others do. Maybe that's why you're a writer. You're very analytical, and little weird, too, for the record."

"I am...hey! Weird?" It felt good to laugh. "I've been told I march to the beat of a different drummer. I don't mind, though. At least I know the tune."

"Weird. I say that with love. I think a lot of people wish they could exist in the world you have created. Remember all the people you have touched. Did you see the excitement at the cafe yesterday? They love you because they know you care about them. You get back hundredfold what you give. I have watched you over the years and learned myself from being by your side."

"I know. Thanks, Shar. Thanks for being here when I need you. You are my anam cara. We learn together."

Shar glanced over in the corner of the room. "The memory barrel is in your presence!"

"Yes. It was here when I woke this morning. Must be Jim brought it in last night while I was gone."

"Speaking of last night, come on. Tell me!"

"Tell you?" she said, playfully avoiding the Jeff topic.

"Yes, how did it go? What did you do?"

"Well," Debby started to explain with a big smile on her face.

"Oh my God!" Shar interrupted. "You should have seen Jim's face when he heard that bike start up. He made a path to the window through O'Connor's. You would have thought God was parting the Red Sea. And that wasn't all. The restaurant was in a stir. It was so funny listening to them and watching the reaction to you leaving with this stranger. Who is he? Is he the one in the book at the end? It was hilarious."

"What did you say? Who was that man you were dancing with, too?"

"I said, 'I don't know. It's a mystery to me.' I enjoyed playing along with them. It was great - the people, not the dancing guy." She laughed as she kicked her shoes off and plopped on the bed.

"I can see by the expression on your face it was pretty entertaining for you."

"All right now, so reality, no novel stuff. How was it? Did he kiss you?"

"Shar, I just met him!" she said with a sneer on her face. Dee could see Shar didn't believe her. *So I will give you what you want,* she thought. *A la...story writer.* "You should have been here a little earlier...actually, he just left."

"No! Really?" Shar winced.

"Mm hum, we had great sex last night. I haven't been that excited in a long time. Maybe by being a doctor, you learn special techniques and points of interest, you know what I mean?" Her eyebrows raised to give the effect.

"Really?" Shar couldn't believe what she was hearing.

"He made my body do things I didn't think were possible!" Debby sighed as she collapsed on the bed."Oh my God! Ohhh..."

Shar's mouth just stayed open watching Debby woo her to her imaginary evening adventures.

Then Deb sat up and stared at the look of sheer admiration on Shar's face.

"Shar?" Debby jumped on the bed and shoved her. "Nothing happened!"

Her mouth snapped shut, and she began swatting Debby with the pillow. "You got me. I was really sucked into it."

"I know...I love it when you're so gullible. I may be weird, but you're gullible, girl. I'm going to call you 'GG,' Gullible Girl!"

They continued to wrestle on the bed. "You really had me thinking you did, he did!"

"I know", Debby said with tears running down her face from laughing. "Okay, okay! I give up!" Guarding herself from the bombardment of pillows. "I'm sorry! I'm sorry!"

"No, you're not, not at all!" Shar howled, laughing almost as hard as Debby was.

They both collapsed next to each other, and the room seemed to calm down.

"You're okay, aren't you?"

Debby smiled as she touched Shar's hand. "My friend, I am more than okay. Truly."

"What happens from here, Deb?"

"I'm not sure yet. I think I'm going to stay a bit longer, relax.

The inn is closing for the season next week."

"Are you thinking of traveling?"

"Now there's an idea. I would love to go to Ireland and Scotland, to see if my book was right. I've heard stories about the castles there."

"Your tale of the one in Scotland was great. Where did that idea come from?"

"Where the whole book came from, silly, inspiration and imagination." She leaned on her elbows and looked out the window. "Shar, can I tell you something?"

"Sure, that's why I'm here. To get the inside scoop. The Enquirer has me on their payroll, but you can't tell them I told you. "

"I'm a bit scared at times with this interviewing thing on the book."

"Why?"

"I've met other authors. It's so hard to talk with them about my book. Talk about how I wrote it."

Shar wanted to comfort her. "They have the typical author questions and are curious. "Why would you be so nervous? You're an excellent writer."

" I had no thought of how to begin or end it. I just started writing."

"So? You went with your dream. Do you realize how many people say they want to write a book and never do?"

"I know, but usually there's a process you go through. I had no process."

"No rules, Deb. You wrote as you live now. Who is to say how you are to write? Who wrote those rules anyway?"

"Although many will really want to run with the 'no rules' concept."

Shar laughed. "Now, that is a good one to play with."

"Yes, I know. I have to explain that when it comes out."

They both laughed.

"This story came to me in so many unlikely places. From writing on a picnic table in a friend's yard as I watched his cattle graze across the road. Then another time, the words came inside the cabin of a friend's boat. My music was playing in the cabin, and the pencil in my hand seemed to flow there as the waves rocked me, saying, 'It has to be written'...I see it now. You know what it is?"

"What?"

"The universal spirit and all its forms of nature, guided me to continue, to get this written."

"Yes, that's a bit unusual. Then, what of you isn't?"

"Oh, thanks."

She avoided thinking of it and directed the conversation in another way. That's what she was good at.

"Jeff did say he wanted to see me again?"

"Did he?"

"Yep."

"When?" Shar knew her well enough to go with the flow.

"I don't know. I gave him my cell number. That seems to be the easiest way to contact me lately." Then her phone rang.

They both looked at each other and laughed, playfully singing together, "It's an Angel thing!"

Debby dashed for the phone. "Hello...hi..." Her voice went up an octave.

Shar covered her mouth to contain her laugh, and Debby did everything she could to stay calm.

"What time did you leave? Wow. That was early. You're making good time. I'll be heading home soon. I live in North Carolina now. Yes, I had a nice time, too. Sure. No, Shar is still here. We're having some girl time. It's been a while since we had time to hang out. Oh, okay. I'll tell her. All right, bye."

She hung up the phone, and Shar glared at her. "Tell me what?"

"He said thanks for giving him the book."

"I let him borrow mine."

"I gave him another one yesterday, at Hattie's request. I even signed it for him."

"Hmm...what did you write?"

"*Everyone meets for a reason...time will tell. We will stay in touch.* Shar, the distance is huge, and you know how I am on long distance dating. He's a nice guy, but -"

The phone rang again.

"Two calls in one day!"

Debby looked at the phone. "It's Bob." She put her finger up to her lips for Shar to be quiet.

"Hey."

"Hey to you, lady. Are you having a good time?"

"Yes, I am. Everything went so well yesterday. I signed books for about seven hours. It was wonderful."

"I just finished talking to Danny. He said all is going so well with the book that it might be translated into a few foreign languages. Did he tell you?"

"Yes, he did. He's so busy getting it out there. It's good for him, though. It keeps him out of trouble."

"I have news for you, too," Bob said.

"Really?"

"I met with a client the other day, he knows someone in Hollywood that happened to mention *The Memory Barrel*. Small world, as we both know."

"Why did they mention my book?"

"It seems he heard someone mentioning that they might want to get some movie rights to it."

"What?" Debby yelled. "You're kidding!"

Shar fell off the bed when Dee jumped up. Debby went over and pulled her arm to get her back up on the bed. It was hard to keep back the explosion of laughter, seeing her fall on the floor.

They were always like that when they were together.

"Are you okay? Am I interrupting something?" Bob brought her back from playing with Shar.

"Oh, no it's fine. Shar is playing monkeys on the bed again. What can I say? Sorry."

He laughed. "Shar's there? Tell her hi for me. I haven't seen her in ages. So, my little author, how about that idea of making a movie? It would be your dream come true. You used to say it would be made into a movie, remember?"

"Yes, but I was dreaming out loud."

*She remembered, when you believe it, you will see it...thank you...
I remember.*

"Dreams sometimes do come true, you know!"

"Oh my gosh, does Danny know?"

"No, I didn't tell him. I thought that was something for you to do with your entire family. I wanted to tell you. To be the first."

"Well, babe, you have made my day."

"That's what I'm here for, *angel*, to make your day."

Debby dodged that statement and went speechless, realizing she'd slipped and called him 'babe'.

"Hey, hey, don't get serious on me now. Ease and flow, missy," Bob said.

"No, I 'm fine."

"I'll let you get on with the day. Call me if you need me, OK?"

"Thanks, Bob."

Shar sat there staring. "What did he say?"

Debby looked out the window at the clear blue sky. "Let's go for a walk."

"Oh, no you don't. What's going on?"

"Bob said he heard someone wants to make *The Memory Barrel* into a movie."

"What???" Shar screamed. "Debby, congratulations!"

"I can't believe it, Shar. So much good is happening. It's one thing after the other."

"Come on, let's go for that walk," she said as she put on her jeans and a sweatshirt. "Let's go down by the water."

As they walked into the lobby, Jim was standing there wearing his old faded overalls. His eyes locked on theirs as they rounded the corner. Helen smacked his arm in an effort to break the gaze he held on Debby.

"Hey, Pops," Deb said.

"You didn't get much sleep last night now, did yah?"

Debby glanced at Shar as if to say, *Should I give him the story I gave you?* Shar's eyes opened wide, and she shook her head no.

"Well…" Debby said, hesitating and looking back at Shar. "I didn't need much," she said with a grin.

"Sounded like a lot of wrestling going on up there this morning."

Shar again looked at Debby, shaking her head no. Debby sighed with a snicker.

"It was Shar's fault. She was beating me with the pillows. Are we grounded?"

Jim laughed his deep laugh. So did Helen; she loved it when Deb teased him. He came around the desk and grabbed her as she was dodging for the back door, scooping her up with his bear hug.

"Ugh," Debby grunted.

"Young lady, you have to be more careful, is all. We didn't lose you to the cancer, and we don't want to lose you to a Harley." He set her down gently, and she gave him a kiss on the cheek. "Now, where are you two off to?"

She sighed. "Questions, questions."

Shar quickly interjected, "For a walk, is all. We won't be long."

The squeaky screen door slammed behind them.

~*~*~*~

Chapter Twenty

Home again

Jeff had made good time. He was already on the outskirts of Ohio. The book sat on the seat beside him. Doc was content, snoring in his normal position with his head on Jeff's lap. *Welcome to Ohio*, the sign read as he crossed the state line.

"Ohio," he said under his breath. *I had her...I had her right in front of me...she is amazing*, he thought, *everything I had hoped she would be.* It was hard for him to tell what was real and what wasn't from reading the book. *It seemed so real having her on my bike.* He didn't want to dwell too much on what had happened; he wanted to get home, see Mary Margaret.

"Hey, Peanut," he said, answering his cell phone. "Yes, I just crossed the state line. I should be there in a few hours. It should be around seven or so. Have you checked on the house? Is it still standing?"

"Yes, Daddy," Melody said. "Uncle Jake has been going over, and so has Paul. All of us have made sure it's fine. You're getting home in time for the holidays. Let's let this year be different from last year, okay?"

"Sure...sure."

The sun had been down for two hours. *This daylight savings time makes the days so short. I hate that.* As he turned onto Holly Brook Pond Road, he was excited to see the old house. His kids were born there; it was his place of memories. Seeing *The Memory Barrel* on his seat made him realize he had his own memories. They were irreplaceable; some good, some bad. *I should ask Debby to paint one of her memory paintings for me. What a unique idea. Everything about her seems to be unique*, he thought.

Doc's sat up, as if he sensed he was home. His nose pushed against the glass window on the door as he whined, as if to say *let me out, let me out.* The truck stopped, and Doc couldn't get out fast enough.

The glow of the full moon lit up the whole yard, but even without it, Doc would have known where every little hole was. He chased the unsuspecting rabbit out of the bushes. The poor rabbit probably was very content with the thought of Doc not returning. Jeff looked around, stretching, taking in a deep breath. It was hard to believe five months had passed. The grass and bushes were trimmed nice. Someone had been taking good care of the place.

The lights from an oncoming car approached the house. The driveway to the house was quite long, so you could see up Holly Brook for any visitors, wanted or otherwise. The car pulled into the driveway, and the horn started tooting.

The driver's door opened. "Sorry," the voice on the driver's side said. "She made me do it."

Melody ran, jumping into her father's arms. "Daddy, you're home!"

"Ahhh," he howled, spinning her around. "Yes, and it feels good, Mels. I've missed you."

Doc ran up, jumping with leaps and bounds to the celebration, almost knocking Jeff over with Mel in his arms. They both laughed. "He's happy to be home, too!"

"Hey there boy." Melody shuffled his hair and kissed his face. "I missed you. Did you take good care of him? I'm sure you would have stories to tell, if only you could talk."

"Oh yes, he would, but that's the best companion to have, the ones that don't tell," Jeff said, laughing.

"Sir," Eric said, extending his hand to Jeff. "Welcome home."

Jeff shook his hand, then grabbed him and gave him a big Nichols bear hug.

A tiny voice echoed in the car. Jeff stopped and froze for a moment; this would be his first time seeing and touching Mary Margaret. *This moment will never come again,* he remembered.

"Go ahead, Daddy...you can get her."

Jeff walked to the door of the car and slowly opened it so as not to startle her. "Hey, Mary Margaret...hey, baby girl," he said, ever so softly.

She was dressed in a warm pink jacket, with a white fluffy hat to keep her warm. *She smells new*, he thought. Mary Margaret's eyes were smeared with a tear from crying. Jeff gently wiped her cheek. "Don't cry, baby girl, Grandpa is here." Her blue eyes sparkled from the moonlight. He gently unhooked her seat belt and pulled her carefully towards him. "Oh my, she smiled at me!" Jeff said.

Melody held Eric as they enjoyed their first encounter as Grandpa and granddaughter.

"Ohh...there she is...he brought her close to his chest."

Doc sat watching, knowing, as if instinctively, it was a baby; our new baby.

Jeff handed the keys to the house to Eric, then carefully walked up the stairs, as if one missed step and he might lose her. Before he could set her down on the couch to remove her coat, another voice came into the room.

"Dad!"

Jeff turned to see Paul standing there, with Pam next to him. *God, he's grown into a man since I was gone.*

"Paul? Oh man, I am so glad to see you, son. Good to see both of you."

"Welcome home," Paul said.

"Thanks. It's good to be back. I should go away more often. Receiving these amazing welcome home moments is great!"

Paul and Melody both simultaneously said, "No!"

"Kidding," Jeff said, "kidding."

~*~*~*~

Chapter Twenty-One

I will walk through the storm with you,
and teach you to dance in the rain…

Debby stayed at the inn a bit longer to relax. It wouldn't be long, though, before the inn closed for the season. She wanted to make sure before she left to contact Arabella; there was something about this beautiful young woman. She called her and arranged to meet the next day at the café.

Arabella was waiting outside as Debby approached. She laughed, seeing Deb walk down the sidewalk doing her "happy dance."

Of course, Deb knew she was watching. Always good to start with a smile. *If it starts out right, it will end up right,* Dee thought to herself.

"Hi, Arabella. Finally, we get a moment alone. How are you?"

"Miss Debby, could you call me Abbey? Arabella is lovely coming from my ancestry, but it would feel so much more relaxed if you called me Abbey."

"Of course, then you call me Dee. Miss Debby is so formal."

Debby learned she had been hiding so much from her family. She thought this was more than her family could have handled.

While in Ireland, cancer had been discovered in her breast. She wanted to come home to start the process of recovery. Hoping success would be the outcome.

Deb sat listening to Abbey share her story. They were there for hours. Hattie knew it was time to keep them separate from everyone. She went out of her way to make sure they weren't disturbed. Hattie had seen Debby do this before.

Everyone loves Debby. She wasn't just an author; she genuinely loved people and went out of her way to help them in whatever manner she felt she had to; sometimes too much, but she would never say it was too much. You could see it in her face when she did. She called it "Angel magic"; not of herself, but from the Source of all that has life, to help us "to be"...be still...and listen.

Debby touched Abbey's hand. "It's normal to be afraid. Pray to the Spirit that encompasses the entire universe, your angels, or whatever you feel is the source of life to you. Release it to the air, the wind, and the earth. It's the fear and uncertainty. Thoughts you have heard from others going through these moments, and not many think positively. I will guide you as much as you allow me, then we can make it through this together."

Her statements were life-giving to Arabella, words she had never heard quite this way before.

"Do you feel there is more for you to do here on this Earth plane?"

Abbey had never heard questions asked with such a sincere attempt to have her examine herself and her life. Without hesitation, she looked at Debby and said, "I am not finished here. I do have more to do."

"Then we must ask. You must ask, let the fear go now, try to see it gone, out of your body..." Debby touched her hands as the soft music played in the background, and her tears flowed as if the dams of pain had broken within her little body.

Hattie stood back watching. The café was empty, and it was almost sunset.

Debby stood up and extended her hand to Abbey. "Will you come with me?"

They drove to the lighthouse. The light in the upper dome was flickering, as if prepared to perform its task of protecting the people at sea. The lighthouse represents so much, if you have the eyes to see. Debby not only saw it, she experienced it, too.

This lighthouse was commonplace to the town people, like familiar things we all get accustomed to when we are around them all the time. We take them for granted or don't even take the time to enjoy them, time to appreciate where you live and the simple, peaceful things in life that cost nothing. Sometimes things are taken from us to give us clarity and we find that we truly did want them and had just forgotten how precious they were until they were gone. She learned this on the island, and she will continue here, take nothing for granted.

Debby knew that she had to give hope to this young woman, to breathe hope into her soul, take away the fear of the unknown and help her think. Think beyond the fear.

Deb patted the ground for Abbey to sit, and they sat face-to-face.

"I…" Debby began. "I have been on your path. I am going to try to explain how I survived it, and then the choices are yours. Do you understand?"

Abbey nodded.

"We have angels that are with us from the moment we enter this realm. They are always there to guide us, to help us. These guides will not tell you what to do, that is your decision. They will give you information to assist you, but the final choice is always yours. They can't help unless we ask. When we ask for their help and they give it, it isn't always according to our time frame, and they aren't here for frivolous things, but for important life moments like this. The first step is to believe that if you ask, you shall receive; it's a huge step of faith. We are shown in our lives to be careful what we ask for…because we just might get it. Thus, you think of this first, make sure it is important."

She went on. "Oh, they can guide you to the little things, too. There is nothing small in the eyes of the Source of life; it is all designed to make you happy. As minuscule as a street light changing just when you think about it or knowing there will be a parking place when you pull into a parking lot. Things that. really aren't important, but they make you smile. You think it, and it happens. Well, do it for this. You can., you have permission, it is your right. The law of life can and will make this happen. Do you believe this?"

Debby paused for a moment and gazed off to the water. She

then took a deep breath to make sure she was clear in her explanation, clear in this moment. The sun cast its last light on the water to rest before turning it over to the moon. The waves continued to flow, breaking on the rocks below.

The air was filled with magic; you could feel it.

"Anything is possible," Deb insisted, her eyes still looking off into the distance as she touched her hand. "Now, I have learned as I listened to many voices in this realm, hearing words that comforted me. By having them brought to me; yes, they were brought to me. By their words, their lessons, I understood life a bit clearer. I will give you the same words.

"Are you okay? I do have a way of carrying on and on with words. They just seem to come. Are you with me, or is this stirring for you, being here by the water, listening to a silly author telling you of life?"

Abbey's eyes shone with a bright glow. "I am here with you, Debby. I was brought to you, as those others were brought to you on your journey. You are or were meant to be a guide to me. I will listen as you did to others, knowing your words will guide me. Then I will, in time, find another who will also need these words. It's like they are waves of life passed from moment to moment. Those who want to hear or know will. Those who have no ears to listen will just endure life. We will live it. I see you...the trueness of the word {Namaste}. I see you, and I know you see me."

Debra wrinkled her nose in shyness; it was still there from time to time. Her hand reached up to touch her heart with the wave gesture she always did, then she touched Abbey's cheek. "I see you as well. I did from the moment you came into the café to meet me. We will be together even after this journey, my friend."

She continued again after taking a deep breath, as if asking for life to give her the right words to share.

"It is a common statement said in the world, 'I will believe it when I see it'...amazing how we humans think or have been convinced. Yet, it truly should be said. 'You will see it when you believe it!' Do you understand? It's like looking in a mirror and seeing it as it really is. Is it real, or a reflection? The power of life and the heart are amazing, more powerful than we can even begin to imagine. Now…close your eyes," she said softly.

Her dear friend taught this to Debby when she went through the cancer. Then a student; now a teacher.

Abbey closed her eyes with no hesitation.

Debby began. "Feel Spirit, the Source of life around you…feel it and breathe. Now, see a white light…it is surrounding you. Take your time, adjust your thoughts, and envision it around you. Do you see it?"

Abbey nodded.

"Good."

"Be calm and breathe slowly…relax."

Abbey sat still with her eyes closed; listening to Debby's calling words.

"The white light is the white light of God. It is surrounding you. While you are taking this path, this light will always be there for you. Any moment, any time, any place. Feel the positive energy coming into your body. Relax and breathe. Feel the love of God enter your body, Abbey.

"As you do this, listen to that still, small voice within you. Words will be shared from time to time that you need to hear. Watch for signs also. Pay attention to all that is around you. Sometimes people come to you; some would say they are angels taking on form for a moment, or a spirit guide. Listen and consider all that is brought to your life circle."

Abbey's eyes were still closed as a tear came down her cheek. She was feeling it.

This is how it was for me so many years ago, Debby thought to herself.

Debby's soft voice continued. "Relax and breathe, my friend, relax and breathe. Your angels are here for you, right beside you. They have been with you since your life here began. You are an eternal being having a physical experience. They will help you, as they always have; however, you need to ask them. If you ask them for help, they will. You have to ask."

Knowing she repeated this lesson again, it was so important

for her to remember and understand. "Trust in the universal love of God, Abbey. Believe in the things you can't see with your eyes, but sense with your heart."

Debby continued to stroke her hand softly. Abbey then opened her eyes and stared at Debby.

"I see."

"Good!" With a deep sigh, she looked around at the star-filled sky, glancing back at Abbey. "It's your strength. Think positive always. Stay in the white light; it is your protection and your strength. Once you understand this, you can do it for others. Keeping them safe with the light, just as the lighthouse keeps boaters safe with its light."

On the rock beside them lay a white feather.
They hadn't noticed it yet.

As they turned to stand, both of them saw it at the same time. Abbey picked it up and held it to her heart. The tears touched their smiling lips. They shared the moment together and knew it would be one they would never forget. Never…

*****

Debby returned to the inn, where she found Helen and Jim waiting by the fire. Both could see she had been crying. Without a word, the three of them embraced.

Jim whispered, "Take some from me, angel."

She did…

Again, the night encompassed her room as she snuggled under the soft blanket.

Dream…remember and dream…be at peace.

As she drifted off she remembered;
My friend, one of my Earthly angels, of that I am sure, came to me
when I needed him most. His gentleness and sincere words brought me
through the darkness of the cancer. Everyone meets for a reason. I
always felt this, and as the years have passed, I have become more
aware. He took the fear away with his Native American ways.
He guided me many times when things became confusing or I was
scared. He was one of my Earthly angels. Drawn to his knowledge, he
shared with me the Native American ways.
His voice I could hear in the darkness of the night…
"Surround yourself with the light; feel it coming from the top of your
head to every part of your body."
Teaching of the knowledge of lighting candles, explaining why this is
done in religious beliefs, continuing with crystals and the energy God
created within them.

~

Yasteeh, what does this mean? I typed as I viewed his profile online.
His reply came the next day.
It means live in 'peace and harmony'.
I replied: Hello. My name is Debby.
    We passed a few emails back and forth. He was a very intelligent and
loving man. I will always remember one particular day. It was a Sunday.
My parents were sleeping, and I was alone in their back room, sitting and
just killing time on the computer. My daughter and I were waiting to go
to our new home. Radiation hadn't started as of yet.
Hello, my new friend whose name was Gentlebear said.
I replied, Hello back.
What is yasteeh? I asked. My screen name was Softbreeze.
Gentlebear: Oops sorry, It is a dine' [Navajo] word that means live in
beauty, peace and harmony.
Softbreeze: Nice, very nice. A good word.
Gentlebear: A good way to live, I wish everyone could find it.
Softbreeze: I think I have, missing a few pieces is all.
Gentlebear: Awesome.
Softbreeze: Yes.

Gentlebear: Now if we could help others find it.

Softbreeze: They have to want it first.

Gentlebear: True. See I knew you were a wise woman.

Softbreeze: Some look in the wrong places.

Gentlebear: Most it seems what a shame.

Softbreeze: Well, sorry to keep you longer, I was just curious about that word...

Gentlebear: Can I ask you a quick question.

Softbreeze: Sure.

Gentlebear: What do you write about?

Softbreeze: I have been writing a novel for about five years. I will attempt to finish it this year.

Gentlebear: Cool, are you going to publish it?

Softbreeze: Yes, or burn it.

Gentlebear: Don't burn it till I have had a chance to read it okay?

Softbreeze: Yes, then we can build a campfire on the mountaintop and let its spirit go where it was supposed to. It was good for me and, well, maybe that is all that it was for who knows?

Gentlebear: I am putting in my order for an autographed copy now, avoid the rush.

Softbreeze: Oh yeah, see me on Oprah.

Gentlebear: Still when I see an eagle fly, it's all better.

Softbreeze: I know what you mean I am that way when I see the sun's rays streak through the clouds on a bad day. I say okay. It will be fine.

Gentlebear: Do you have a favorite animal?

Softbreeze: A dove has always been my favorite.

Gentlebear: Feminine energy strength and wisdom good choice. I love their call.

Softbreeze: How do you know that is what it means?

Gentlebear: I have researched it and learned from a Shaman.

Softbreeze: Where do you find this information?

Gentlebear: All animals share energies with us. They are our protectors. In a way we learn from them they are guides to us. By reading, asking questions, listening. I also sought out healers to learn from them.

Softbreeze: Really?

Gentlebear: Yes.

Softbreeze: God I am so interested.

Gentlebear: You have but to listen to yourself, you have much knowledge it shows in what you write and how you think.

Softbreeze: There is more to learn I do feel like there is some missing for me.

Gentlebear: Funny thing is the more you learn the more you realize you don't know.

What do you feel is missing?

Softbreeze: Let me explain it this way. I go by the water and find a lot of strength there.

Gentlebear: You are opening yourself a good thing. Water is an essence of feminine energy.

Everything is your family, we are all a part of the one, interconnected and reliant on each other.

Softbreeze: I do know that.

Gentlebear: Knowing and feeling are two different things. Are you able to let yourself do that?

Softbreeze: Maybe that is what I am lacking.

Gentlebear: I wouldn't say lacking you are just finding this oneness slowly.

Softbreeze: I have so much to be happy for and I've made it through some very hard moments in my life. It's okay because all of them made me who I am today, I know that's a good thing. I do need to understand this better.

Gentlebear: You see, most people don't realize it's a good thing to be themselves. You understand much, you will more when you learn to share and by that I mean find a way to trust others and then yourself with what lies in your spirit.

Softbreeze: Yes, fear.

Gentlebear: It's sort of like a warm ray of sunshine surrounding you on a dark damp day. You have conquered much fear in your life.

Softbreeze: Expect nothing, no expectations no disappointments. If good happens it's wonderful, but you didn't expect it or doubt it.

Softbreeze: My sons are very spiritual and so is my daughter they recognize this. This year I said to them, this is the whole statement, I can now finish it. Expect nothing, hope for everything. They smiled when I said that to them. It made it less harsh. Do you understand?

Gentlebear: Yes, I do, I would say to you, though, that as we put energies out into the universe you will have them returned in a like manner. You have given tremendous amounts of love and of yourself in general over this walk. You will find it coming back to you now.

Gentlebear: When more of the pain heals, you will open more to it.

Softbreeze: Really? Hmm.

Gentlebear: Listen to your heart and from there you will know your truth, okay? God does love you.

Softbreeze: I feel everyone crosses each other's paths for a reason. It isn't an accident. I have been searching in myself and trying to understand what to do with my life now that I am not Mom 24/7. I would really love to learn these things, and understand them more.

Gentlebear: You are looking at different paths, be a little patient. You will know when to start. I will share all that I know and help you find your own direction, whatever that is.

Softbreeze: How did you learn all this?

Gentlebear: This could be a book lol.

Softbreeze: Haha another chapter, okay let me ask this.

Gentlebear: For many years growing up I didn't feel like I fit in anywhere. I always saw things differently. I have some friends who I share with now and again my pathway is my own though if that makes any sense they opened doors for me.

But it was my decision to walk through, I would warn you though to listen to your inner voice.

Softbreeze: I do, all the time.

Gentlebear: Not all doors are right for everyone.

Now she understood why she always felt so safe and comforted being near the water. There are many things in this creation for us to learn from. It isn't from organized religious beliefs. The creation soothes, comforts, and teaches us daily. We need to consider these things.

It was nurturing. She was being guided all those years, and finally now she was becoming aware of why. He became her friend, but maybe they knew each other in a previous time. In her lifetime, she had met both demons and angels.

I love him. He is my friend, one of my angels, for forever and a day. I will never forget.

Chapter Twenty-Two

Change the way you look at things, and the things you look at change.

The phone rang. "I'll get it."

"Okay…"

"Yes, I'll have her call them."

Danny turned the phone off.

Pillows surrounded Deb as she lay with her journal face down on her chest, staring out the window of the apartment. She had an amazing view of her world. The ocean was outside her door, the fishing pier within a few steps. This was her safe place, her nest.

She lay there lost in thought, listening to her music.

"Look at you!"

Debby was startled by the tone of voice that broke her concentration.

"What?" she whined back. "Can't I relax?"

"Mom, you've been in a state since your friend passed."

She sat up cross-legged on the floor. "Your point is?"

"Mom, she walked with it for three years; it was her time."

"I know, I know," Deb said. "The time seems to have passed so quickly. I am reflecting back, remembering."

"You always say look at the positive."

"I'm fine." Her whining did nothing to convince her.

"Have you heard from Jeff lately?"

Her eyes rolled. "Nope, and he hasn't heard from me."

"Why not? You liked him a lot."

"Yes, I did."

"You had some great times together."

"I know, I know. Sometimes things aren't always as they seem."

Remembering:...

Dear Journal,

It was so easy to go to him. He knew my best friend. One call, and it started.

"Want to come for a visit and play with me on my boat?" the voice on the other end of the phone said.

"Really?"

"Yes, I bought a boat, traded in my bike."

"When?"

"This weekend, come be with me."

I hadn't been with him since Maine. I wanted to see him again, and I could hear in his voice that he wanted to be with me, too. He sounded well.

When I arrived, his boat was docked at a small pier, with all the other boats lined up.

It was an older cruise boat. He stood there next to the boat, with his jeans and green jacket on. God, he looked like eye candy for sure.

"Hey, you," I said.

"Welcome to my new world, Debra Pratt."

Jeff told me the first night on the water he had finished reading my book. I laughed. He then told me about his recollection of moments in my book that occurred while recovering from his injury on his bike, explaining how he had envisioned himself as the one on the bike with Debra. It's amazing how the mind and imagination seem to make things real that aren't. Or were they?

Maybe at some moment in time it happened. Who's to say?

We spent our time together revisiting the past, talking about the future, relaxing, and not thinking about anyone but each other. Dinner on the boat was so pleasant. The feeling of the wind on my face felt just like being on the bike as we soared across the top of the water. He pulled me close to him as he kept us on course.

Moments, memories, faces, and places in time.

It has been two years. It seemed perfect for us, but after returning from Scotland, it all seemed to fade. Yes, I went to meet his Scottish family and journeyed through the hills. His family was amazing on the Isle. I met them during my international trip with my staff. He wasn't able to come with me. I should go back sometime to visit Sean and Margaret, and maybe I'll take the girls with me. Lilly and Savannah would love it there. I loved feeling the magic; it was in every shop and on every face you came in contact with. Similar to Pemaquid, but it was across the water. Sean even reminded me of Jim. They say everyone has a twin, but it wasn't in their appearance; it was who they are. Two separate people, oceans apart, yet similar. How one's imagination could go with that idea.

It wasn't meant to be for me and Jeff, that's all. He still loved his wife, and I could see it in his eyes. She still loved him, too; you could see it when they were in the same room. Everything happens for a reason. Sometimes being separated will eventually bring you back together.

Families; it's all about our families and staying together for the love. Our family circle gives us the life energy we need to have a successful, abundant life.

I have no regrets for the moments we shared, nor does he. He felt the magic of life. Sometimes we need to go back and do it again, do it right this time. We can be given a second chance.

That's how it worked for him. It can work that way for all of us.

I remember, I remember.

Bob? Where did he go? What happened? Was it me that made the choice? Was I thinking and learning all this with Jeff to see if I was to go back, too? To do it again?

The last few years have been like a whirlwind. They seemed to blend into each other. Jeff and the book have separated us, seeming to divide our friendship. I know he would want me to be happy and would stay away so I would be. It has been years.

Timing; it was synchronized timing. They say when you are ready for your dreams to come true, they come to you. But first you have to be ready.

I was in a new beginning, a new world opened for me so quickly after releasing the book to the world. Was I procrastinating? They say procrastination is the absence of readiness. I wasn't ready then for what he wanted. I had so much clutter in my heart from past relationships.

The timing is arranged through the universe. Is he waiting for me now? Is this what I am being shown?

I'll have to see if I can find his number. Leah must have it; she was very close to him. She probably has stayed in touch with him without telling me.

Oh, he is probably re-married now and very content with his life. Maybe I should just leave well enough alone. Yet the words "Let's do it again" keep echoing in my mind. Why?

The doorbell rang.

Saved by the bell! She thought to herself, thankful the internal chatter about Bob would stop.

"Debby Pratt?" A man stood at the door, with an envelope in his hand.

"Yes."

"This is for you," he said as he handed her the envelope. "Please sign here."

He nodded his head, gave her a kindly wink, and walked towards his car.

Debby leaned out to see what he was driving. She had her shorts on and as always, bare feet. No one seeing her would know she was an author by any shade of the imagination. She chuckled and thought to herself, *Hmm...he's cute.*

Danny stood at the top of the stairs. "Who was that?"

She spun, looking up the steps. "Ohh...my Mr. wonderful. Oh baby, oh baby."

Danny laughed; he loved to see his mom playful.

"No really, Mom, who was it?"

She raised an envelope. "A bearer of gifts." Deb sat on the couch and opened the envelope.

My dearest friend,

I am inviting you to visit one more time the Isle of Skye. I remember the joy in your eyes when you were here two years ago. We miss you and would love to have another opportunity to have you stay at our inn.

We have contacted your publisher, and your book will be here in large quantities for you to give others the pleasure of your acquaintance.

Sincerely,

Sean Roberts

#3Kelargen Path
Isle of Skye, Scotland
P.S. Enclosed is your voucher I purchased. Please notify of date of arrival.
Lass, we miss ya!
Love, Sean and Margaret

Debby smiled and looked at Danny, her eyes filled with emotion. She covered her mouth with the letter and looked out the window. "I'm going on a trip."

"Where?"

"Back to Scotland." She sat still. It was hard to hold back the tears.

"When?"

She handed the letter to Danny.

"You need to do this, Mom."

"I know."

Just then, Leah came in the door. "Hey, what's all the racket about?"

"Mom's going back to Scotland for a visit."

"Really?" she said. "When did you decide this?"

"Now," she said as she handed her the letter.

Leah read it and smiled. "Cool, Mom. Maybe you'll meet your Mr. Wonderful there." They both started laughing.

Danny didn't get the joke. He just stood there smiling, watching the two of them do their playful game.

"Interesting you say that. I was just teasing your brother, saying the mail carrier was my Mr. Wonderful."

This will make you laugh, Danny. Deb explained why this was so hilarious.

"Leah and I had bought a doll a few years back. We found him at the local store. He was our icon, Mr. Wonderful. He said all the right things. It was so funny. Lilly and I took the doll to Mom's since Lilly liked playing with him. When Lilly left the room, I said, 'Look, Mom, Leah and I found Mr. Wonderful.' I started pushing his controls, so he said all his programmed comments:

'Let me go shopping with you, I can carry the bags!'

'Here, honey, you can have the controller, I don't need to watch the football game.'

On and on...

Then I said to your grandmother, 'Look, Mom, he has huge feet. You know what they say about guys with big feet!'

She laughed until her eyes filled with tears. Oh my God, I thought, my mom is 79 years old and she knows what this means...how funny; how shockingly funny."

Danny and Leah started laughing.

"Gram said that she knew?" Danny asked.

Leah and I looked at each other, then back at Danny. We all just roared with laughter.

*****

Years have passed. So many things have changed, and I have learned about myself. I feel better now than I ever have. My little book was published; it was an enormous success. What appreciation I have for this experience. I never imagined it would be made into a movie. Then when the offer came to be on Oprah, to talk of how it was written. I am beyond appreciation.

Out of all the bad, out of all the nightmares, out of all the trauma in our life, we now were good. My little book brought us all the beginning of an amazing life. It has been a blessing. Words given to me that I was allowed to share with others, even if it was just for one person. It would be a success in my heart. It was.

One person said to me, "Debra, it isn't just the book. The book opened the doors for you to step into the world. It is you! You needed to come out and live your life and share with others."

This was going to be a long flight. I don't mind. I have my music, my books, and oh, I almost forgot. Kathy wanted me to go over this.

The notebook of her business companion Kathy was sitting

beside her on the plane. She placed her headset on, and opened the first page. I wonder how she perceives things ....she began to read the words written.

Meredith, New Hampshire:
By Kathy Williams

I remember this! Her heart felt the excitement as the words took her back to the auditorium.

Entry:
Meredith, New Hampshire. A national group called "Women for Life" contacted Debra on October 2012. Would you come be with us? Our group met this last week, and many suggested asking you to come, since seeing you on Oprah. We would love it if you could find the time and present your unique way of looking at life.

It took no time for her response. I know her so well; she never says no to anyone.

.

*****

Meredith, New Hampshire

Deb stood nervously on the side of the stage. It was common for her to feel this way. She took a deep breath, familiar with what to do, closing her eyes and seeing this experience as fun and teaching, with all she had been given. It was easy for her.

The essence within her just made all fear and concerns disappear.

"Hello..." Her voice filled the room. "Well, are you ready to have fun?"

The audience of mostly women responded enthusiastically, "Yes!"

Her eyes sparkled, and her smile lit up the room. Everyone knew this would be a presentation they would enjoy; some for the first time, others coming from a great distance to be with Debra Pratt...

She was a teacher of life...and loved every moment.

"How many of you have had an exciting new moment happen for you in the last year or so?"

Some hands rose, and the chatter began within the group...

"Well..." De's voice raised an octave. "Let's talk about them, if you don't mind." Her laugh seemed to say, *Get ready for this.*

"New moments, maybe a relationship, a home, a new job, children. All of these moments are life-changing. Each is a new chapter. Now this is for you to examine and consider, give you a wee bit of clarity," she said in her playful Irish accent. "What are you bringing with you to it?" She paused for a moment to allow them to think of what she just asked them. "Yes, what are you bringing with you to it? What is necessary for the expansion of it, and to enjoy it with all your dreams being manifested within it?

"So let's just take one of the many new moments in your life, one you can pretty much see clearly within your mind. Since words don't teach, they only guide, you need to be able to walk into this lesson with your mind able to visualize it. Let's say you have found a new home to move into. Yes, you have a new home. It doesn't matter if it is an apartment or a house. It's new to you, and you're looking at it with a new outlook. It's going to be better than where you are. It has more possibilities for your life expansion. It is NEW!

"Now, you're standing in your present home or moment and have to get ready. How to get ready...first you need to walk around your home, area by area, room by room, closet to closet. It seems like a lot, doesn't it?"

Deb marched around the stage, taking full control of the moment.

"Keep the vision in your mind; this is going to be a new beginning for you. You have always wanted this, and it's here. Right now, in this moment, it is here. Okay, you say...I'm ready. You gather boxes and begin segment by segment packing."

She reached under the table and pulled out a box, then she pulled out another box. Everyone laughed with her entertaining way of visual learning. Then the curtain behind her opened, and there were tables filled with clothing, books, items most of us have buried in our homes. The fun was now going to begin. It was her way.

"Now we begin," she said. "You may start with your closet, your bookshelf, your cabinets in your bathroom. But you do need to begin."

She began to dig into the "treasures on the table."

"Oh look, I love this!" she said as she held a box that was given to her by her grandmother. "This comes!" Digging deeper into the items...an old candy bar wrapper? "Oops," she laughed and threw it on the floor. "Sometimes we don't even realize what is there, now do we?"

Again laughter.

She reached to the back of the table.

"Hmmm...where did this come from?" She pretended acting out, holding a piece of wood with a heart on it. The words *I love you* were painted across the top. "Hmm...I must have kept it all these years for a reason."

"Oh, I remember.....'John' bought me this on our first anniversary."

Now she goes into an act like she is this woman married to someone named John.

She entranced the audience with her actions and playful scenario as she started reflecting. Going back to the moment by the lake, she continued her creative story:

"He poured a glass of wine to show me how much he loved me and gave me this. My heart's racing," she said as she put her hand on her heart to feel it. "Why is it racing so?" she said. "Ohhh, I remember," as her voice carried even louder in the auditorium, "because he is now with another woman and celebrating probably with the same intentions he did with me. Oh God...this goes."

She entertainingly quickly dropped it into the "let go of it" box.

The audience was getting her intended reason of being so visual, to be so blunt. The lesson was coming across loud and clear.

"As you touch each thing, say, "Do I need this? or Oh, I so love this.' Many emotions come into thought as you begin to get ready. Now, I'm not going to go into every segment of your home. My goodness, we would be here for hours. But each thing, each article, each memory, each reason for bringing it...think this...is it necessary to carry to my next chapter? If the answer is YES, then pack it for the 'take with me' box. If not, let it go. Just let it go. You don't need more clutter in your next chapter. The clutter of your old way of thinking and the old stuff that just took up space don't make room for the new. New trinkets, new memories. Do you see?"

"So, are you entering a relationship with old clutter, or good thoughts to bring into it? Are you moving into any moment with clutter and just stuff that isn't necessary? If so, then you're just re-creating exactly what you are trying to leave behind. Make it a new story. You are the author and the facilitator of it. You're creating it. It's your life, your experience."

"Now get those boxes out and examine what goes, and what comes..."

*****

She caught it every moment; Kathy is such a dear friend and help. She gets it she gets me.

She had a long flight ahead of her, her book rested beside her as she closed her eyes to be ready for this new journey.

Chapter Twenty-Three

Come back...let's do it again.

My plane landed at 9:30 pm. It was dark in the airport, only a few faces walking through. Traveling alone was a huge transition for me. I wouldn't even go into restaurants alone, let alone fly anywhere.

Remembering, remembering...

"Leah, guess where I am?" I felt so confident holding my cell phone in my hand and sitting totally alone. Yet truthfully, I felt as if I were breaking an unwritten rule. My hand shook as I spoke.

"Where?"

"At a restaurant, The Golden Corral!"

"By yourself?" she asked.

"Yes, all by myself!"

"Good for you, Mom," she said, almost like a mother encouraging her child to go forth in the world.

What was I afraid of? Why is it such an ordeal for a woman to walk into a restaurant alone? No one would hurt me. I knew that.

Maybe because it was something we all do with someone; it's a social acceptance or non-acceptance. I took my book and papers to read as I ate dinner, and no one thought badly of me being there. I did get looks from time to time, questioning faces inquiring as to a single woman alone? Why? No one would ask, but if they did, I would say, "Because I wanted to."

How silly; we build walls for ourselves, and society has a preordained way we are supposed to socialize. I decided that I was having a relationship with myself. To do what I wanted to do, to go where I wanted to go, to see what I wanted to see... just to be...

I overcame the wall, now I remember where I came from and knew where I was going. Forward...downstream with the flow of life. That's my direction.

Esther, Abraham, Wayne Dyer, Louise Haye, teachers that were guided to me so that I could see my story of life had to change. It was so easy to hear and learn what they were saying.

I could change it, by just allowing and believing. Asking and allowing with no resistance it would all come. All the good would come and surround me, and my family.

*****

A horn blew, and I glanced at the swinging door in the small airport. My driver stood there, waving his hand to flag my attention. I waved, letting him know I saw him.

"Hi," he said in a lovely accent, or was it me that had the accent?

"Hello. Thank you for being so patient. I have my bags over there, pointing towards the counter."

"Aye, I'll get them for you, ma'am."

I took a deep breath, and my heart raced. I was here, actually here again. A cool breeze surrounded me as I left the small airport. I could smell the ocean. We were so close to it. Inn of the Isle, next destination.

"Please?" the gentleman said, taking my bags and pointing to his car. "How long will ya be stayin'?" he said as he opened the door for me.

"I'm not sure. I want to relax and take some time to enjoy your world for a bit."

"Aye," he said, "'tis a grand world here. The Isle is a magical place."

"I know," I said, thinking back to when I came here before.

The Isle of Skye was a land few people were aware of. A treasure hidden in the midst of the water, it was. Off in the distance, you could see lights shimmering from cottage windows hidden in the crest of the hills from the small villages.

This was a place of peace, a sense of calm for me. The world of concrete didn't exist on this little island. My eyes closed, going to a place where there are no worries. The rhythmic thumps from beneath the car were lulling me to sleep as it passed over the brick-covered road. The time passed, but I had no perception of it. I was in my second home, driving a road that I was somewhat familiar with, knowing the destination would bring me joy. That was all I needed to know.

We pulled in front of my familiar place. Nothing had changed since my last time here. The same white three-story house, flowers surrounding it. A familiar face appeared at the door. I had written to her so often, I felt as if we were family. Her gray hair was pulled back into a bun, her appearance just as I remembered.

"Margaret," I said softly, with a hint of sheer solace.

"Debby! 'Tis me Debby!" Her arms extended to scoop me up. "Oh my." Her soft Gaelic voice chanted. "Oh my...welcome, love. Welcome."

"Thank you. I am so very happy to be here again. I have missed you more than words can say."

The driver extended his hand to me as he came out of the Inn from bringing my bags inside. "Miss Debby," he said as he touched the brim of his cap. "I hope ya find what ya be lookin' for."

I smiled, shaking his hand, then looked at Margaret. She laughed, and so did I.

"Aww, he remembered from your book, when you said you sat by the water you were lookin' for something ya lost. Do ya remember, lass?"

"I remember." My heart raced just to think back to when I wrote that in my book.

*****

Celtic music was playing on the old phonograph in the corner of the parlor. The décor of the room was peaceful, with soft, comfortable chairs placed close together to allow for good conversations as the logs burned in the fireplace. *This is so familiar to me, similar to Jim and Helen's Inn at Pemaquid Point.* Deb had never connected the two before.

There were many connections coming she had never made before

It was more than I remembered. I felt as if I were home. *Someday,* she thought, *I am going to have a fireplace like this in my cabin buried in the woods.*

"Margaret, I have to make a quick call back home."

She smiled and said, "'Ere ya go, love," handing me the phone on the desk top. "Take as long as ya need."

She dialed the phone, not even thinking of the time back home.

"Hey," a sweet voice said on the other end.

"Hi, baby girl, I am here."

"Yes, I 'm more than okay. I have so many mixed feelings, but I am fine."

"How's Lacey?"

"Oh, she's fine, Mom. She keeps asking where Meme is."

"Tell her I will be home soon and I'll bring her a gift from a magical island I am visiting. That will make her smile. Be sure to tell Lilly and Sav, too, okay?"

"Yes, that will for sure make her smile. The three of them will love whatever you bring."

"Angel, where are your brothers?"

"They're waiting to hear if you made it to the Isle."

"Tell them I love them. I will call in a few days. Leah, this place is so good for me. I'm excited about tomorrow."

"I'm glad you were able to go back, Mom. Just be safe. Tell Sean and Margaret hello for me, give them my love. Do you have your other book with you? You might be inspired there. You know what the castles and the water do for your imagination," Leah joked with her mom.

"No, but I have a pencil and paper, as always. I wanted to take a break from the book writing for now." She started laughing.

"Call when you can, and make sure you relax."

"Oh, I will, don't worry. Bye."

*****

Margaret took the phone from her hand and softly placing her hand on Debs hand, "Sooo, love, ya think this place has the answers for ya now?"

"Margaret, I'm not sure what it has, but I am anxious to see. I had to come as soon as I received your invitation. I love it here. If I have found or gained anything from all this experience, I have gained you and Sean and the magic of the Isle.

She reached softly, touching my face. Her eyes were holding back the tears. "Aye, you're very dear to us. I have shared your book with so many, we all are praying for ya. Ya know we'd like you to get back with the lad from here. He was the one. We all think that ya know."

The door opened, and Margaret's face lit up.

I turned to see who came in. I think I expected Bobby to walk in. I am not sure why, but he has been on my mind lately.

"Aye, she's here, finally here." The deep Gaelic voice I remembered so well. His white beard a little longer, his eyes a little wiser.

I could hardly contain myself when I saw him. "Sean, how wonderful, how truly wonderful to see you again, my friend."

Sean squeezed me so hard, it took my breath away. "Lassie, it as been a spell since we saw yer pretty face. Glad you took up our invitation."

"I couldn't turn ya down." She said in her Gaelic drawl.

Everyone laughed at her attempt to speak with the accent. It appeared more Irish than Scots.

The phone rang. Margaret answered, giving Sean a look.

Sean nodded and said, "Debra, come over here, let's sit by the fire. Ya must be exhausted."

"I am, it was a long flight."

*****

Margaret continued with her private conversation. "Yes, she is here."

The voice on the other end said, "How does she look?"

"She's fine. She looks tired, but she is fine."

"She…is she…" He hesitated.

"Come on, lad, ya know what ya have to do. Are ya ready?"

"Yes, I'm fine. I am a bit nervous. She can be pretty stubborn, as I recall. Her fear of marriage…well, I am going all the way this time. I know the angels are on my side.

"Aye, they are, but we are here to help ya if ya need it."

"Are the books in yet?"

"Boxes and boxes arrived the other day."

"Good."

"I'm in Ireland right now. My cousins have made room for me in Dublin. I will be there in two days. Margaret?"

"Aye?"

"Thank you. Thank you so much for this."

"Ah, laddie. Sean and me, we know ya love her. She has been through so much. You're an amazing man to organize this, to be with her. She will say it was angel magic. We are glad to be a part of the magic, is all. It's like a chapter of her book is coming to life right before our eyes."

"She does look well…and is….?" He stumbled with his words.

Margaret laughed aloud, sensing his nervousness, so loud that Sean looked at her, and so did Debby.

"Lad," she said softly. "She's angelic, as always."

They hung up the phone.

He stood there, looking around his room.

How was he going to pull this off? He wanted to come back into her life. He met her such a long time ago and patiently followed her, watching, making sure she was okay.

Would she be upset the family kept me informed?

Oh, stop worrying; it will be fine, he thought to himself and dropped on the soft bed.

It had been a long day.

~*~*~*~

Chapter Twenty-Four

The Blending

They had met online a few years after her divorce. It seemed like it took forever to get to this time and place. This was it; this was the moment he waited for. The right time to come back.

She always said to expect the unexpected. So many of her cute little *Deb-isms* crossed his mind. Well, she better practice what she teaches. We shall see.

The moment it began....
As the realm of spirit orchestrated and watched it all take place...signs are given to guide you to what you have asked for.
These two people, being only two lives, are very significant in the energy of life. You see, they will touch thousands, as it is taking place right now.
We always hear the words that are said, and silent words from the heart.
They both wanted this.
So it is...
{We are always here, dear one...always...it is an angel thing}

Allow us to share with you how this meeting began...
We will take you back..So you can understand where they are and where they are going. But mostly important what you will learn from their experiences.

Hey you, he typed on the computer after seeing she was online.
Deb: Hey you back...
How are you?
Deb: Oh, keeping busy with work and the kids. They are always into

something.

So are you ready for the drink you promised me?

Deb: When?

What are you doing right now?

Deb: Hmmm, nothing, actually nothing...

How's the book coming?

Deb: The book? I don't know. It seems to be taking its own time.

No worries, it will be perfect, I am sure, when it is finished...

Sooo, when will you be ready?

Deb: They say there is a storm coming, seems to be quite a nasty one.

It doesn't scare me, I can handle it

Deb: Ok, then. How about 7? Is that ok?

Sure, he typed.

Deb: Good, hey...can I ask something?

Yes? He could sense she was nervous. They had been writing off and on for over a year.

Deb: This is friends, right? I mean, well, you know what I mean.

Friends, of course...no worries. We will always be friends.

Deb: Okay. See you at 7.

Deb turned off the computer.

Leah could see that she was concerned. "What's the matter, Mom?"

"You know the person I told you about that lived in Watertown?"

"Yes."

"We're meeting tonight."

"Good, you need to get out. Things have been stressful for you lately."

"Yes, but we're doing fine."

"I know. Still, you need to relax."

"I can't believe I'm finally meeting him. We have shared so many moments together being playful online. He was always so busy with his life. I never felt he would actually be serious and want to meet."

*****

I was early, as usual. I looked at all the cars in the lot and wondered which would be his.

A tap came on my window; it startled me for a moment.

The smile on his face made my heart skip a beat. I wasn't disappointed at all in his appearance, or his personality. He was everything I had hoped he would be. I was also quite relieved; he looked like his pictures he had shared with me.

(Online dating teaches you to never know what to expect, since many times truth isn't visible in the eye of the beholder. Or is it?). Whenever that happened, I would have a cup of coffee and wish them well in life. I never saw them again. It was my safe mechanism. I had many safe mechanisms acquired over the years.

We spent the evening talking and discovering even more of each other moment by moment. He shared of his travels, and to my amazement, his family was from the Isle of Skye in Scotland. Scotland?

"You're from Scotland?"

"My grandparents live there. I've gone back from time to time. I have family in Ireland, too."

"How lovely. I would love to go to Scotland someday, and Ireland. I'm writing about it in my book

"What's the name of your book?"

I started to answer...

He stopped me and pointed to the weather outside. The snow was coming down, the blizzard had arrived. We still sat totally warm and comforted by each other's passion for life. It was a walk down a memory path for both of us.

All of us in the world of dating have to do this from time to time. Until we find that one last time, we don't have to say it again. No more questions, no more answers; just being with each other, being what each other would desire. I call it the blending...

Not expecting perfection, but we each enhance the other's life. That is my analogy of dating.

Bumps disappear in time, as with all blending relationships.

"So...when can I see you again?" he said.

"I am not sure. I have to go out of town on business, but I will return in a few days."

"Good, then," he said. "Let's stay in touch. I won't ask you for your number yet."

Debby smiled. "Yes, yes, that would be fine. I appreciate your patience."

"As my Granddad always said, 'Good things come to those who wait.' Timing is everything."

She smiled. "He sounds like a very wise man. Is this the Irish, or the Scottish Grandfather...?"

He laughed.

"I should get home." Looking out at the storm, the snow was getting deeper by the minute.

"Me, too," he said.

"Okay," they both said simultaneously, standing.

He walked her to the car and touched her cheek, "Thank you, Milady. I have waited for this for a long time, Debby."

She shyly looked away from him and opened the door, not daring to think more than it was.

*****

The next morning, her writing seemed to glide across the page...this, she had learned, was *her* time; when words just come easily and flow, unerring and perfect. The peace within her and the happiness she was feeling opened the doors and windows of her mind to make whatever she wanted to be created on that page with her hand. It was her happy place within.

They both had shared so many things last night, and she felt comfortable writing an imaginary story. This would be enticing and humorous; nothing like an imaginary story between two friends to quicken the mind.

Focusing back on her mission, her fingers slid across the keyboard.

Subject: Sunday Morn imagination and dream from the Irish Lass
Ahh, a day where there is no rushing around. Now this is my imagination; maybe I will make it an entry in my book...kidding.

She continued to write

Let's see. You like country music. It's just sunrise. The window is open, and you can hear the sounds of the birds waking outside. We have been spooned most of the night. I can't sleep without touching you. I know you love to relax, so I softly turn over and touch your cheek with my finger. You smile slightly. I know you're awake, but you want me to show you I'm glad you're beside me.

Oh God, I can't write this. Ha-ha. I'm getting pretty caught up in it, and...well, it has been a while since I woke with anyone beside me, so another story...

Hmm...she clears her mind...

Story two: try it again...

It's the day before Christmas. We have been together now for what seems not long enough. We feel that life is so good together. How did we breathe without the other, before that first meeting...?

The kids will all be coming tomorrow, but we make this day our day. It's the one day we go into "our own" world.

Today, you planned a special day for me. I had no idea what to expect, and now writing about it just makes me remember even more how wonderful you are.

When I woke, the coldness in the air through our window felt so amazing (you had already gotten up). The snow covered the ground overnight. I was so excited to see it. I started to get out of bed, reaching for your shirt.

I smiled as you came into the room and said, "Good morning, beautiful, how was your night?" You said that all the time, since our first morning together.

You said, "Come on, baby, we have things to do! Get your shower and meet me outside in thirty minutes."

I said, "Okay." I loved it when you surprised me.

My heart was racing. What was he up to?

I fixed my hair perfect, not being too particular; you liked to mess it up anyways...

I slipped on my jeans and boots...the khaki jacket and scarf you bought for me last Christmas. Sprayed myself with your favorite perfume and made sure I tucked my special gift for you in my pocket.

As I came to the back door and you were standing with your hands up to cover my eyes. "Don't look," you said, laughing. "Just listen..."

I could hear something like bells coming up the road. *What is it?* I thought. Then I heard clamoring. I had heard that before because the Amish lived close by. I was so excited.

I loved you more than anything.

You stood in front of me, so I couldn't see. Your eyes looking in mine. You loved my eyes, and I knew it...you could read my thoughts from my eyes...

You said, "Today is our fifth Christmas Eve..."

I said, "Yes, I know."

"I wanted to make it special..."

I smiled and said, "They are always special..."

"What are you planning?"

You smiled, and the noise stopped. You said, "I love you!"

With a tear coming down my cheek, I said, "I love you more..."

You stepped to the side so I could see. I couldn't believe my eyes.

A sleigh sat in front of our home, with an elderly gentleman as the driver. It was like a photo from Norman Rockwell. If this is a dream, I don't want to wake up.

Our laughter echoed in the air. Our home was always filled with and surrounded by laughter. I wondered what the neighbors must have thought, yet knowing within their minds they must wish they had what we had. I wish they did, too.

"Come on, babe, this is the beginning. It's our day."

You held my hand as I stepped into the sleigh. You even had a blanket to cover my legs. I felt like I was in heaven. The wind went through my hair. I snuggled as close to you as I could. You are my everything. We rode for miles, then the elderly gent steered the horse to turn on to what seemed to be a road less traveled...I wasn't familiar with it. Why hadn't I noticed this road before?

The sleigh was slowing now, the trees surrounding us swaying with the cold snow on their branches. The gentleman turned and said, "To the right, sir?"

"Yes."

The sleigh turned up a very narrow pre-plowed path...there it was, this amazing cabin. Smoke appeared from the top of the stone chimney, and lights were in all the windows. You could see a Christmas tree decorated set close to the window inside.

This is for us tonight, baby; then tomorrow will be for the kids.

Our day and night was filled with more love, more joy and laughter, than I had ever experienced. We were brought together by the Spirit of Life, and there wasn't anything we couldn't have, as long as we were together.

I most definitely have to stop now. I create things sometimes so easily. The words come as I am surrounded in the moment of my imagination. That is what a good writer does, I am learning. If my books contain words and experiences like this, it will be lovely for others to have a glimmer of it in their lives.

I pray it happens for me and for them.

Everyone has to be in love; it is what creates the magic in the air…

I hope you enjoyed my story.

Debby

His email reply in the same early morn hours didn't surprise her at all.

My dearest Debby

Upon reading this amazing story, I have to admit, I was feeling many emotions. One, of amazement by the way you have been able to express your deepest thoughts in words, which say so little, yet say so much. You do have a gift to write. I anxiously await the opportunity to get to know the woman behind these words.

Can I have a signed copy when it is completed?

For the purpose of your remembering this, I can make this come true.

Debby read his reply with complete satisfaction. He liked it, she thought. Should I put this in my book? I have never written anything like this, but it is tasteful.

The message came up *you have mail*…**she smiled, thinking it must be him again.**

You are cordially invited to meet me at:
1245 Mount Haven Place
Canandaigua, New York
Time: 4pm
Attire: Snow boots, scarf, and warm coat

Purpose:

To totally enchant you in the new snow-covered ground. To allow you to sit in the sun beside me under this amazing tree, feeling the breeze touch your beautiful face. I will provide beverage and amusement upon your arrival.

I anxiously await your reply, sweet lass.

She laughed after reading his invitation. He was getting to know her. Getting to know how she thought and wanted to continue.

"Leah?" Debby called to her from the living room. "Did you have anything you needed me for today?"

"No, why? What's up?"

"Oh, nothing. I am going to go play in the snow for a bit this afternoon."

Leah shook her head with a smile and said, "Okay, Mom, have fun."

She went back to the computer to reply:

Dear Sir:

I accept your sweet invitation, my friend. I will arrive at the time you requested, with a bit of curiosity for the amusement you have stated you will provide.

You have my attention.

Debra

*****

The years have passed, and she had disappeared into her world and he couldn't reach her 'til now. He could sense it, feel that the time was right.

Do it again, be playmates again.

It was to be...now you the reader will see it more clearly.

*****

With Sean and Margaret's help, he finally had the opportunity, this one last time to do it right. To capture the magic. Would he be able to pull it off?

His phone rang.

"Yes, angel, I'm here. No, she doesn't suspect anything. Yes, you and the boys did great. Thanks for doing this for me. Did you have a chance to look at the property I bought for us? She admired this big old tree on it when we went there for a bike ride a few years ago. I know, I know. I spoke to Margaret. She said your mom looks great, just a bit tired. When? In two days. Yes, I'm going to ask her." He laughed, hearing the words from Leah. She sounded more like her mom every day. "I know angel. I love you, too. It's time for us now."

Chapter Twenty-Five

Living the dream

Margaret and Sean visited with Debby for a bit longer, sipping tea and talking about all that has taken place in her life. Her last visit was so involved, with book signings and talks with large gatherings, there wasn't much time just to have her relax. She was on her journey, touching so many. Now they could see in her eyes that she was in a different place. She came back to them again. Sean knew he had words that were given to him to share with her and would easily be given the time. He had the same connection with the spirit realm as Debra, and soon she would experience it.

"Well, love, Margaret said it seems like a lifetime since you were with us before. How have you been holding up? Life was taking you for an amazing ride then. The wind was in your sails, and there was no stopping you."

"I'm fine; a bit tired. Things fell into place so quickly, it was a bit overwhelming.

"Aye, lassie," Sean said. "Ya hardly had time to breathe. Jeff stayed in touch with us and filled in the news your letters didn't cover."

Margaret could see Debby was exhausted; she was staring at the logs in the fireplace as if she were somewhere else. They shared with her that they knew Jeff went back with his wife.

Deb let out a sigh of relief. "It..." She hesitated a bit. "We weren't meant to be more than friends." Her eyes were still captivated by the flame and the soft music soothing her to that peaceful place within herself.

Sean stood up, tapping his pipe softly on the edge of the mantel. "Lassie, I can see ya need a bit of shut-eye. Ya need to get some rest," he said softly. "I would like to take ya to the village tomorrow and 'ave some of the locals get a chance to say hello to ya. You put the Isle on the map since your book, ya know."

Debby smiled and stared at the floor, shaking her head with an apologetic gesture."The same reaction took place at the Point."

"Not to worry, love," Margaret said. "The Isle needed a bit more excitement anyways."

Sean helped her up from the chair. Still holding her close, he said, "You're not dreamin', angel; this is what you were always meant to do. I will come get you in the mid-morn, and we will go have tea by the brook."

"I will be ready."

He started to reach for her hand, but he continued and hugged her so tight. It was like a father's loving hug for his daughter. If he had said, "Take some from me," it would have been perfect. But she felt it from him. Words weren't necessary for her to know what was in his heart.

She had no idea what the next few days were going to bring...

"Alright, missy, let's get you settled in. Come on." Margaret helped her up from the chair.

She had the most wonderful Scottish accent. It was like listening to a melody when she spoke.

*****

Dee's room was simply decorated, pretty framed photos on the wall of family and friends. The bed was beautifully arranged with handmade tapestry pillows. An oil lamp burned on the antique desk that overlooked the view outside. Darkness covered the street below. But the light from her room reflected on the stone path below.

Her thoughts began to imagine what the next few days would be like.

"Think it and create it," she said out loud.

I created this moment, I wanted to come back, and I did. I need to experience the magic of this land. I have heard so much over the years. Castles, along with the fun so many reported they shared here. When I would listen to them, there was a familiarity to it all. I could sense the life here. It was as if the angels set this Island here so I would believe. Believe anything is possible, and...

She stopped her thoughts.

I'm just going to flow with what is here. Not be the one creating, but the one experiencing what life is bringing to me. I know there is so much more. I need to just be. Be here now...and enjoy.

Deb felt a little shaky in the knees, and the last thing she remembered was crawling under the soft blue bedspread. Sleep came quickly.

Tap, tap...

A soft knock at the door...she thought she heard a soft voice.

It's time to wake; you have so much to do.
You came to do it again. Now open your eyes. I am here.

Another knock at the door.

"Deb, love, are ya okay?"

She thought she was dreaming, and it took a moment for her to get her thoughts gathered. Then another tap.

"Oh, Margaret!" She jumped up and ran to the door. "Oh my gosh, I am so sorry. What time is it? I didn't mean to worry you."

Margaret's face lit up with relief, then a huge smile. Her eyes examined Deb from head to toe. "At least ya got your shoes off, love," she teased her about her appearance.

Debby looked down...well, that was all she had taken off; she was still fully dressed.

"What time is it?"

"It's half past nine, love. But not to worry. Sean will be back in an hour or so. We both knew it would be hard for you to get up, especially with the time change and all."

"Okay, I'll be ready."

Margaret reached for something on a table in the hall. She handed Debby a flask. "Here, love, this will open those blue eyes."

The aroma from it was heavenly. "My own special brew. You won't find it anywhere else like this."

This sounds just like Hattie, again her thoughts seeing another connection

She gave Margaret a hug and quickly prepared for her quest of the Isle.

The sky was as blue as the water. "Crystal water blue," she said out loud. You are so lovely today, and I am going to enjoy the sight of you, every moment I am here.

Water was her element,
Her strength and energy always came from the water.

The view was grand from her window, the mountains were full and green, as if an artist's hand stroked the fullness of the trees with only perfection in mind. The sea touching the shores of the Isle with the gentle stroke of his waves, caressing the Island as if it were his love. There is magic here...I can feel it.

Slipping on her jeans and sneakers. No suits this trip; casual and relax. She felt the excitement as a child beating in her soul, to experience this place inch by inch, breath by breath. She ran down the stairs, jumping the last two steps to land perfectly like a dancing fairy on the hardwood floor.

Debby could sense that someone was watching her. She glanced playfully to the side of the staircase. There he was...sitting in an overstuffed chair by the fireplace. His stature was of strength as he seemed to pretend not to hear her. His glasses rested on his nose as he looked at her over the rim of them, with a smirk on his face.

"Feeling kind of playful, lassie!!"

"Sean, I'm sorry I'm late."

He stood up and stretched with a growl. "No rules, no time."

I thought I had heard that before. It echoed in my mind so often lately.

Sean took her by the hand, leading her out the door. He knew the plan and was aware of what he had to accomplish today.

Her heart raced with anticipation, like a little girl going on a journey with her father. No words were said from her; she was taking every moment like a breath within her. Never to forget, always to remember this time. It was for her, and she felt it.

The street was paved with cobblestones. The sight of the small village took her breath away. Debby remembered being there before, but she hadn't felt this way.

It was like an imaginary village lifted from a book. Stone covered shops, flowers lining the sidewalks everywhere. There were no large crowds of people, only small gatherings here and there.

As they walked down the street, Debby could see faces catching a glimpse of her and Sean. They waved, and Sean returned the favor. Debby smiled, thinking, *I wish they knew me. I wish I knew them.*

Not far from the inn was a café, near a small stone path. On each side of the path were small white tables, a flower in a vase on each of them. There was a brook coming down from the mountain. The café was intentionally built by the brook. Sean pulled a chair up for Debby and waved to the waitress.

"Feasgar math, Sean. What can I get ya today?" She then glanced at Debby and softly said, "Halò, we're glad yer here."

"Tapadh leat," Debby replied, with her limited Scottish. She wondered to herself, *how did so many know I was coming? This is so strange.* Having the feeling again as if someone were watching her, but dismissing it as just her imagination.

"Deb, do ya want some sweet lace with your tea today?" Sean asked, trying to distract Debby from the obvious.

"Umm, yes, sure...what is it?"

The waitress closed her eyes and swayed from side to side, saying, "It is the most delicately scrumptious morsel you will ever put on yer lips.."

"Oh my, really?"

"Aye, they say the recipe was given to the fairies and passed on through a dream."

"Unbelievable!! Who has the recipe?"

"The fairies, of course," she answered, with a smile and a wink, and then danced away from the table.

Sean lit his pipe as if he already knew this tidbit of information and it didn't surprise him at all.

"The fairies, Sean?"

Sean smiled, with his pipe resting to the side of his mouth.

"Now, you of all humans should know as far as I could surmise from your book and your written words that things are not always as they seem." His head tilted to the side, with his eyebrows slightly raised.

Debby loved this...a town filled with magical imaginations and tales to be told...

"Hey, missy, are ya here with me?" Sean said.

"Oh yes, I'm sorry."

As they enjoyed the splendor of this unique café, a wonderful sound came from around the corner: a young man appeared, playing his mandolin. It was a Scottish serenade, telling of the love of the land. His kilt swayed with the movement of his dance as the small black tam held tightly to his head.

He seemed to recognize them and approached the table, still playing as he nodded to Sean and acknowledged Debby with a smile, then gave a slight bow. When the serenade ended, everyone whistled and clapped.

"Look to your right," Sean directed.

There were women of age and wisdom sitting around a large round table.

"Now look at what you are seeing and sense what is taking place."

"I see peace with them, contentment being together."

"Yes, they are. Now wait a moment."

They suddenly all started singing "Happy Birthday" to one of their friends. Her face glowed with delight as she was given the gift of being with them and having them in her life. Her lovely, aged face came to life. Her eyes twinkled as if she were hearing the song for the first time, as she did when she was young.

She felt as if she were hovering over their moment, experiencing it with them.

How lovely to take the time to see and listen to life. They had celebrated this day that echoed through time, for more years than some have forgotten. Now the day of their *beginning* is coming very soon to the close of their book. They authored and created their story just before they came forth.

"What are you thinking?" Sean said.

"I'm thinking, I hope they know there is a continuum of life. Steps we have taken continue on, taking another form. The form of life they have always had within, but it had been encased in the form of flesh and bones for a time, for a season."

"Ahh, yes," Sean commented as he watched Deb's face. "You are seeing and understanding. That is why you have been a good teacher to so many. You have been given the gift of interpreting life. Do you see?"

"Yes!!!" She remembered now a dream, a dream that seemed so clear and vivid as she woke. This one stayed longer than others, maybe since it touched her soul so deeply to her purpose. But the words Sean spoke had been heard in another place, another time. In my dream.

A being not of flesh stood beside me.
What is happening? How can this be...?

Where I was, I have no recollection. The sight was of paintings of all colors in frames, setting on shelves lining a wall. I couldn't see what they were of, but I could at a distance see the colors of the frames surrounding each one were a variety of designs.

"What are they?" I asked.

Well, in order to understand them, you need to step closer.

So we did. He beside me, or sensing the maleness of him, we spoke to each other, but not with verbal communication. It was an exchange of thought, understood very clearly.

I looked closer....with surprise. "They are memory paintings!"

"Yes, they are. It is now time for you to understand why you have been painting them. Each is different and unique, as all lives are. Each life encased with different frames.

He paused so I would have time to understand my life, my purpose.

"You hear words of their life as each individually shares their story. Then you blend it in a lovely, colorful piece of art. An artistic creation for only them to enjoy, since others would have no connection to the story that is shared. It is for them and their family alone."

"I see. Yes, I see!!!"

"You, my Iroquois princess, are as your ancestors painting their story on canvas in this time. Yet in another life and time, the stories were painted on deer skin of the teepees they lived within."

I listened and understood.

"Now this is for you to take with you from this moment. You are an interpreter of life, listening, watching, and putting it visually in front of the seeker to understand how colorful their life has been. The joy and sorrow they have experienced was all for their own personal journey. Not to learn some lesson or to overcome some moment to show they were worthy of a reward. It was for them to see the beauty of being alive and participating in life."

My heart was more alive within now. I realized with total clarity I was important and a part of this universal experience.

"Ahh, lass, that was such a wonderful dream." His hand touched mine to bring me back to the café.

"Sean, I...I..."

He touched my mouth. "No words are necessary. You are here with us on this island, to see it all was for a purpose. Just as their lives are," he pointed to the women. "As chair by chair becomes vacant, they, too, will see in time, it is still truly filled. Not seen with the view of natural eyes, but sensed with the eyes of the soul within them. Are ya ready to continue the day?"

"Where are we going, Sean?"

"Ah, lassie, you have so much to see in such a short time. Let's make every moment count, feel the life around you, always pay attention. Isn't that what you shared with Arabella as you both sat with her beside the water?"

Sean shared words and wisdom with her that she had never heard or seen before. She wasn't going to question; just observe and learn. He was her guide this day. The saying 'When the student is ready, the teacher appears' Maybe he has been beside me all along?

They walked down the path to the oceanfront.

"See over there?" He said as he pointed to a small area of land, where all that could be seen were trees, with a tower peeking out from above the umbrella of the leaves. "Tomorrow night, we will be going there it is Glenora Castle."

"We will?"

"Yes, that is what this is all about."

"What?"

"Your book. It always has been about your book, the timely trip, the whole adventure."

"Really?" Her mind still trying to comprehend what was taking place.

"Your memories are in that book, are they not?"

"Yes."

"It's the life experiences you share. You lived your life and gave your children and grandchildren their special lessons along with your memories. Your words my child, are what is important now. It's time. Are you ready?"

"Sean, I am ready."

The entire town will celebrate tomorrow; it's the feast of the Harvest Moon."

"It is?" Her eyes glassed over. "I forgot."

"No, my child, you didn't forget. Times have changed for this moment. This time needed to be. It is a gift so you understand. You truly created this story, as those women did theirs. Yours is different, though; it is being shared with the world. "

Her silence was as of a child listening, to truly see what she was to learn.

"Who will be there?"

"Everyone…now that's enough questions. Let me explain Glenora to you. But then maybe you already know of Glenora."

Her mind was racing, trying to understand. "I thought…I thought I came for a book signing?"

"We ave' many of your books over there in the Laddin's Bookstore. Ya can do them today if ya like."

His voice was being so playful with her, enjoying this moment,
knowing what was coming but carefully protecting the surprise.

Debby's heart was racing. "I'm excited, I've never been to this castle."

"I told you it's a magical place. You did imagine and create this one in your book, now didn't you? The story behind the castle is one of true love. Do you remember?"

"Yes, yes, I remember."

"So you have been there in your mind...felt it, knew of it. Created it and believed others would believe in love and of it. Is this true, Debra Pratt?"

She just felt totally elated.

Again he said, "Is this true, your story you created? Did you want it to be enjoyable and magical?"

A tear slid down her cheek. "Yes, of course. It was a dream I was shown as I sat by my large old oak. I wrote it from that moment that experience. "

"Yes, you did. Now let's go see how your story ends. Are you ready?"

She laughed as she jumped up, a tingling sensation vibrating through her back, the feeling when her angels surrounded her. "I am...I am ready!!!"

"Yes, you are...let's continue, shall we?"

*****

The flutes and drums echoed in the village as their moment continued.

Sean recited the story as if it were a historical event that had been shared many times over as they walked together through the paths of Skye, towards the view of the castle on the water's edge.

"Back in the days of the Vikings, there were wars everywhere in Ireland. Here in Scotland, it was a very dark, dark time. A young lad from Ireland came here to the Isle and wanted to build a safe place for his love, to keep her safe from the terror of the war. He had planned his construction of it, and all the town's people gathered to build his haven of stone. It was not an easy task, but the young captain never tired, selling all his possessions to buy more supplies to build their castle.

"It wasn't as big as Glenora is now. It was a small home for his family. But it was on the side of the mountain and hidden under the trees. No one would see it unless the lights were lit in the windows. As the last stone was laid, the village gathered in merriment. The celebration of renewing their vows was to be soon, and all celebrated the love of the two young people. It was a time that magic and love would overcome the darkness surrounding the land."

Debby listened intently.

"Allon and his beautiful wife Adara moved into the castle. It was small, but in their eyes it was a mansion. The village residents now were their family.

"Music filled the air from Glenora. Adara would sing melodies that echoed through the trees. They were safe, they were living life with such joy.

"In time, Allon bought a small ship and went out in it to catch some fish for their winter stock. Adara was going to tell him she was with child, yet planned to have a surprise when he returned. Actually, it was around now this same time of year.

"He sailed off full sail, and that was the last she saw of him. Their son was born the following spring, at sunrise. She always sensed Allon with her when the little babe snuggled in her arms. It's said his love still filled the castle. and every night the candles in the windows would light. No one lit them. The legend is that Allon is the one that does the lighting."

"I...why do I feel..." Debby felt the sadness that Adara endured it was so familiar.

"Because you, too, will be touched with this magic. It's what you have dreamt of, you write of, yet you understand there is no ending. You have been adjusting to where you are now. You have come back to do it again. It continues, it continues, it always does. It never ends. Humans don't see beyond this. You do, now you must show him as you are. "

Debby sat on the ground, looking at the castle, holding the tears back. *What is he saying?. ...*

Sean sat beside her, realizing his words were stirring her. "Debra Pratt," he said softly, "it is a legend, so they say, but is it? It's a wonderful love story. Lights come on in Glenora still from time to time, when true love has come to the castle."

They sat on the rocks, looking out over the water to see Glenora.

You were Adara in another time with your Irishman. Sean put his arm around her to comfort her heart. Now you are to be with your Scotsman. A new journey you experienced and created love.

He stood, reaching for her hand to pull her up. You could only write of true love because you experienced true love. Your Irishman was a match made in heaven hundreds of years ago. The light of that love still glows in the castle. Now your words in your books shine a light on the magic of life.

It can appear again. As life is never ending and a new journey so is each love.

Debby was awakened now by this revelation. "Thank you, Sean, for sharing this with me. I do see it clearly now. Where is Allon? Is he as I?"

"Tá fáilte romhat. Maybe ye can put a glimmer of him in your next book. Once our souls touch we always are visible one way or another."

"My next book?" Debby laughed.

Sean took her by the hand. "Yes you are a writer of words and that too will continue. Now let's get back to Margaret, on the morrow is the celebration. I know Margaret wants to spend some time with ya, doin' them girl things."

Debby renewed in her soul said, "I am ready."

*****

They returned to the inn to find Margaret busy in the kitchen.

"What ya makin'?" Sean asked as he dodged her and tried to touch the food that was scattered all over her counter.

"Oh, never you mind, Sean Donald. You keep your nose outta me kitchen." She slapped his hand, giggling at his playfulness.

Sean laughed his deep laugh.

"Did you have a good walk, Debra?" Margaret said.

"Yes. It was...well, it was beyond explanation."

"Ahh yes, Sean has a way of makin' the ladies speechless." She chuckled and flipped the dough she was working on on the counter.

Debby enjoyed watching and seeing them enjoying life. "Sean said there is a celebration tomorrow...the Harvest Moon..."

"Aye, that it is...and we need to be getting you to the House of Pearl!"

"The House of Pearl?" she said.

"Aye, she is waiting for us...well, for you...ya need to be fitted."

She felt so foolish; she had no idea all these things were being planned for her..

"Let me roll this dough out and set it on the sill to rise, then we'll be on our way."

"All right," she said. "I think I will go call home for a moment."

"Yah...you do that, lass."

Margaret watched as Debby left the kitchen, making sure she was gone. She then opened the door to the pantry. "Laddie, she almost caught ya...you have to be more careful. It would ruin everything."

He laughed. "I see you're good at hiding men in the pantry, Maggie. Had practice doing that, maybe?"

"Awe, be gone with ya," she said, slapping him on the butt. "Keep yer face hid and outta site; she might see ya."

"No, she hasn't seen me yet! You have the dress I picked out ready, right?"

"Aye, what else would we be doing at Pearl's? The whole town is in on this with ya."

He jumped in the air, swinging his arms. "I can't wait to see her face! She loves surprises, and this is the best one ever."

"Do the kids know?" Margaret said.

"Yes, they helped me with everything. 'Tis the magic of the Isle...'tis the magic of the Isle," he played in his Irish accent. Out the back door he ran. In time, the door to the kitchen opened.

Margaret breathed a sigh of relief. She thought, *He has to get better timing, or maybe not. It seems to be working for him.*

A smile came to her face as she shook her head in disbelief. "Is everyone safe at home?" Margaret said, with a quick glance, wondering if Debby saw the door close.

"Everyone is fine. Well, I hope...I left a message on the machine. They will be excited when they listen to my message of my harvest moon celebration."

"As they should be. Now, princess, let's get to Pearl's. I know she is waiting."

The walk to Pearl's was lovely. Everyone was preparing for the celebration.

A soft yellow peasant dress hung on the first rack of clothing as she walked in the door. It was lovely, a dress she has always envisioned within her mind. When she tried it on, Margaret and Pearl hugged each other and squealed. Debby was a little taken aback by all the attention, but she loved every moment of it...a perfect day from beginning to end.

*****

The next day came, and Debby woke to the sound of music outside the inn. Her windows were open, and you could hear the violins playing, people laughing, and clamoring everywhere. She was amazed...where did all these people come from? She could see old and young gathering together; it was a celebration. Boats were coming into the cove, filling the shoreline, and there were horns blasting and the tapping and shuffling of dancing feet going up and down the brick streets.

"There's the angel by the water," a voice yelled from the sidewalk below.

She was startled that someone saw her watching from her window.

"Get dressed and come play with me!" the voice below playfully chimed.

She thought she recognized the voice. She stared closer...it was Arabella! "Abbey, what are you doing here?" she called to her.

"I was in Ireland, sweetie. I live there, you know that! What? I can't come here to celebrate with you?"

"I will be right down." *Celebrate with me? How did she know I was here?*

Debby took her shower as quick as she could. She laughed, remembering how she would always call the shower her waterfalls. *I love my life,* she thought, not noticing her body no longer had scars.

The dress hung on the door. She took a moment just to admire it, then sighed and shook her head in disbelief. *I think...I think I saw that at...no, it can't be the same one,* her thoughts filled her mind.

Arabella came to the kitchen door. "Guid' mornin, Miss Maggie," she said, popping her head inside.

"Angel!" she called. "My angel is here."

Arabella laughed at her excitement, "I missed you. Is everything ready?"

"Aye, it 'tis...she has no idea, none."

*****

The day was filled with food, music, and laughter.

Debby signed a few books for the locals and some tourists that came up to her, saying, "You're an author?"

She laughed and said, "Why, yes..."

"Would you sign one for me?"

It was a day that no one worried about anything. Just enjoying the sunshine, dancing to the music, and eating to your heart's content.

"Look at her. She is so happy. I love to hear her laugh," he said.

"Sae, whaur wull ye be at gloaming?" Sean said.

"Making sure th' horses ur duin o' coorse."

The gent knew his Scottish slang very well. His family traveled between there and Ireland for generations.

"Ur th' bairns aff tae be 'ere?" Sean inquired of the children.

"Aye, a' o' thaim wull be 'ere aroond five, they're oan thair wey noo fae th' airport...she haes na idea."

"Are your children coming, too?" he said as he smiled; the lad knew his Scots way.

"Yes, they are coming too. It is a family memory moment...as Debby says; it's an 'angel thing'."

*****

Dee wrote in her journal:

If this is a dream, may the ones I love share it with me? Somehow, I feel I should be writing. Journaling, it's what I do. I've been able to capture so many moments with words written so they are not lost. I have been allowed to interpret and see things that come not from me, but are given to me.

How do I explain that to anyone? They would think I was crazy...and maybe I am. I don't mind if I think not as others, as long as it enhanced their life to think as they thought before they came to this realm.

Time has hidden so much from us. So many layers of life are worn that conceal the magic of being alive.

Did I create this moment? The letter from Sean, my friend transitioning, and feeling her with me? The words Sean shared of my life before this. This is why the castles and Ireland are so deep within my soul. It began then.

I forgot to take time for me. Is this what this is about?

Music carried from the street to her open window, the smell of the sea air filled her lungs.

Maybe this is what heaven is like. It just comes; there is no waiting for it to come. I just walked into heaven.. My heart is so filled with peace; it must be...I must be here. Does my family know? Are they missing me...? It seems there is no time here.

"*I haven't seen a clock!*" she thought. Is this the place of no rules, no time I have always heard about?

"Oh my God, I see it!" She no sooner said this as the voice within her shared.

Love surrounds you now, as it always has, Debra...

She reached for her dress, which was lying on her bed. She held it close, repeating the words she heard from within...

Love surrounds you...Love surrounds you...

Spinning in place, holding it, as if dancing to a song only she could hear. "I get it…I get it!!"

She dropped her robe and slid the dress over her head. As it rested on her body, she looked in the mirror. It reflected a woman she had never truly seen…she looked different, ageless. "No time, no rules," she whispered, as if a secret were being revealed. "Of course, this is going to be my first harvest moon…alone, but yet not alone."

Remember; don't let your eyes deceive you, sweet one…
You are surrounded with many that love you.

She closed her eyes. "*Thank you,*" *she said as tears filled her eyes.* "*Thank you…*"

As she was making sure she had everything she would need, especially her journal. She was reaching for the door and heard voices outside…she hesitated, but she knew there was not anything to fear in the world of the Isle.

"Shhh," someone said.

"Are we to go in, or wait here?"

"Shhh," another voice said.

"Oh, come on. She won't care."

Debby opened the door.

"Mom!" they yelled. "Happy harvest moon!"

She started to cry. "I am…oh…when did you?" She just kept stuttering.

They all started laughing. "We were coming from the beginning, Mom."

Dan hugged her, trying to calm her and explain. "Sean and Margaret knew you would be surprised."

"When did you get here?" Her mind raced with questions as they all came down the hall, laughing and talking at the same time.

Standing at the bottom of the stairs was Sean, looking up at Debby. His face glowed as he saw her in her beautiful yellow gown. "Ya look lovely. A true princess you are, our very own

Irish Iroquois princess." His eyes filled with tears to see her smile light up the room. "Happy harvest moon, Debra."

She nodded and curtseyed.

"I...I don't know how to thank you, Sean."

"Then don't, lass. Just keep smilin' and laughin'. It fits ya well. Sae, ur ye duin'?"

"I am ready, my dear sweet Scotsman!"

He handed her a piece of paper rolled in a ribbon. "I was told to hand ya' this."

Deb looked at it...it looked like a scroll.

"Don't open it yet!"Everyone insisted together. The townspeople standing by the door, watching her begin the moment, called out, too, "Ye cannae open it yit!!"

Dee was surprised everyone knew and seemed to be so aware. She held the scroll in her hand, following as everyone guided her outside.

Sean stood in front of her and said, "Wait right there. Don't move, just listen."

She couldn't see around him, but she heard the sound of the beating of many hearts simultaneously on the brick road...then it stopped. Sean stood to the side as he pointed towards her ride.

"Your chariot awaits, sweet lass," he said.

Everyone was standing there, enjoying the moment. She looked elegant as the tears started to come down her cheek.

"I don't understand," she said, looking to Leah for answers. Leah touched her heart to tell her mom, *I love you.* It was a symbol they always did when they were across the room. Debra did it back.

Danny and Rob took their mothers' hands and walked her to the carriage. "We love you, Mom," they said as they held back the tears.

"I love you, too. Why is this happening? What is happening?"

The carriage pulled away. An elderly man with a white beard was driving.

I feel like Cinderella, she thought. *This is a dream...this can't be happening. I didn't do anything to deserve this.*

The townspeople seemed to follow as she tried to understand, glancing back and waving, then looking up to the star-filled night sky.

The moon was magical. Full and elegant.

It guided the way for all of them to come to the final chapter of her story...but is it?

> *You're reading this, and have been since the first page.*
> *Emotions are flowing in wonderment within you right now?*
> *This could be your story.*
> *Is it? Or a piece of it.. I think so.*

The carriage reached the edge of the shoreline. The driver said, "Now, madam, you are to read the parchment."

She almost forgot it was in her hand. Carefully releasing the ribbon that kept it tight, she rolled it open. A white feather floated from within and the soft breeze caught it up as it danced on the air above.

It read:

To my dearest love... you sent this to me many years ago. I have saved it to this day...

We all have had moments in our life; some storms, some rainbows.

My storms have passed, and now is the time for my rainbows.

I feel you create what you desire or feel you deserve. I have learned this now. Maybe that's why my life 'til a few years ago was so enduring. I felt I had to be a warrior...a warrior princess...defending and protecting those I loved and were in my life circle.

I realized this way of thinking, always being prepared for battle, wasn't one of a becoming spirit. Life isn't battles and wars, waiting for the next battle, ready always to take it on with my arrows, my confidence, my endurance, and warrior patience to protect and defend. Maybe it wouldn't have been so difficult.

Now I look at every day as a gift. When I hear the echoes of war in someone's camp, I don't put my warrior clothing or arrows on my back. I stand and be still and say, 'Please protect them'... and it is so.

I let God and the Universe do what has to be done for others' paths.

They have lessons they have to learn. I am not the almighty fixer. I am an guide. I feel to extend hope and comfort and a different outlook on life. To give someone positive energy, to say, "This will pass, feel the love of God surround you; He isn't pain and suffering. You will live, but live strong and always positive. That it is all good. Even to what some would call bad...it is good".

Me? I have met so many men, my friend. Over these last six years of revolving around the sun...I loved a few, just a few, all falling short (maybe for my shortcomings, requiring more of them than they were able to provide). Not from a physical, materialistic view, but of the heart.

I will not allow myself to hurt you; that is why we will meet this weekend, hand to hand, sit across from each other and walk through time. Our worlds have many pictures of the past, but I am looking to find this one man. Maybe he is only in my dream, of my imagination. I don't know his face. I do know his heart, and he knows mine. For me to desire him so in depth, I must have known him before.

I so look forward to seeing you, my friend...to stand in front of you and say hello.. Have we met before? Or is this our first meeting? I will know...

So, please be patient...

Lass, I have been patient...
Now listen to the driver and follow his directions.

Debby looked at the driver with questions in her eyes. I sent this to one man, and he always called me 'lass'...*she knew who it was...*

The driver said, "Milady," and held his hand out to her to guide her down the steps of the carriage. She could hear the music playing in the town, and rows of people were watching as a small boat pulled up to the shore.

The driver guided her again with his hand toward the boat and helped her in. The engine starts, and the shoreline is getting further and further away...

She watches in disbelief what is happening...

A soft, familiar voice says,
"All things are possible, Debby... It's your angel thing."

Debby looked to the shore...the lights were on in Glenora Castle. "Ohhh...the lights are on!" She took a deep breath, wiping her eyes to see the view.

The music echoed in the air...it sounded like angels singing.

A glow of light shot through the sky, its flash blinding her for a moment. She looked around; she was on a different boat, the wind was blowing through her hair, and the sails were at full sail.

Where...where am I? She could see the shore. She still had on her elegant yellow dress.

"Are you okay?" a male voice said. "You seem to be somewhere else."

Debra looked but couldn't make out his face, but she did seem to recognize his voice; she had heard it before. "Yes, yes, of course I'm fine."

"Did you enjoy your party, babe?" the voice asked. "We do play well together, don't we?"

"Yes...yes, of course." She thought to herself,

I have lost my mind. What's happening? Am I dreaming?

"Look, angel, the moon is full," he continued. "See how the light touches and glows on the water over there? Let's go there!!" He quickly pulled the ropes of the sails to have them catch the wind.

"I...I...see the light," Debby said. "Yes, it's beautiful."

He started laughing. "Look over to the shore, the light from the lighthouse; it adds to the moment, doesn't it?"

She spun quickly, looking and seeing the lighthouse on the shore. "The lighthouse.."she said softly. "The lighthouse?" she whispered again.

The voice came closer, and she felt his arms surround her. He whispered, "I love you, my angel by the water. This time, you're living the dream."

She melted, putting her head back on his chest, overwhelmed, but understanding the moment. Angel magic in its true form.

"I see...I remember..." she said."

His heart raced as he reached in his pocket.

Debra turned. "I missed you. I wondered if you forgot me, Bobby."

He touched her face, softly wiping the tear slipping down her cheek. Trying to keep her warm, he draped her tan coat over her shoulders. Her dress swayed from the ocean's breeze.

"I see you have your dress. The one you admired in Pemaquid."

"Yes, yes...I knew it was familiar. You were there?

"I was never far...ever! No rules, no time, because we have the magic, lass. We are to be forever and a day. Distance of miles and realms never keeps us apart," he said as he placed her ring on her finger.

"We are truly forever, then?" she sighed.

He laughed that amazing laugh. "We have always been, babe. We just came back and did it again. The way it should have been before."

"The kids will be so excited!"

"They already are."

She smiled, realizing he had planned all this out...

As the boat reached the glow of the moon on the ocean,
A small white object floated in the water, tapped on the bow of the boat.
It appeared to be a white crumpled a paper, throw into the water from the shore.
Discarded thoughts or dreams shared with the ocean.

The voice whispered within her:
"You have been adjusting to where you are. You have come back to,
"Do it again."
It doesn't matter which realm you're in; they intermingle and are interchangeable.
We in this realm know it, and you did as well before you came to your human form.

*One exists, and so does the other. One is the forever, and the other just
a place your spirit wants to take part in.*

Why?

For the experience.

This was your surprise I promised you.

Now you see.

*It never ends, the cycle of life. As the circle of the sun and moon, or the
orbits, the planets come around to where it began. At that point, is it
an ending or a beginning?*

Both.

Humans don't see beyond the world that is of them.

You do.

Now you understand, angel, continue to live well.

As it was meant to be.

As your first writing needed to go back and do it again.

So you have.

This is the reality…that was a dream.

Chapter Twenty-Six

Heaven made the match; it was written in the stars.

The phone rang. "Is this Leah Robinson?"

"Yes."

"Hi, Leah. This is Judith Howland, from Woman's Life magazine. I was just reconfirming our appointment, to make sure the time was still the same for our interview."

"Of course, I am ready. How long will this interview take, Judith?"

"Oh, it won't be very long. Is it okay if I bring my cameraman so we can include a few visuals with the article?"

"Sure, that's fine. I don't want any taken of my daughter, though."

"No, we understand.."

"Good. Then see you at 1:30."

Leah smiled and laid the book down on the stand. "Well, here we go, Momma. The journey continues. Angels, stick around; I think this is going to be a fun ride."

The phone rang again.

"Hey, Dan... She will be here at one o'clock or so. No, it will be fine. I'm ready. Sure, come over anytime tonight. Make sure you bring Reesie and Lilly Anna. When you and Michael get going with your guy talk, she and I can do our thing with the girls."

The morning passed quickly. Lacey was determined to make Leah forget anything other than entertaining her. Between the dog and Lacey, downtime was limited, unless they were sleeping.

Early mornings and late nights were Leah's *me time*.

*****

Debra and Bob were admiring the soft-covered book resting on the foot stool.
"She did a good job, didn't she, babe?
"Yes, siree...quite the talented lass, like her momma."
"I know it was hard on them for a bit, with us both coming here within a few days of each other.
They did it, though."
"I liked how she created the ending, didn't you?"
"Like I said, she has quite an imagination, just like her momma. To take us back to our boat near the lighthouse.
It was magical."
"Hey, maybe she saw us doing it again, ya think?"
"I think she was told of it, just like you were when near your tree. She is your daughter and thinks just as you did."
"Like I 'do"...
"Yes, lass, like you do. You taught her, and her actions reflect she believes it all."
Deb snuggled close to feel his breath.
"Well, it was fun. My friend Nathaniel said to have fun, and we did!"
"Nice touch, by the way, with the horse and carriage.
I loved that; it was like when we were at our cabin.
Remember? You took me for a ride to another cabin hidden in the woods."
"Of course I remember, my angel. You are my reminder if I ever forget."

She snuggled closer to him.

"We did it again, walked it again,
it turned out as it was supposed to be.
Just like the book.

Do you think everyone will understand the book?"
"Those who are supposed to will.
Others will learn in time.
Life and Life."

*****

Judith walked slowly from her car. It was familiar to her as she stared at the garage and the little house in the woods. Another thing she noticed was the old oak tree as she came around to the front door.

"Are you ready?" she asked her companion.

"Yes, I'm ready."

Leah answered the door quickly, with a welcoming smile. "Come in. Welcome to our home."

The camera was capturing Leah's facial expressions and gestures, and the recording every word.

Then, of course, Judith saw the canvas memory painting. Leah had it framed and hung above the fireplace. On the edge of the framed glass, there it was: the acceptance envelope. On the other side, the handwritten first page of Debra's dream. Perfectly placed just below were the journals. Her journals. All of different colors, and worn by time.

Judy pointed to the pink slip of paper that extended off the page edge. "Is this...?"

"Yes, it's the original. She wrote on them all 'for the book'."

"Is this how you knew to create *The Memory Barrel*?"

"Yes, but not just by reading the journals. I lived most of this with her. It's silly, I know, but though my mom never went to a counselor, I actually became her counselor over time; so was my brother. We are a very close family."

Bob put his arm around Deb as she listened to her daughter share their life.

"She had a real hard time walking through the cancer, and

just before that having my father walk away."

Judy said, "I know. I could sense that as I read your book. There are so many hidden messages in there. Were they from you or her?"

"Oh, her. Most assuredly, they came from her."

"Where did Jeff Nichols come from? Was he a real person in her life?"

Leah giggled. "No...he was my creation. It was fun to add that part. I could understand what Mom was trying to say about finding a place. When you're writing there, the words will come to you. That's how Jeff came to be. Out there by the tree is actually where I sat. I think she gave it to me."

Judith smiled. "It sounds like mother, like daughter."

Leah sighed. "Yes, I guess that is truer than even I realized. I am the oldest woman now from my mother's generation, so I will do what she did for me: pass the stories and lessons of life down to each other. Yet her life and lessons....well, she wanted to share it all with the world. Thus, The Memory Barrel...*her Memory Barrel.*

"Jeff was symbolic of the men Mom met after Tom. Some thought they were the mountain man. They would try to be him in silly ways. She had been writing for years, creating certain segments of the book, just never putting it all together. That's what I did. I put it together for her. Kind of like when she was with me, she helped me put life together, and I did with her, too. Jeff was imagination; he fit perfectly."

"Well, it seemed because he was from Scotland and the Isle of Skye, it was going to be him at the end. He would be the one."

"Yes, I knew that, but sometimes it is a wee bit more fun to create a bit of mystery to share at the end of the story. Don't ya think?" she said playfully, in an Irish accent. "Bob was from Scotland, too, but was hidden in the mountains of New York. Jeff was from Ohio."

"Ahh, I see," as her face lit up with a smile. "You were very creative. It's almost a love-mystery story."

"Some might see it as that. It touches each person differently."

Leah reached on the mantle for a wooden box that contained

letters from readers. It was filled to the brim. She shuffled through the envelopes.

"Yes, here it is. This came just the other day from a reader."

Judith moved to sit by Leah to hold the letter in her hand. She gently lifted the handwritten paper from the envelope.

Leah,

Thank you so much for gifting me your book! I felt ready to listen as much as you felt I was ready to hear the words.

I can tell you I was pulled in right from the start, with my tears flowing steadily from page to page. It took a lot longer than expected to finish your book. It took time to process all of the emotions that were brought to light from the words on the pages.

The story line kept me coming back for more. I would become totally immersed in the book, and then...out of the blue...BAM! It was like someone turned the tables, and I was the one they were looking at! Immediately, I would slam the book shut, as if someone were going to jump out of the pages and make me look into my own mirror. A "hot potato" hitting too close home.

I can say that I have never read a book that has caused me to feel so uncomfortable, and yet so deeply loved. It saw through my smoke screen, made no apologies, and loved me anyway.

It shines a bright light into the dark, forgotten places I had built long ago. I was comfortable and familiar living with my darkness, but your book would not have me stay there for long.

Lori

*****

Leah looked, waiting for her response.

"I don't know what to say," she said. "I must admit, I had my own personal experience reading it. But being a reporter, I have to stay unbiased and unaffected. Sometimes it is hard keep an open mind without swaying one way or the other. This book was one of those moments for me."

Leah answered quickly, sensing more needed to be said. "Yes, I know but..." Then she boldly looked at the cameraman. "Can you turn that off for a moment, please?"

He lowered the lens.

"Sure, just give us a moment here privately. Take a step outside for a minute, Okay?"

The door closed behind him..

"It's just you and me now."

"Okay," she took a deep breath, hesitating to let this out. Her hand reached into the box filled with envelopes. "Look at these letters. They came from Germany, England, Texas, all over the United States. This book has circum-navigated the world, hasn't it?"

Leah smiled. "It was 'a message in the bottle', my mom called it."

Suddenly, the sound of Celtic music began to play on the computer. It startled Judith.

"Oh, sorry," Leah said. "I had it on pause. It must have just begun again."

"I don't know if I agree with that, since reading your book."

They both laughed so hard.

Judith continued. "I believe and could relate to so many things in the book. I really didn't want it to end. I could hardly put the book down! When I went away from it to do something, it was as if it pulled me back into the story." She laughed so hard.

"I have never, ever had that happen to me reading a book. How in the world did you write this? It was as if I had my own angel or guide taking me on a journey of life. The words in it reflecting into my life. Just as Lori tried to explain in her letter."

Leah smiled. "It was a personal experience for you, between you and the Source of life, Judy. As I was writing this book and pulling it all together, like a well-woven fabric of life, it captivated me, too! It seems to be a book, but it is so much more. Whether author or reader, it truly affected all who touched it."

"There is so much we have to learn. As my mom wrote and tried to share through Nathaniel, to whom she referred so often . Our journey here at the beginning was totally uncluttered with man's thoughts. We came from Spirit and were very much aware of life. No one made us fear or believe this or that. It was 'taught' by people inundating us with their way of thinking. *Their choices.* Whether religious or just how we are to think. If we don't succumb to it, then we are going to answer to them or a higher power. Our life has been surrounded by fear.

"Now it has been awakened by so many teachers that stand tall to say, 'Live your life in joy.' The Bible quotes confirm this supposedly new way of thinking. That it isn't new at all, it's timeless. Quotes such as 'As you think, so shall you be.' Does that sound familiar?"

Judith nodded her head in acknowledgement.

"So when people such as, mom, Louise Haye, Esther Hickes or Wayne Dyer say, "Your thoughts are creating your life." Those words are red flagged by many who say, 'it isn't true. We don't have the power to create our life!'"

"Well…" Leah laughed. "Yes, we do, and it comes to us as we always are talking about. Like the beat of a drum. We beat the drum saying:

"Life is hard, life is hard, life is always hard. Then it is!"

or

"If we say, everything is always working out for me. My life is filled with abundance. Then it comes.

So many corrections need to be made of how humans think. If you worry of sickness, you pull it to you. It is the law of attraction in action.

What you worry of, you expand, and the universe gives it to you. As you think, so shall it be."

"Now, we need to teach by our experiences what we have learned by living it to our children, and their children's children."

Judith sat silent, listening to Leah's voice as it changed with excitement. She smiled. "You do have your mother in you. You both think and teach just the same. I see the excitement and confidence in your words. I will be anxious when Lacey grows to see and hear her story."

Leah laughed. "So will I! She and her grandmother have a special connection.

Judith, just please watch for your own personal signs. They will guide you on your journey. You, too, shall touch this realm with your words. I understand you're here for seemingly this interview, but it truly was for more. We were supposed to meet. So can we stay in contact? Who knows, maybe you will be interviewing Lacey or her daughter in the years ahead."

Judy walked back to the door for her partner, but not without first giving Leah a hug. "I get it, and I see," she said. She opened the front door. "You can come in now."

He smirked and followed her back to the fireplace.

Deb and Bob were sitting on the floor, listening intently.
"Did you turn the music on?" Bob asked.
"Who me?"
"Well, they will be friends now. That makes me happy."
They both laughed.
Then she listened..
"I hear Lacey…ya wanna?"
"You don't have to ask me twice, baby doll."
"Leah is fine, she is going to be just fine."
"She gets it."
"Yes, she does."
"Yayy!
{Deb squealed as she did her happy dance to the kitchen.}

The camera light came on to show they were recording again. Leah winked at Judith, and she winked back.

"So your mom was, like, the 'ghost writer' of the book."

Leah laughed. "I guess you could say that. I would describe her more of a 'spirit writer', though."

They both laughed.

"I see you didn't put your name on the book."

"No, I used the first page she had written. Her intention was to have a book named this and for her name to be there with it."

Leah pulled the framed, handwritten paper from the fireplace.

The Memory Barrel
by Debra Pratt

Judith continued her interview. The light glowed on the camera, showing it was on. *Capturing this moment.*

"Leah, are you going to continue with your writing? Is there another book to come?"

"Oh, I don't think, so but as they say, never say never. This one was one of a kind. I don't think I can write about what will be in the future, as she did with Bob. To create their life the way she did in her words. That was a gift I think few have. Some people had a tough time figuring her out. She loved her gifts and played with the world with them. My gift is this, I can tell the stories. Of our family, it's the way of our women, passing the stories from one to the other. Memories stay alive when they are shared."

Leah continued. "I can't say for sure, but I think that might be something Lacey or her daughter will decide when it is time to write. It's our heritage, the way of the Iroquois. Wisdom that is learned by words."

"Well, it was a pleasure, and great success to you with your first novel, Leah. Oh, by the way, I heard a producer has contacted you for the rights to make it into a movie?"

"Isn't that just amazing? I did write that in the book. I see it as a play in my mind. Mom talked about that occasionally and gave me some interesting ideas on how to create it."

She shook her head, so you're creating this movie moment so to speak?! Well, I will definitely stay in touch. Who knows, maybe a door will open for that from my magazine."

"Something will come from this, I am sure. Thank you, Judith."

Judith parted, a little more enlightened than when she entered that little cabin. Her eyes seemed to sparkle as she turned the key in her car. *I will see you again, my friend,* she thought as they pulled down the driveway. *I will see you again.*

Leah went towards the kitchen to find Lacey. "Lacey, come on, baby girl, let's take a walk."

"Okay, Momma." You could hear her giggling in the kitchen.

"What are you doing in there?"

"Oh, nothing, just playing with Jessie." Laughter continued to fill the room. She loved to hear her laugh.

As Leah entered the kitchen, she saw Lacey on the floor with Jessie, their puppy. What a sight to see. Her mom would have loved to be here, watching her.

She stepped forward and felt something hit her shoe. When she looked down, there it was. She could hardly believe it.

A muffin lay on the floor

"Oops," Dee said playfully.

Bob took hold of Deb's hand, both of them chuckling like kids as they walked out the door.

Their voices whispered in the air,
"I love it when you do that, babe."
She giggled and said, "Angel magic."
"Now who are we going to play with?" he growled, grabbing her and spinning her around.
"Lilly Anna and Savanna! They love their Poppa!"
"And their Meme..."

Their laughter filled the air.
It was as it should have been. They did it again.

There comes a time...when you finally get it.

"THE AWAKENING"

Now it continues…

~*~*~*~

Forever and a day.

~*~*~*~

Believe it and you shall see it.

Let it be so.......

~*~*~*~

DBLorgan

21242503R00169

Made in the USA
Middletown, DE
22 June 2015